UNDERSTANDING
by DESIGN

Professional Development
Workbook

ASCD

Alexandria, Virginia USA

JAY MCTIGHE AND GRANT WIGGINS

1703 N. Beauregard St. • Alexandria, VA 22311-1714 USA
Telephone: 800-933-2723 or 703-578-9600 • Fax: 703-575-5400
Web site: http://www.ascd.org • E-mail: member@ascd.org
Author guidelines: www.ascd.org/write

Gene R. Carter, *Executive Director*
Nancy Modrak, *Director of Publishing*
Julie Houtz, *Director of Book Editing & Production*
Darcie Russell, *Project Manager*
Reece Quiñones, *Senior Graphic Designer*
Barton Matheson Willse & Worthington, *Typesetter*
Tracey A. Smith, *Production Manager*

All Web links in this book are correct as of the publication date below but may have become inactive or otherwise modified since that time. If you notice a deactivated or changed link, please e-mail books@ascd.org with the words "Link Update" in the subject line. In your message, please specify the Web link, the book title, and the page number on which the link appears.

Printed in the United States of America.

s3/04

ISBN-13: 978-0-87120-855-2

Paperback ISBN: 0-87120-855-5   ASCD product no.: 103056

Also available as an e-book through ebrary, netLibrary, and many online booksellers
(see Books in Print for the ISBNs).

13 12 11 10   12 11 10 9 8 7 6

UNDERSTANDING by DESIGN
Professional Development Workbook

Stage 2—Evidence: Design Tools and Samples

Contents

**Stage 3—Learning Plan: Design Tools
and Samples**

Introduction—

The Logic of Backward Design

Introduction

The *Understanding by Design Professional Development Workbook* is designed primarily as a resource for participants in *Understanding by Design* (UbD) workshops and undergraduate and graduate-level courses. It is also intended to support educators developing curricula and assessments with a focus on developing and deepening students' understanding of important ideas. The workbook builds on the ideas presented in its companion publication, *Understanding by Design,* with an emphasis on the practical issues of curriculum design.

To support learning and applying the ideas of *Understanding by Design*, the workbook contains the following six categories of materials:

1. **Design Templates**—practical organizers based on the three stages of backward design for use in developing a unit or course. One-, two-, and six-page versions of the UbD Template are provided.
2. **Design Standards**—criteria for reviewing curricular designs as a means of continuous improvement. The UbD Standards guide self-assessment and peer reviews, whereby colleagues provide feedback and guidance on each other's designs.
3. **Exercises and Process Tools**—thought-provoking workshop activities for developing and deepening participants' understanding of the key ideas of UbD. A set of review and reflection tools is included.
4. **Design Tools**—a variety of practical worksheets and graphic organizers are available to assist designers in each stage of backward design.
5. **Examples**—multiple examples from diverse subject areas and levels illustrate the various elements of understanding-based designs.
6. **Glossary**—definitions of key terms.

We recommend that readers also access the Understanding by Design Exchange Web site (http://ubdexchange.org). The site features electronic design templates based on backward design, a searchable database of curriculum units and assessment tasks created in the UbD format, and an online review process based on the Design Standards.

Introduction

Stage 1

Stage 2

Stage 3

Peer review

Exercises

Process sheets

Glossary

Additional resources, such as hot links to other supportive Web sites, answers to Frequently Asked Questions, and expert reviews are offered to members.

Product Versus Process

It is important for users of this workbook to distinguish between the *goal* of their design work—producing a coherent design with clear alignment among the three stages—and the *process* of achieving it. To use an analogy, think of curriculum design in terms of two bookends. The first, a completed design in the UbD Template form; the second, a set of design standards for reviewing (and improving) the design. Everything in between—including the tools used, design sequence, and examples studied—is process. You'll notice that the design tools contain letter codes linked to the corresponding field on the Design Template to help users see the process–product connection.

We were inclusive in selecting examples, exercises, and design tools for the *UbD Workbook* because one size does not fit all. After all, curriculum design work is idiosyncratic: the preferred starting points, the sequences, and the tools used will be as varied as there are individual users in unique settings.

We have found that different people resonate with various approaches and tools, depending on the content and their own preferred style. For example, in Stage 1 there are six different design tools for prioritizing the curriculum and identifying the "big ideas" worth understanding. Although each tool has proven useful to some people some of the time, rarely would a single designer use them all.

Thus, users are encouraged to be selective and choose only those approaches and tools that work for them. Resist the urge to work on *every* page or to fill in *all* of the blanks on a design sheet. In other words, always keep the end result in mind, and don't get lost in the details!

Sequence

Curriculum design is not only idiosyncratic, but iterative. Although there is a clear logic embodied in the three stages of backward design, the process is not rigidly linear or step-by-step. Therefore, users of the *UbD Workbook* should not feel compelled to work through the materials in a rigid sequence. Indeed, successful designers find themselves constantly circling back to aspects of the design that need to be revised or rethought entirely in light of reflection, feedback from others, and experience with learners.

Building a unit or course design is thus more like painting from a blank canvas than painting by numbers, more like cooking from available ingredients than following cookbook recipes. As educational designers, we are like architects developing a blueprint. The architect cannot (in one fell swoop) listen to the client, review the building codes, research materials and labor costs, and develop a blueprint by following a step-by-step recipe. The blueprint emerges through a process of trying out ideas, getting feedback, matching the proposed ideas to the reality of the available space and client wishes. Each design idea affects other design ideas—and leads to a new, perhaps unexpected reaction by the client, who requires more changes.

On the other hand, there are some crucial givens in architecture: building codes, budget, and the number of rooms. The challenge in design is to keep playing with the

Introduction
Stage 1
Stage 2
Stage 3
Peer review
Exercises
Process sheets
Glossary

imaginative possibilities while ensuring that all the givens are honored. So, too, in curricular design. The designer can imagine all sorts of wonderful possibilities, but a new idea about learning activities may require a rethinking of the proposed assessment plan. Givens exist here, as well, including state content standards, realistic time and resource constraints, student achievement levels, and interest—all of which must be balanced with our imagination.

Thus, this workbook cannot and does not provide a step-by-step procedure for constructing a unit or course, any more than there is a foolproof procedure for developing architectural blueprints. What we have done is to organize the book according to the three stages of backward design, while allowing designers to begin in different places and follow varied pathways to achieve the same end—a complete design that meets standards.

We do not intend for participants in professional development workshops and university courses to march through the workbook page by page. Instead, think of this publication as a toolbox, and choose the tools for the job in a sequence that works for you.

We hope and trust that the Exercises, Examples, Templates, Design Tools, and Standards will lead to improved curriculum designs—units and courses focused explicitly on important questions and big ideas worthy of understanding, more convincing evidence of understanding by students, and more engaging instruction and learning for students and teachers alike. Ultimately, observable and measurable improvements in learning and performance will result.

Introduction

Stage 1

Stage 2

Stage 3

Peer review

Exercises

Process sheets

Glossary

A Social Studies Unit

Topic
Topic: Westward Movement and Pioneer Life Social Studies—3rd Grade

Activities

1. Read textbook section—"Life on the Prairie." Answer the end-of-chapter questions.

2. Read and discuss *Sarah Plain and Tall*. Complete a word-search puzzle of pioneer vocabulary terms from the story.

3. Create a pioneer-life memory box with artifacts that reflect what life might be like for a child traveling west or living on the prairie.

4. Pioneer Day activities: Dress in pioneer clothes and complete the learning stations.

    a. Churn butter

    b. Play 19th-century game

    c. Send letter home with sealing wax

    d. Play "dress the pioneer" computer game

    e. Make a corn husk doll

    f. Quilting

    g. Tin punching

Assessments

1. Quiz on pioneer vocabulary terms from *Sarah Plain and Tall*

2. Answers to end-of-chapter questions on pioneer life

3. Show and tell for memory-box contents

4. Completion of seven learning stations during Pioneer Day

5. Student reflections on the unit

Introduction

Stage 1

Stage 2

Stage 3

Peer review

Exercises

Process sheets

Glossary

Activity-Oriented Design
(Before Backward Design)

Introduction

Stage 1

Stage 2

Stage 3

Peer review

Exercises

Process sheets

Glossary

Stage 1—Desired Results	
Established Goals: **G** Topic: Westward Movement and Pioneer Life	
Understandings: **U** *Students will understand that . . .*	**Essential Questions:** **Q**
Students will know. . . **K** • Factual information about prairie life • Pioneer vocabulary terms • The story, *Sarah Plain and Tall*	*Students will be able to. . .* **S**

Stage 2—Assessment Evidence	
Performance Tasks: **T**	**Other Evidence:** **OE** a. Show and tell for the memory box and its contents: What would you put in it? Why? b. Quiz on pioneer vocabulary from *Sarah Plain and Tall* c. Answers to factual questions on *Sarah Plain and Tall* and from the textbook chapter d. Written unit reflection

Stage 3—Learning Plan

Learning Activities: **L**

a. Read textbook section "Life on the Prairie." Answer the end-of-chapter questions.

b. Read *Sarah Plain and Tall*. Complete word search on pioneer vocabulary.

c. Create a pioneer life trunk with artifacts you might take on a journey to a new life.

d. Prairie Day activities:
   1. Churn butter
   2. Play a 19th-century game
   3. Seal a letter with sealing wax
   4. Play "dress the pioneer" computer game
   5. Make a corn husk doll
   6. Quilting
   7. Tin punching

Introduction

Stage 1

Stage 2

Stage 3

Peer review

Exercises

Process sheets

Glossary

After Backward Design

Stage 1—Desired Results

Established Goals: **G**

2D—Explain the lure of the West while comparing the illusions of migrants with the reality of the frontier.

5A—Demonstrate understanding of the movements of large groups of people in the United States now and long ago.

Source: National Standards for United States History

Understandings: **U**	**Essential Questions:** **Q**
Students will understand that . . .	
• Many pioneers had naive ideas about the opportunities and difficulties of moving West.	• Why do people move? Why did the pioneers leave their homes to head west?
• People move for a variety of reasons—for new economic opportunities, greater freedoms, or to flee something.	• How do geography and topography affect travel and settlement?
• Successful pioneers rely on courage, ingenuity, and collaboration to overcome hardships and challenges.	• Why did some pioneers survive and prosper while others did not?
	• What is a pioneer? What is "pioneer spirit"?

Students will know . . . **K**	*Students will be able to . . .* **S**
• Key facts about the westward movement and pioneer life on the prairie	• Recognize, define, and use pioneer vocabulary in context
• Pioneer vocabulary terms	• Use research skills (with guidance) to find out about life on the wagon train and prairie
• Basic geography (i.e., the travel routes of pioneers and location of their settlements)	• Express their findings orally and in writing

Stage 2—Assessment Evidence

Performance Tasks: **T**	**Other Evidence:** **OE**
• Create a museum display, including artifacts, pictures, and diary entries, depicting a week in the life of a family of settlers living on the prairie. (What common misunderstandings do folks today have about prairie life and westward settlement?)	• Oral or written response to one of the Essential Questions
	• Drawings showing hardships of pioneer life
• Write one letter a day (each representing a month of travel) to a friend "back east" describing your life on the wagon train and the prairie. Tell about your hopes and dreams, then explain what life on the frontier was *really* like. (Students may also draw pictures and explain orally.)	• Test on facts about westward expansion, life on the prairie, and basic geography
	• Using pioneer vocabulary in context
	• Explanation of the memory box contents

Stage 3—Learning Plan

Learning Activities: **L**

- Use K-W-L to assess students' prior knowledge and identify learning goals for the unit.
- Revise Prairie Day activities (e.g., substitute *Oregon Trail 2* computer simulation for "dress the pioneer" and ask for journal entries while the simulation is played).
- Include other fictional readings linked to the identified content standards or understandings (e.g., *Little House on the Prairie, Butter in the Well*).
- Create a timeline map of a pioneer family's journey west.
- Add nonfiction sources to accommodate various reading levels, such as *Life on the Oregon Trail, Diaries of Pioneer Women* and *Dakota Dugout*. Guide students in using a variety of resources to research the period.
- Review the scoring rubrics for memory box, museum display, letters, and journals before students begin the performance tasks. Include opportunities for students to study examples of these products.

After Backward Design (continued)

Stage 1—Desired Results

Established Goals: 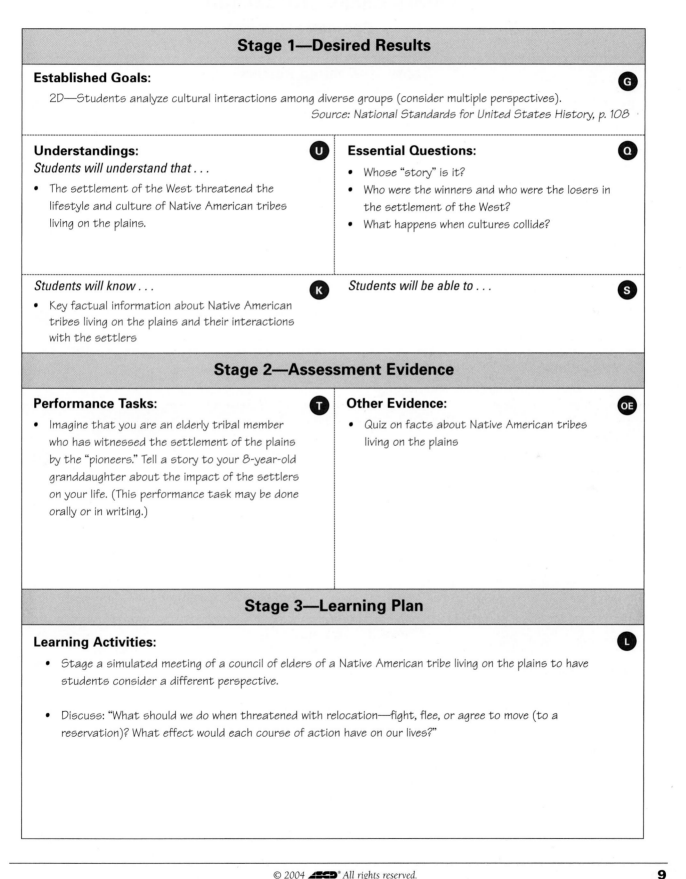 **G**

2D—Students analyze cultural interactions among diverse groups (consider multiple perspectives).

Source: National Standards for United States History, p. 108

Understandings: **U**	**Essential Questions:** **Q**
Students will understand that . . .	• Whose "story" is it?
• The settlement of the West threatened the lifestyle and culture of Native American tribes living on the plains.	• Who were the winners and who were the losers in the settlement of the West?
	• What happens when cultures collide?

Students will know . . . **K**	*Students will be able to . . .* **S**
• Key factual information about Native American tribes living on the plains and their interactions with the settlers	

Stage 2—Assessment Evidence

Performance Tasks: **T**	**Other Evidence:** **OE**
• Imagine that you are an elderly tribal member who has witnessed the settlement of the plains by the "pioneers." Tell a story to your 8-year-old granddaughter about the impact of the settlers on your life. (This performance task may be done orally or in writing.)	• Quiz on facts about Native American tribes living on the plains

Stage 3—Learning Plan

Learning Activities: **L**

• Stage a simulated meeting of a council of elders of a Native American tribe living on the plains to have students consider a different perspective.

• Discuss: "What should we do when threatened with relocation—fight, flee, or agree to move (to a reservation)? What effect would each course of action have on our lives?"

Introduction

Stage 1

Stage 2

Stage 3

Peer review

Exercises

Process sheets

Glossary

Introduction

Stage 1

Stage 2

Stage 3

Peer review

Exercises

Process sheets

Glossary

Textbook-Oriented Design
(Before Backward Design)
Geometry

Stage 1—Desired Results

Established Goals: **G**

Topic: Surface Area and Volume (geometry)

Understandings: **U**	**Essential Questions:** **Q**
Students will understand that . . .	

Students will know . . .   **K**

- How to calculate surface area and volume for various 3-dimensional figures
- Cavalieri's Principle
- Other volume and surface-area formulas

Students will be able to . . .   **S**

- Use Cavalieri's Principle to compare volumes
- Use other volume and surface-area formulas to compare shapes

Stage 2—Assessment Evidence

Performance Tasks: **T**

Other Evidence: **OE**

a. Odd-numbered problems in full Chapter Review, pp. 516–519

b. Progress on self-test, p. 515

c. Homework: each third question in subchapter reviews and all explorations

Stage 3—Learning Plan

Learning Activities: **L**

- Read Chapter 10 in UCSMP Geometry.
- Exploration 22, p. 482: "Containers holding small amounts can be made to appear to hold more than they do by making them long and thin. Give some examples."
- Exploration 25, p. 509: "Unlike a cone or cylinder, it is impossible to make an accurate two-dimensional net for a sphere. For this reason, maps of earth are distorted. The Mercator projection is one way to show the earth. How is this projection made?"

After Backward Design

Geometry

Introduction

Stage 1

Stage 2

Stage 3

Peer review

Exercises

Process sheets

Glossary

Stage 1—Desired Results

Established Goals: **G**

IL MATH 7C3b, 4b: Use models and formulas to find surface areas and volumes.
IL MATH 9A: Construct models in 2D/3D; make perspective drawings.

Source: Illinois Mathematics Standards

Understandings: **U**

Students will understand that . . .

- The adaptation of mathematical models and ideas to human problems requires careful judgment and sensitivity to impact.
- Mapping three dimensions onto two (or two onto three) may introduce distortions.
- Sometimes the best mathematical answer is not the best solution to real-world problems.

Essential Questions: **Q**

- How well can pure mathematics model messy, real-world situations?
- When is the best mathematical answer not the best solution to a problem?

Students will know . . . **K**

- Formulas for calculating surface area and volume
- Cavalieri's Principle

Students will be able to . . . **S**

- Calculate surface area and volume for various 3-dimensional figures
- Use Cavalieri's Principle to compare volumes

Stage 2—Assessment Evidence

Performance Tasks: **T**

- Packaging problem: What is the ideal container for shipping bulk quantities of M&M's packages cost-effectively to stores? (Note: the "best" mathematical answer—a sphere—is not the best solution to this problem.)
- As a consultant to the United Nations, propose the least controversial 2-dimensional map of the world. Explain your mathematical reasoning.

Other Evidence: **OE**

a. Odd-numbered problems in full Chapter Review, pp. 516–519

b. Progress on self-test, p. 515

c. Homework: each third question in subchapter reviews and all explorations

Stage 3—Learning Plan

Learning Activities: **L**

- Investigate the relationship of surface areas and volume of various containers (e.g., tuna fish cans, cereal boxes, Pringles, candy packages).

- Investigate different map projections to determine their mathematical accuracy (i.e., degree of distortion).

a. Read Chapter 10 in UCSMP Geometry

b. Exploration 22, p. 504

c. Exploration 22, p. 482

d. Exploration 25, p. 509

Introduction
Stage 1
Stage 2
Stage 3
Peer review
Exercises
Process sheets
Glossary

UbD: Stages of Backward Design

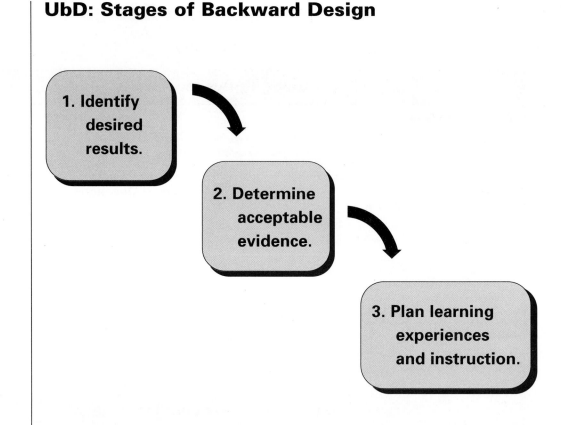

The backward design approach consists of three general stages:

Stage 1. Identify Desired Results. In Stage 1 we consider the goals. What should students know, understand, and be able to do? What big ideas are worthy of understanding and implied in the established goals (e.g., content standards, curriculum objectives)? What "enduring" understandings are desired? What provocative questions are worth pursuing to guide student inquiry into these big ideas? What specific knowledge and skills are targeted in the goals and needed for effective performance?

Stage 2. Determine Acceptable Evidence. In the second stage we consider evidence of learning. How will we know if students have achieved the desired results and met the content standards? How will we know that students *really* understand the identified big ideas? What will we accept as evidence of proficiency? The backward design orientation suggests that we think about our design in terms of the collected assessment evidence needed to document and validate that the desired results of Stage 1 have been achieved.

Stage 3. Plan Learning Experiences and Instruction. With identified results and appropriate evidence of understanding in mind, it is now time to finalize a plan for the learning activities. What will need to be taught and coached, and how should it best be taught, in light of the performance goals? What sequence of activity best suits the desired results? In planning the learning activities, we consider the WHERETO elements (described later) as guidelines. Those guidelines can be summed up in a question: How will we make learning both engaging *and* effective, given the goals and needed evidence?

1-Page Template

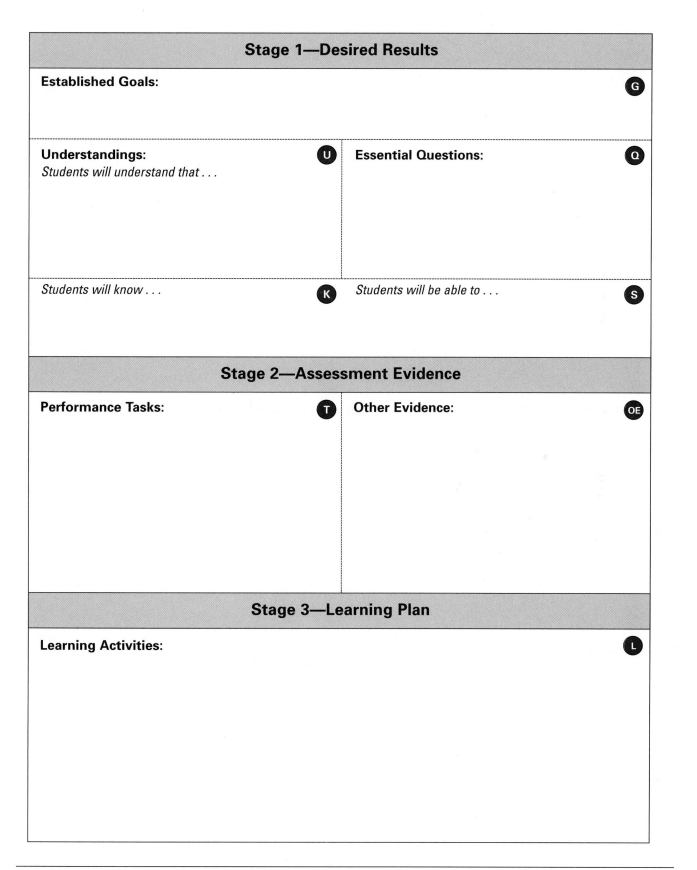

Stage 1—Desired Results

Established Goals: **G**

Understandings: **U**
Students will understand that . . .

Essential Questions: **Q**

Students will know . . .   **K**

Students will be able to . . .   **S**

Stage 2—Assessment Evidence

Performance Tasks: **T**

Other Evidence: **OE**

Stage 3—Learning Plan

Learning Activities: **L**

Introduction · Stage 1 · Stage 2 · Stage 3 · Peer review · Exercises · Process sheets · Glossary

Introduction

Stage 1

Stage 2

Stage 3

Peer review

Exercises

Process sheets

Glossary

1-Page Template with Design Questions

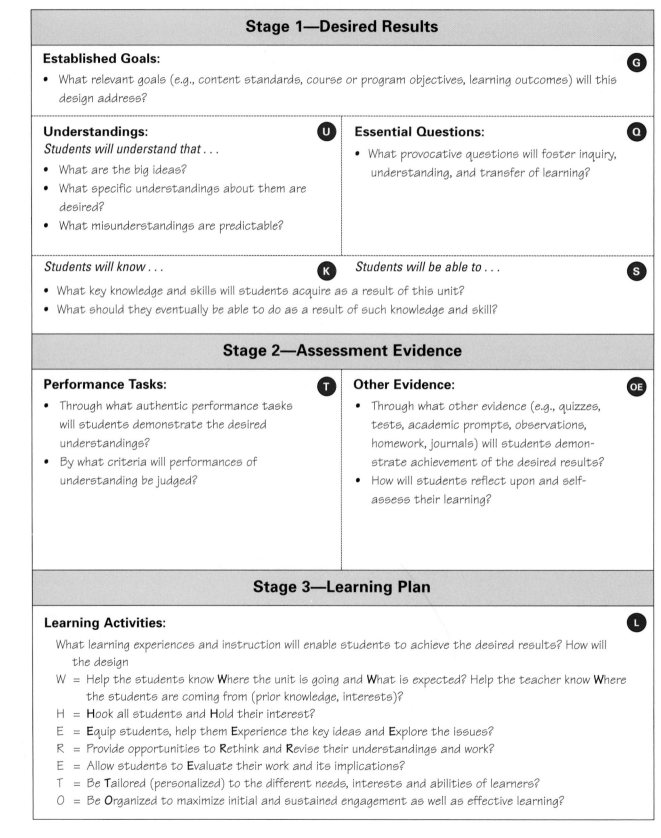

Stage 1—Desired Results

Established Goals: **G**

- What relevant goals (e.g., content standards, course or program objectives, learning outcomes) will this design address?

Understandings: **U**
Students will understand that . . .

- What are the big ideas?
- What specific understandings about them are desired?
- What misunderstandings are predictable?

Essential Questions: **Q**

- What provocative questions will foster inquiry, understanding, and transfer of learning?

Students will know . . . **K**

- What key knowledge and skills will students acquire as a result of this unit?
- What should they eventually be able to do as a result of such knowledge and skill?

Students will be able to . . . **S**

Stage 2—Assessment Evidence

Performance Tasks: **T**

- Through what authentic performance tasks will students demonstrate the desired understandings?
- By what criteria will performances of understanding be judged?

Other Evidence: **OE**

- Through what other evidence (e.g., quizzes, tests, academic prompts, observations, homework, journals) will students demonstrate achievement of the desired results?
- How will students reflect upon and self-assess their learning?

Stage 3—Learning Plan

Learning Activities: **L**

What learning experiences and instruction will enable students to achieve the desired results? How will the design

W = Help the students know **W**here the unit is going and **W**hat is expected? Help the teacher know **W**here the students are coming from (prior knowledge, interests)?

H = **H**ook all students and **H**old their interest?

E = **E**quip students, help them **E**xperience the key ideas and **E**xplore the issues?

R = Provide opportunities to **R**ethink and **R**evise their understandings and work?

E = Allow students to **E**valuate their work and its implications?

T = Be **T**ailored (personalized) to the different needs, interests and abilities of learners?

O = Be **O**rganized to maximize initial and sustained engagement as well as effective learning?

Alignment: The Logic of Backward Design
Westward Expansion and Pioneer Life
(What Do the Desired Results Imply?)

Stage 1	Stage 2	Stage 3
If the desired result is for learners to . . .	*Then, you need evidence of the students' ability to . . .*	*Then, the learning activities need to . . .*
Understand that . . . (U) • Many lives were sacrificed and hardships endured to settle the West. • Many pioneers had naive ideas about the opportunities and difficulties of moving west. • All pioneers display great ingenuity, courage, and collaboration in overcoming obstacles. **And thoughtfully consider the questions . . .** (Q) • Why do people move? Why did pioneers leave their homes to head west? • What is a pioneer? • Why did some pioneers survive and prosper while others did not?	• Infer from examining primary and secondary accounts why the migrants left home to travel west and what pioneers' lives were *really* like. • Find and select appropriate information sources about westward movement and pioneer life (e.g., in the library and on the Internet). • Use pioneer terms and historical facts accurately in various contexts. **Then, the tasks to be assessed need to include some things like . . .** (T) • Create a museum display, including artifacts, pictures, and diary entries, depicting a week in the life of a family of settlers living on the prairie. (What common misunderstandings do folks today have about prairie life?) • Write one letter a day (each representing a month of travel) to a friend "back east" describing life on the wagon train and the prairie. • Pass a test on basic facts about westward expansion and prairie life. (OE) • Respond orally or in writing to one of the Essential Questions. • Create drawings showing hardships of pioneer life.	*Help students* (L) 1. Learn about westward movement and prairie life, 2. Empathize with the pioneers and their challenges and 3. Show what they have learned by: • Reading, viewing, and discussing primary and secondary information sources. • Reading and discussing relevant literature, such as *Little House on the Prairie.* • Using computer simulations, such as *Oregon Trail 2.* • Making the big ideas real through experiential activities (e.g., Prairie Day) near the outset of the unit and discussing and reflecting on the meaning of the experiences. • Gathering additional information through research. • Showing what an interesting and effective museum display is like. • Offering models and providing guided practice in writing letters and journals. • Providing feedback on the performance and product work under construction.

Introduction　Stage 1　Stage 2　Stage 3　Peer review　Exercises　Process sheets　Glossary

Alignment: The Logic of Backward Design Template

(What Do the Desired Results Imply?)

Stage 1	Stage 2	Stage 3
If the desired result is for learners to . . .	*Then, you need evidence of the students' ability to . . .*	*Then, the learning activities need to . . .*
Understand that . . . U		L
And thoughtfully consider the questions . . . Q	**Then, the tasks to be assessed need to include some things like . . .** T	
	OE	

Introduction
Stage 1
Stage 2
Stage 3
Peer review
Exercises
Process sheets
Glossary

Sample Design for a UbD Workshop

Stage 1—Desired Results

Understandings: (U)

Students will understand that . . .

- Effective curriculum design evolves backward from clear goals and is aligned across all three stages.
- UbD is a way of thinking more carefully about curriculum design; it is not a prescriptive program.
- Using design standards improves quality.
- The UbD design process is nonlinear and iterative.
- Teaching and assessing for understanding enhances learning of content standards.

Essential Questions: (Q)

- Why are the best curriculum designs backward?
- What is good design? How does UbD support effective curriculum design?
- How does continuous improvement apply to curriculum design?
- Why teach for understanding?
- How will we know that students *really* understand?
- What is the difference between understanding and knowing?

Students will know . . . (K)

- The three stages of backward design
- Characteristics of big ideas and essential questions
- The six facets of understanding and GRASPS
- The WHERETO elements of instructional planning
- Design standards for UbD

Students will be able to . . . (S)

- Develop understandings, essential questions, and assessment evidence
- Draft a unit in the template
- Review designs against the design standards

Stage 2—Assessment Evidence

Performance Tasks: (T)

- Develop a draft design using the UbD template and tools. (Design meets most of the UbD design standards.)
- Participate in a peer review process using design standards and provide feedback to designers.

Other Evidence: (OE)

- Pre- and post-workshop surveys
- Observations of participants' understandings, questions, misconceptions, frustrations
- Quality of responses on exercises and worksheets
- Participant self-assessments and reflections on their understandings and design
- Written and oral feedback to presenter

Stage 3—Learning Plan

Learning Activities: (L)

- Overview of session; performance goal; meet in role-alike groups
- Exercise on good design
- Study and discuss before and after design examples
- Guided design work on each stage
- Watch and discuss relevant video clips
- Gallery walk to review participants' designs
- Lecture and discussion on key design elements and issues
- Peer review against design standards
- Action planning for UbD (classroom, school, or district level)

Introduction

Stage 1

Stage 2

Stage 3

Peer review

Exercises

Process sheets

Glossary

Developing a UbD Action Plan
Using Backward Design

Stage 1—Desired Results

Established Goals: **G**

What are our goals (e.g., what would be seen in classrooms, schools, and the district if designing, teaching, and assessing for understanding were the norm)?

Understandings: **U**

To achieve our goals, what understandings will be needed (e.g., by teachers, administrators, policymakers, parents, students)?

Essential Questions: **Q**

What essential questions will focus our goals, stimulate conversation, and guide our actions?

K **S**

To achieve our goals, what knowledge and skills will be needed (e.g., by teachers, administrators, policymakers, parents, students)?

Stage 2—Assessment Evidence

E

What will count as evidence of our success?

What baseline data (e.g., student achievement gaps; staff understandings, attitudes, and practices; organizational capacity) should be collected?

What are key indicators of our short-term and long-term progress?

Stage 3—Action Plan

Actions: **L**

What actions will help us realize our goals efficiently?

What short- and long-term actions will we take?

Who should be involved? informed? responsible?

What predictable concerns will be raised? How will we address them?

Introduction

Stage 1

Stage 2

Stage 3

Peer review

Exercises

Process sheets

Glossary

UbD Curriculum Framework: The Macro View

Understanding by Design offers a 3-stage backward design framework for developing units of study (micro level). The same process guides larger-scale curriculum development for courses and programs (macro level). The following visual represents a UbD curriculum structure for building a coherent curriculum, spiraling around big ideas, essential questions, and core assessments.

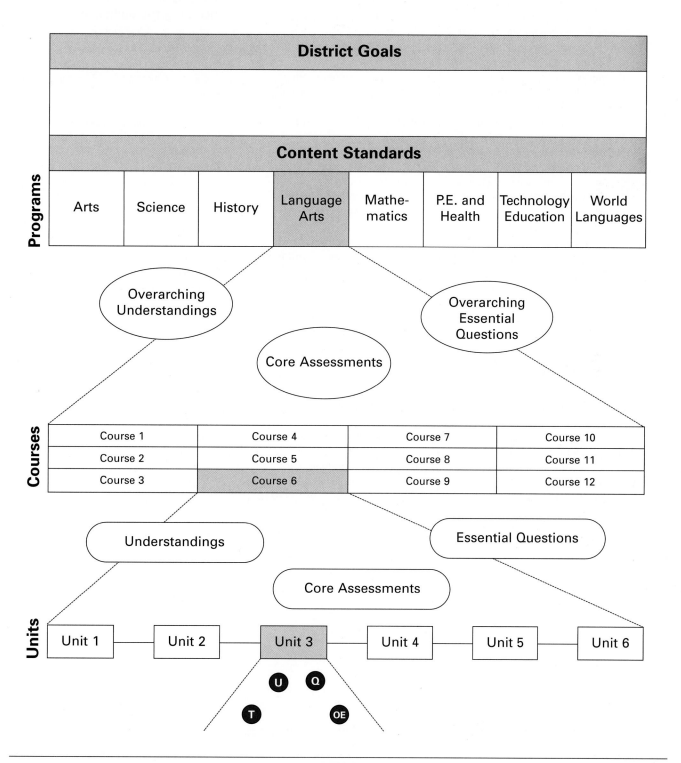

UbD Curriculum Map for Stage 1
U.S. History, Grade 7

Course Understanding	Course Essential Questions	Course Skills
Students will understand that...	**Are we becoming the nation we set out to be?**	**Students will develop skills for historical and geographical analysis, including the ability to**
• The preambles to the Declaration of Independence and the Constitution establish the ideal for why we need government and principles that should guide the government's decision-making—providing a framework by which we can evaluate our nation's progress and suggest means for improvement. • Progress often comes at a price—the extent of which allows history to judge its success. • Individuals, even outside of elected leaders, can have a profound impact on history. • The United States abandoned its isolationist policy as economic and geopolitical interests began to change, becoming the dominant world power with new challenges and responsibilities. • To promote the general welfare, the government has attempted to balance the need to let the market operate freely with the need to regulate it in order to safeguard public interests. • Geography continues to influence the economic, political, and social development of our nation. • Throughout U.S. history, war-time fears and perceived threats to security have led to the denial of certain civil liberties. • U.S. culture reflects the events of the day and shapes how we perceive ourselves. • Ratification of the Constitution did not end the debate on governmental power; rather, economic, regional, social, and ideological tensions that emerged, and continue to emerge, further debates over the meaning of the Constitution and the proper balance between federal and state power. • The government and public commitment to civil and equal rights has advanced.	• What price progress? • How do individuals make a difference? • How did the United States become *the* world power? • What issues determine our involvement in foreign affairs? • Why did the United States abandon its traditional isolationist foreign policy? • Should commitment to the ideals in the Constitution extend beyond our borders? • What is the government's responsibility to promote the general welfare? • Should the government be more hands-on or hands-off with regard to the economy? • How does geography influence history? • Why is there a struggle between security and liberty? • How has the cultural identity of the United States changed over time? • How has the struggle between states' rights and federal power played out over time? • How has the government's commitment to establish justice changed over time? • How has the definition of justice changed to become more inclusive?	• Identify, examine, and interpret primary and secondary source documents to increase understanding of events and life in U.S. history. • Make connections between the past and the present. • Sequence significant events in U.S. history from Constitutional times to present. • Interpret ideas and events from different historical perspectives. • Evaluate and discuss issues orally and in writing. • Create and explain maps, diagrams, tables, charts, and graphs. • Analyze and interpret maps to explain relationships among landforms, water features, climatic characteristics, and historical events. • Analyze political cartoons, political advertisements, pictures, and other graphic media. • Distinguish between relevant and irrelevant information. • Review information for accuracy, separating fact from opinion. • Identify a problem and recommend solutions. • Select and defend positions in writing, discussion, and debate.

UbD Curriculum Map for Stage 1 (continued)
U.S. History, Grade 7

Unit Understandings	Unit Essential Questions
Students will understand that . . .	
1. The Declaration of Independence and Constitution establish the ideal for why we need government and principles that should guide the government's decision-making.	1. Why do we need a constitution? *Related Course EQs: How do individuals make a difference? What is the government's responsibility to promote the general welfare?*
2. The Constitution was written in reaction to the inadequacy of government (under the Articles of Confederation) to provide for the protection of natural rights and to promote democratic ideals.	2. Why is the constitution structured the way it is? *Related Course EQs: How do individuals make a difference? What price progress? What is the government's responsibility to promote the general welfare? How does geography influence history? How has the struggle between states' rights and federal power played out over time?*
3. Geography influenced the economic, political, and social concerns of the founders, which was reflected in the compromises made within the Constitution.	3. Why is the U.S. Constitution called a living document? Related Course EQs: *What is the government's responsibility to promote the general welfare? How has the government's commitment to "establish justice" changed over time? How has the cultural identity of America changed over time?*
4. The U.S. Constitution is the most enduring and successful blueprint for self-government in human history because it established a government that derives its power from the people, shares power between national and state governments, protects the rights of individuals, and provides a system for orderly change through amendments and interpretation.	
Individuals Who Made a Difference	**Resources**
John Locke, Charles-Louis de Secondat Montesquieu, Jean-Jacques Rousseau, Daniel Shays, George Washington, Thomas Jefferson, Ben Franklin, James Madison, Alexander Hamilton	*History Alive! The Constitution in a New Nation*—The Roots of Government (1.1, 1.2, 1.3, 1.4); The Creation of the Constitution (2.1, 2.2, 2.3, 2.4, 1.4); The Creation of the Bill of Rights (3.1, 3.2, 3.3, 1.4); The Constitution in Action 1789–1820 (4.1, 4.2, 1.4); The Constitution in Action Today (5.1, 5.2, 5.3)
	Primary Source Documents
	• John Locke's writings on natural rights
	• The Declaration of Independence
	• The U.S. Constitution
	• Federalist Papers 10 and 51
	Courtesy of Mark Wise and the Middle School Social Studies Team, West Windsor-Plainsboro, NJ

Introduction · Stage 1 · Stage 2 · Stage 3 · Peer review · Exercises · Process sheets · Glossary

Introduction

Stage 1

Stage 2

Stage 3

Peer review

Exercises

Process sheets

Glossary

Curriculum Alignment Through Assessment

Quarterly Assessments, Grades 6–12

Grade	Expository	Persuasive	Literary Analysis	Creative and Expressive
6	Research paper	Position paper	Literary essay on setting or conflict	Original myth
7	Autobiography	Policy evaluation	Literary essay on character	Literary persona
8	Research report	Problem/ solution essay	Literary essay on symbolism	Narrative fiction
9	Cause and effect essay	Editorial	Analysis of multiple literary elements	Poetry
10	Research paper	Social issue essay	Critical lens essay	Historical persona
11	Definition essay	Argumentative essay	Comparative genre essay	Parody or satire
12	Research paper	Position paper	Response to literary criticism	Irony

Courtesy of Greece Central School District, New York

The Six Facets of Understanding

Facet 1—EXPLANATION

Sophisticated and apt explanations and theories that provide knowledgeable and justified accounts of events, actions, and ideas. Why is that so? What explains such events? What accounts for such action? How can we prove it? To what is the action connected? How does this work?

Facet 2—INTERPRETATION

Narratives, translations, metaphors, images, and artistry that provide meaning. What does it mean? Why does it matter? What of it? What does it illustrate or illuminate in human experience? How does it relate to me? What makes sense?

Facet 3—APPLICATION

Ability to use knowledge effectively in new situations and diverse contexts. How and where can we apply this knowledge, skill, process? How should my thinking and action be modified to meet the demands of this particular situation?

Facet 4—PERSPECTIVE

Critical and insightful points of view. From whose point of view? From which vantage point? What is assumed or tacit that needs to be made explicit and considered? What is justified or warranted? Is there adequate evidence? Is it reasonable? What are the strengths and weaknesses of the idea? Is it plausible? What are its limits? What is a novel way to look at this?

Facet 5—EMPATHY

The ability to get inside another person's feelings and worldview. How does it seem to you? What do they see that I don't? What do I need to experience if I am to understand? What was the author, artist or performer feeling, seeing, and trying to make me feel and see?

Facet 6—SELF-KNOWLEDGE

The wisdom to know one's ignorance and how one's patterns of thought and action inform as well as prejudice understanding. How does who I am shape my views? What are the limits of my understanding? What are my blind spots? What am I prone to misunderstand because of prejudice, habit, and style? How do I learn best? What strategies work for me?

Introduction · Stage 1 · Stage 2 · Stage 3 · Peer review · Exercises · Process sheets · Glossary

Introduction

Stage 1

Stage 2

Stage 3

Peer review

Exercises

Process sheets

Glossary

UbD Design Standards

Stage 1—To what extent does the design focus on the big ideas of targeted content?

Consider: Are . . .

○ The targeted understandings enduring, based on transferable, big ideas at the heart of the discipline and in need of uncoverage?

○ The targeted understandings framed by questions that spark meaningful connections, provoke genuine inquiry and deep thought, and encourage transfer?

○ The essential questions provocative, arguable, and likely to generate inquiry around the central ideas (rather than a "pat" answer)?

○ Appropriate goals (e.g., content standards, benchmarks, curriculum objectives) identified?

○ Valid and unit-relevant knowledge and skills identified?

Stage 2—To what extent do the assessments provide fair, valid, reliable and sufficient measures of the desired results?

Consider: Are . . .

○ Students asked to exhibit their understanding through authentic performance tasks?

○ Appropriate criterion-based scoring tools used to evaluate student products and performances?

○ A variety of appropriate assessment formats used to provide additional evidence of learning?

○ The assessments used as feedback for students and teachers, as well as for evaluation?

○ Students encouraged to self-assess?

Stage 3—To what extent is the learning plan effective and engaging?

Consider: Will the students . . .

○ Know *where* they're going (the learning goals), *why* the material is important (reason for learning the content) and *what* is required of them (unit goal, performance requirements and evaluative criteria)?

○ Be *hooked*—engaged in digging into the big ideas (e.g., through inquiry, research, problem solving, and experimentation)?

○ Have adequate opportunities to *explore* and *experience* big ideas and receive instruction to *equip* them for the required performances?

○ Have sufficient opportunities to *rethink, rehearse, revise* and *refine* their work based upon timely feedback?

○ Have an opportunity to *evaluate* their work, reflect on their learning, and set goals?

Consider: Is the learning plan . . .

○ *Tailored* and flexible to address the interests and learning styles of all students?

○ *Organized* and sequenced to maximize engagement and effectiveness?

Overall Design—To what extent is the entire unit coherent, with the elements of all three stages aligned?

Frequently Asked Questions About Backward Design

This three-stage approach makes sense. So, why do you call it "backward" design?

We use the term "backward" in two ways.

First, plan with the "end in mind" by first clarifying the learning you seek; that is, the desired learning results (Stage 1). Then, think about the evidence needed to certify that students have achieved those desired learnings (Stage 2). Finally, plan the means to the end; that is, the teaching and learning activities and resources to help students achieve the goals (Stage 3). We have found that backward design, whether applied by individual teachers or district curriculum committees, helps to avoid the twin sins of activity-oriented and coverage-oriented curriculum planning.

Our second use of the term refers to the fact that this approach is backward relative to the way some educators plan. For years, we have observed that curriculum planning often translates into listing activities (Stage 3), with only a general sense of intended results and little, if any, attention to assessment evidence (Stage 2). Many teachers have commented that the UbD planning template makes sense but feels awkward, given that it requires a break from comfortable planning habits.

Backward design is not a new concept. In 1948 Ralph Tyler articulated a similar approach to curriclum planning. In more recent times, outcome-based education advocates, such as William Spady, recommended that curriculum be "designed down" from desired outcomes. In the best-selling book 7 *Habits of Highly Effective People,* Stephen Covey conveys a similar finding: Effective people plan with the end in mind (Covey, 1989).

Do you have to follow the template order (top to bottom) when you design?

No. Backward design does not demand a rigid sequence. The process is inherently non-linear with various entry points that lead to an organized product. The final design is presented in a logical format, via the UbD template. While the final *product* reflects the

Introduction

Stage 1

Stage 2

Stage 3

Peer review

Exercises

Process sheets

Glossary

Introduction

Stage 1

Stage 2

Stage 3

Peer review

Exercises

Process sheets

Glossary

three-stage logic, the designing *process* typically unfolds in an iterative and unpredictable way, with the end result in mind. Think of the difference between cooks experimenting in the kitchen and their final product: a new recipe. They may be inspired to start in various ways: with a fresh seasonal ingredient, a specific audience for whom to cook or the desire to test out new preparations. Much trial and error is likely as various combinations of ingredients, spices, temperatures, and timings are tried. But the final product is presented to others in an efficient step-by-step form. Similarly, while the UbD template provides a format for sharing the final design "recipe," it does not specify the sequence of the design process. (And, of course, designs as well as recipes will often be revised following feedback from peer review and use with students.)

Fill the template with your ideas as they come to you. We have observed that certain variables, such as subject area, topic, and a teacher's style, seem to influence the design sequence. (See page 276 for specific entry points that may be helpful as you work within the three stages.) Regardless of approach, designers should complete the template and routinely check the emerging design against the UbD Design Standards to ensure that the process yields the desired high-quality design.

Is Understanding by Design appropriate for all grades and subjects?

Yes—as long as the goals involve some big ideas worth understanding as opposed to those requiring only drill and recall (e.g., touch typing).

Can you use the three stages of backward design (and the UbD template) for lesson planning?

We have chosen the unit as a focus for design because the key elements of UbD—big ideas, enduring understandings, essential questions, and performances of understanding—are too complex and multifaceted to be satisfactorily addressed within a single lesson. For instance, essential questions are meant to be revisited over time, not answered by the end of a class period.

Nonetheless, we have found that the larger unit goals provide the context in which individual lessons are planned. Teachers often report that careful attention to Stages 1 and 2 sharpens their lesson planning, resulting in more purposeful teaching and improved learning.

How does a unit fit into an entire course or K–12 program?

While backward design certainly applies to the design of individual units, the process is also an effective way of mapping a coherent curriculum. When applying backward design to curriculum mapping, we consider our desired results—including content standards and other exit outcomes—and then map backward (e.g., 12 to K) to ensure that all the important results are explicitly addressed through the courses and units. Backward mapping helps to identify any gaps and redundancies in the curriculum, and to target needed curriculum revisions and additions.

Understanding by Design suggests a particular spin on the mapping process: Instead of simply listing the topics taught, a UbD map specifies the big ideas and essential questions that are addressed at various points in the curriculum. This approach helps to identify the overarching ideas and essential questions that provide important throughlines in the curriculum. Throughlines are big ideas, not necessarily interdisciplinary, that run vertically throughout the curriculum. For example, in social studies an overarching EQ might be, *Why do people move?* This same question would then be examined in 3rd grade for the westward movement, 5th grade when we study the explorers, and 10th grade with immigration.

Additionally, we propose that a UbD map should include core assessment tasks that all students would perform to demonstrate their understanding of key ideas and processes. (Of course, these tasks would be accompanied by agreed-upon scoring rubrics.) We believe that such curriculum mapping brings conceptual clarity and coherence to the curriculum.

The UbD Web site (ubdexchange.org) enables electronic curriculum mapping and the linking of individual UbD units to the map. The maps can be generated online, easily amended, and printed on Excel spreadsheets.

Introduction

Stage 1

Stage 2

Stage 3

Peer review

Exercises

Process sheets

Glossary

Templates

1-, 2-, and 6-page Versions with Samples

1-Page Template with Questions

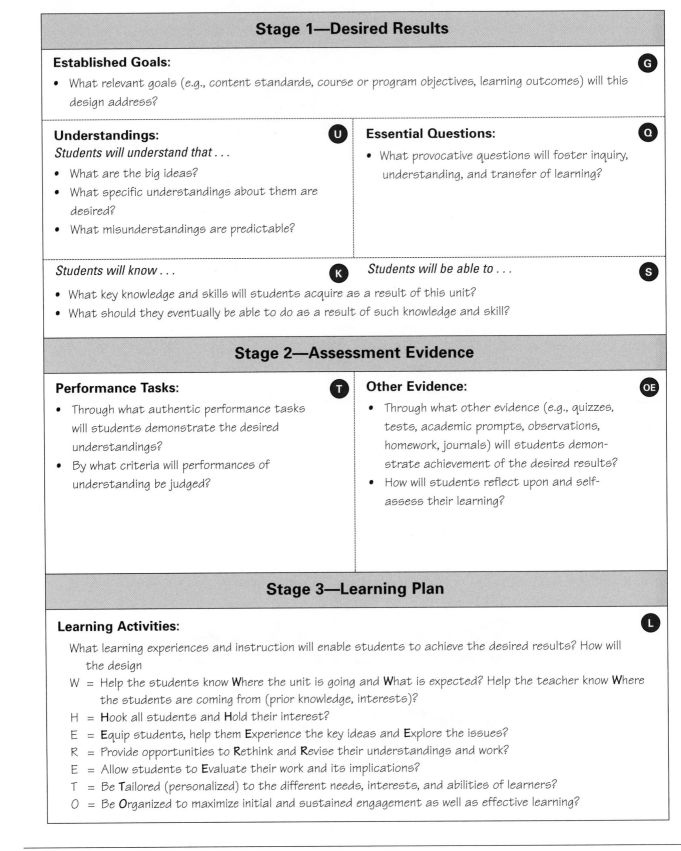

Stage 1—Desired Results

Established Goals: **G**

- What relevant goals (e.g., content standards, course or program objectives, learning outcomes) will this design address?

Understandings: **U**
Students will understand that . . .

- What are the big ideas?
- What specific understandings about them are desired?
- What misunderstandings are predictable?

Essential Questions: **Q**

- What provocative questions will foster inquiry, understanding, and transfer of learning?

Students will know . . . **K**

- What key knowledge and skills will students acquire as a result of this unit?
- What should they eventually be able to do as a result of such knowledge and skill?

Students will be able to . . . **S**

Stage 2—Assessment Evidence

Performance Tasks: **T**

- Through what authentic performance tasks will students demonstrate the desired understandings?
- By what criteria will performances of understanding be judged?

Other Evidence: **OE**

- Through what other evidence (e.g., quizzes, tests, academic prompts, observations, homework, journals) will students demonstrate achievement of the desired results?
- How will students reflect upon and self-assess their learning?

Stage 3—Learning Plan

Learning Activities: **L**

What learning experiences and instruction will enable students to achieve the desired results? How will the design

W = Help the students know **W**here the unit is going and **W**hat is expected? Help the teacher know **W**here the students are coming from (prior knowledge, interests)?

H = **H**ook all students and **H**old their interest?

E = **E**quip students, help them **E**xperience the key ideas and **E**xplore the issues?

R = Provide opportunities to **R**ethink and **R**evise their understandings and work?

E = Allow students to **E**valuate their work and its implications?

T = Be **T**ailored (personalized) to the different needs, interests, and abilities of learners?

O = Be **O**rganized to maximize initial and sustained engagement as well as effective learning?

Templates
Stage 1
Stage 2
Stage 3
Peer review
Exercises
Process sheets
Glossary

1-Page Template

Templates

Stage 1

Stage 2

Stage 3

Peer review

Exercises

Process sheets

Glossary

Stage 1—Desired Results

Established Goals: **G**

Understandings: **U**
Students will understand that . . .

Essential Questions: **Q**

Students will know . . . **K**

Students will be able to . . . **S**

Stage 2—Assessment Evidence

Performance Tasks: **T**

Other Evidence: **OE**

Stage 3—Learning Plan

Learning Activities: **L**

Sample 1-Page Template
Science, Grades 5–8

Templates

Stage 1—Desired Results

Established Goals: **G**

Tennessee Science Standard 4.5c—Limited resources dictate a need for prioritization. 4.5d—The total impact of developments in science and technology on the economy is seldom known at the time of development. 4.6d—The risks and cost benefits must be carefully considered when developing new technology or curtailing existing technology.

Tennessee Science, developed by Joyce Tatum

Understandings: **U**   **Essential Questions:**   **Q**
Students will understand that . . .
- A balance must exist in the environment that should allow for clean air, fresh water, and soil capable of producing food.
- All people are responsible for maintaining the balance.
- Wetlands must be protected to maintain clean water.
- Each citizen can take action to maintain a clean water supply.

- Why is the environmental balance necessary to continue life?
- How much clean air and water is enough?
- If natural resources are so important to a healthy planet, why is conservation such an issue?
- Why are wetlands necessary?
- How can we balance economic progress and protection of wetlands?

Students will know . . .   **K**   *Students will be able to . . .*   **S**
- The importance and relationships of phases of the water cycle; consequences of misuse of wetlands; interconnectedness of the food chain; decision-making models.

- Analyze environmental priorities.
- Discuss pros and cons of environmental and economic decision making at the community and personal levels; compare and contrast a variety of environmental sites.

Stage 2—Assessment Evidence

Performance Tasks: **T**

Goal: As a member of a research team, you will gather environmental evidence about your site.
Audience: The Nature Conservancy will convene a panel of citizens to review the case studies to determine the highest quality study. *Situation:* The Nature Conservancy is contracting research teams to compile environmental and economic evidence about several locations. The Conservancy has received a $20 million grant from Bill Gates to present both economic and environmental issues to the general population of these locations and to U.S. citizens.

  Participants will develop a case study for one of seven sites across the country. The case study will include recently published newspaper articles with analysis, community statements and comments, scientific data, and an analysis of key economic developments, a timeline of events, and a recommended decision-making model. (Other tasks: TVA task force member to assess impact on a local site. Voice your opinion locally in a letter to the editor. Written prompts on the literature studied.)

Stage 3—Learning Plan

Learning Activities: **L**

Introductory Activity: Students read and review five recent news articles about flood-plain regulation in the Brainerd area. Students answer who? what? when? where? why? so what? what else? These articles will be shared through a jig-saw strategy and followed by organizing questions suggested by the groups. A timeline of events will be established from the events in the articles. *Journal responses:* How do these events affect me, you, and us? *Research topics:* development of Eastgate Mall, golf course development, East Ridge house on the flood plain, Flood of 1971. *TVA and Brainerd Socratic Seminars:* Mummy, Oh Mummy, Chattanooga Goo, Sarah Cynthia Sylvia Stout, Brother Eagle, Sister Sky, topographic maps. *Scientific Investigations:* Runoff: What happens to water and asphalt? We All Live Down Stream: What are our choices? Water and Oil: Do they mix? *Looking at Both Sides:* How much clean water is enough?

Sample 1-Page Template
Mathematics, High School

Stage 1—Desired Results

Established Goals: **G**
Students will . . .
- Determine the conditional probability of two events (Bayes' law).
- Solve probability problems involving permutations, combinations, and conditional probability.

From the Alberta (Canada) Mathematics Program of Studies

Understandings: **U**
Students will understand that . . .
- Probability and expectation can be used to make (not always obvious) predictions.
- The best way to count is often not by counting.

Essential Questions: **Q**
- How can we predict the outcomes of events?
- How can we quantify our predictions about outcomes occurring?
- How is expectation different from probability?
- What is the best way of making predictions?

Students will know . . .   **K**
- How to count using fundamental counting principle, permutations, and combinations.

Students will be able to . . .   **S**
- Calculate probabilities, z-scores for using normal distribution, and tables.
- Calculate probabilities using binomial distribution.

Stage 2—Assessment Evidence

Performance Tasks: **T**
- Performance Assessment Outline: Design a game that you know you will win (in the long run). Convince us by using combinatorics, probability, and the expectation that you are guaranteed to win. Your game should be easy to describe to potential players, and the outcome of the game should be ambiguous at first glance, or it should seem like the other players will win.

Other Evidence: **OE**
- Have students assess their own game as well as several others for fairness and according to a provided rubric.
- Journal entries: Compare and contrast combinations and permutations; How is expectation different from probability?
- Quizzes and assignments including constructed response tasks.

Stage 3—Learning Plan

Learning Activities: **L**
- Bus problem to motivate and initiate unit: given an *n* x *m* grid, how many ways are there to get from the farthest SW corner to the farthest NE corner, traveling only north or east? This leads to the use of combinations, permutations including repetition, and Pascal's Triangle and the binomial theorem. (Problem-based learning)
- Play a game (students can start thinking about performance task). Bet 1 cent, then roll 4 die. I pay you the total of your four die, in cents, unless you roll one or more pairs. In that case, you pay me the total shown on your four die.
- Plinko (from the Price is Right)—another opportunity for problem-based learning. Students will have to analyze Plinko-type games and the expected results.
- Probability distributions: How can predictions be made for large groups of people. (Why does car insurance cost more for boys than girls?)
- Complete exercises from chapters 7–9 of Mathpower.

Sample 1-Page Template
English, High School

Stage 1—Desired Results

Established Goals: **G**

NJ English/Language Arts
Standard 3.4—All students will read various materials and texts with comprehension and critical analysis.

The Catcher in the Rye developed by David Grant

Understandings: **U**
Students will understand that . . .

- Novelists often provide insights about human experience and inner life through fictional means.
- Writers use a variety of stylistic techniques to engage and persuade their readers.
- Holden Caulfield reflects common adolescent experiences but masks deep-seated personal problems about growing up and relating to others.

Essential Questions: **Q**

- What is the relationship between fiction and truth? What truths can best be rendered fictionally?
- Does Holden represent adolescence? Is he abnormal, or are all adolescents "abnormal"? Who is genuine and who is "phony"? Why do people act phony?
- How do authors hook and hold readers? How does J. D. Salinger engage you?
- How do writers persuade their readers?

Students will know . . . **K**

- The plot and characters of *Catcher in the Rye.*
- Various stylistic techniques that J. D. Salinger employed.

Students will be able to . . . **S**

- Apply interpretive reading strategies.
- Develop a well-reasoned hypothesis.
- Apply the writing process to produce a draft and a revision of persuasive writing.

Stage 2—Assessment Evidence

Performance Tasks: **T**

<u>What's Wrong with Holden?</u> You are a member of an advisory committee for the hospital where Holden Caulfield is telling his story. After a close reading and discussion of Holden's account of the events of the preceding December, your task is to write (1) a summary report for the hospital, and (2) a letter to Holden's parents explaining what is wrong with him. You should prepare for a meeting with the parents to explain and justify your analysis of Holden's behavior.

Other Evidence: **OE**

1. <u>Essay</u>—Students write to explain Holden's concern for authenticity.

2. <u>Letter</u>—Each student writes a one-page letter describing Holden from the point of view of another character.

3. <u>Quizzes</u>—three quizzes on plot details during the course of the unit

4. <u>Journal</u>—responses to readings

Stage 3—Learning Plan

Learning Activities: **L**

- Introduce Essential Questions as well as the final task and rubrics.
- Read and discuss the text.
- Write daily journal entries on prompted and unprompted questions.
- Research underlying psychiatric issues (depression, denial of death, alienation).
- Read and study the John Burns song that gives the book its title.
- Role-play a case worker dealing with various family members and friends.
- Review writing process.

Sample 1-Page Template
Language Arts, Grades 3–5 (Gifted)

Stage 1—Desired Results

Established Goals: **G**

NJ Language Arts   *Cinderella—grades 3–5 (Gifted and Talented)*
Standard 3.4, 3.5—All students will read various materials and text with comprehension and critical analysis.

Developed by John Brown

Understandings: **U**
Students will understand that . . .

- Fairy tales and other folk literature capture universal patterns and recurrent aspects of the human condition.

- Cinderella is a story appearing in many guises around the world and over time.

Essential Questions: **Q**

- What do different versions of the Cinderella story reveal about culture and the story?
- What can fairy tales from around the world teach us about what it means to be human?
- What are the universal or archetypal patterns that manifest in fairy tales and other forms of folk literature?

Students will know . . . **K**

- Key vocabulary terms.
- Characteristics of fairy tales.

Students will be able to . . . **S**

- Classify and compare using a matrix.
- Use writing process skills—idea generation, organizing, drafting, editing, revising.

Stage 2—Assessment Evidence

Performance Tasks: **T**

Now that you and your classmates have completed this study of Cinderella stories from around the world, develop your own version of the story. Your version and those of your classmates will be compiled into a class anthology to be presented to your library media center. Your version should describe and narrate the experiences of a "modern Cinderella" from a culture or society with which you are familiar. Make certain that you include all of the universal characters, events, and symbols encountered in the four other versions you studied. But make certain that your version has a tone, voice, and "feel" of the world you have chosen. Be prepared to share your original version of Cinderella with students in other classrooms, particularly students in kindergarten and first grade.

Stage 3—Learning Plan

Learning Activities: **L**

- Create a classification web, identifying recurrent categories (e.g., characters, events, settings) and their attributes.
- Discuss key questions: What generalizations and principles can you abstract from these four tales? In what ways do all versions confirm or allude to universal experiences and events?
- Identify differing attitudes and reactions presented about similar events depicted in different versions of the tale. Analyze reasons for the differences, including potential causes extending from cultural traditions and norms.

Templates Stage 1 Stage 2 Stage 3 Peer review Exercises Process sheets Glossary

2-Page Template, Page 1

Title: _____ Subject/Course: _____

Topic: _____ Grades: _____ Designers: _____

Stage 1—Desired Results

Established Goals: **G**

Understandings: **U**
Students will understand that . . .

Essential Questions: **Q**

Students will know . . . **K**

Students will be able to . . . **S**

Stage 2—Assessment Evidence

Performance Tasks: *Summary in GRASPS form* **T**

Key Criteria

Other Evidence **OE**

Templates

Stage 1

Stage 2

Stage 3

Peer review

Exercises

Process sheets

Glossary

2-Page Template, Page 2

Stage 3—Learning Plan
Learning Activities   *Consider the WHERETO elements.*   Ⓛ

Templates

Stage 1

Stage 2

Stage 3

Peer review

Exercises

Process sheets

Glossary

Sample 2-Page Template, Page 1
Life Cycles—Interdisciplinary, Grade 2

Title: Life Cycles   Subject/Course: Interdisciplinary

Topic: Needs of Living Things   Grades: 2   Designers: Marie Adams

Stage 1—Desired Results

Established Goals: **(G)**

NY   Math, Science, Technology 4.1, 4.3, 4.4–4.7; Technology 5.1, 5.2, 5.5; Interconnectedness 6.1–6.4; ELA 1.1, 1.2, 2.1; Social Studies 3.1

Understandings: **(U)**
Students will understand that . . .

- All living things have needs and must depend on and interact with resources in their environments in order to survive.
- Living things grow and change, sometimes in predictable patterns—yet often, the adherence to a strict pattern weakens the organism's ability to survive.
- Living things are designed to survive as individuals and as a species, yet survival of an individual or community often requires the death of another living thing.

Essential Questions: **(Q)**

- How is a pea, a prairie dog, a praying mantis or a peacock like a person?
- What do living things need to survive?
- How do living things interact with their environments in order to survive?

Students will know . . . **(K)**

- Life-cycle patterns of insects, plants, and mammals.
- A specific food chain within each region.
- The connection between plants and animals and our own needs for clothing, food, and shelter.
- Characteristics of desert, forest, pond, and ocean environments, including climate and natural resources.

Students will be able to . . . **(S)**

- Use graphic organizers to record and analyze data.
- Apply understandings to design a human habitat in a given environment that meets basic needs.

Stage 2—Assessment Evidence

Performance Tasks: *Summary in GRASPS form* **(T)**

Survivor

This task is a simulation of a survival experience in the wilderness within one of five different environmental regions. Given a collection of materials in imitation of natural resources, students will design and build a model of a human habitat specific to the resources and dangers of the region. The model will show how the student will meet his needs for shelter, food, water, clothing, freedom, power, fun, and belonging.

Key Criteria

- Appropriate habitat for environment
- Meets basic needs for food, clothing, shelter, and defense
- Carefully and neatly crafted

Other Evidence **(OE)**

- Unit Vocabulary Test
- Chapter test from Science/Social Studies Texts
- Review of student science journals
- Project self assessment

38

Templates   Stage 1   Stage 2   Stage 3   Peer review   Exercises   Process sheets   Glossary

Sample 2-Page Template, Page 2
Life Cycles—Interdisciplinary, Grade 2

Stage 3—Learning Plan

Learning Activities ⓛ

Students will

- Plant peas and beans, measure and observe; record observations in a journal; determine stages of growth in the life cycle of plants; apply knowledge to other plants through a cut-and-paste life-cycle activity.
- Observe class monarch caterpillar culture. Read *Caterpillar Diary*.
- Raise mealworms and fruit flies; observe and record stages of growth; determine life cycle of insects.
- Manipulate systems affecting survival (food, water, light, space, and temperature); record observations in journal; look for patterns and draw conclusions.
- View and discuss videotapes about life cycles and basic needs of plants and each animal class.
- Read and discuss chapters on life cycles and basic needs in science and social studies texts; complete worksheets.
- Collect flowers and fruits to find seeds; read fact sheet about how seeds travel; sort seeds into groups according to how they travel; make a poster.
- View the video "Bread: From Farm to Table." Choose a favorite food. Draw the steps you think are used to get your food from farm to table.
- Examine fungi and ferns to learn about spores.
- Listen to and discuss books about plants and animals read aloud by the teacher such as *Plants That Never Ever Bloom, The Popcorn Book, Chickens Aren't The Only Ones*.
- Read *The Pilgrims' First Thanksgiving*. Complete a graphic organizer to identify the ways basic needs were met. Visit the *Mayflower* Web site to view the list of supplies purchased for the voyage. Make a list of items you would take to a new world. Read *Over the River and Through the Wood*. Complete a graphic organizer to identify the ways basic needs were met. Use a Venn diagram to compare the lifestyles of the people in the two books.
- Write a book review comparing the lifestyles of the people in the two books.
- View videos about Native American peoples; hear read-aloud books about Native tribes; use books, Web sites, and posters to research food, shelters, clothing, tools, transportation, and fun of native peoples.
- Read *Legend of the Indian Paintbrush*. Read and hear about other Native American legends and identify common elements; write in the style of a legend to explain something that happens in nature.
- Write a letter to the main character in *Indian Paintbrush* telling him about your region, and how you meet your basic needs using natural resources.
- Read *A House Is a House for Me*. Examine posters and local architecture to determine structure, shape, and materials used in building homes in various regions of the world. Find out why some roofs are flat, some sloped. Find out why Adirondack homes are built with the first floor 3–4 feet off the ground.
- Read in social studies and science texts and supplemental materials about forests, ponds, oceans, deserts and grasslands in the United States. Identify the physical characteristics of each region, and its plant and animal life, and note natural resources that meet basic needs; make a poster to demonstrate what you've learned.
- Choose one region and native animal whose characteristics you admire; research the animal's habitat, food, and life cycle. Write a report about the animal.
- Read *Time to Sleep* and listen to the read-aloud book *Animals in Winter*.
- View bulletin board display to learn about adaptation, hibernation, and migration; complete worksheets about each.
- Practice vocabulary words associated with the unit through reading, writing, listening, speaking, and worksheets.

The teacher will

Post the big questions; Gather and prepare materials and visual displays; Order videos and books; Make and post vocabulary cards; Lead discussions; Teach mini-lesson on each subtopic; Prepare and share with students the exemplars, graphic organizers and rubrics for writing assignments; Prepare goals statements, vocabulary lists, and skills to be learned for weekly communication with parents; Prepare practice activities, graphic organizers and quizzes; Observe and record individual participation in activities; Assess individual progress toward unit goals; and Provide instructional intervention.

Templates

Stage 1

Stage 2

Stage 3

Peer review

Exercises

Process sheets

Glossary

Sample 2-Page Template, Page 1
History and Photography, Grade 4

Title: _History? Whose Story?_   Subject/Course: _History, Photography_

Topic: _VA History—Early 20th_   Grades: _4_   Designers: _Amy_

Stage 1—Desired Results

Established Goals: **G**

<u>VA History Standard, Number 9:</u>
   Describe social transitions and diversity in 20th-century Virginia

<u>National Art Standards—Visual Arts:</u>
   Analyze historic meaning in artworks through inquiry

Understandings: **U**
Students will understand that . . .

- Perception is reality.
- One's experiences influence one's view of history.
- Photography can document universal themes of human existence.
- Photographs can reveal but also mislead.
- Race and gender are two important elements in history and influence historical interpretation.

Essential Questions: **Q**

- History—Whose story is it?
- How do we know what *really* happened in the past?
- How do photographers capture the subject?
- What can a photograph tell about a society?
- How can we "read" a photograph? Can we trust it?
- What roles do race and gender have in creating and interpreting history?

Students will know . . .   **K**

- Key historical events during early 20th-century Virginia, including decline of agricultural society, move from rural to urban society, segregation, and desegregation.
- Basic principles of visual design.

Students will be able to . . .   **S**

- Interpret ideas and actions from different perspectives.
- Compare and contrast primary and secondary information sources.
- Conduct four-part art criticism process.

Stage 2—Assessment Evidence

Performance Tasks: *Summary in GRASPS form*   **T**

The Virginia Historical Society invites you to prepare an exhibit to inform the public about significant transitions that occurred in early 20th-century Virginia society and various points of view through which this history can be seen. The history will be shown through photographs. We have included the photos for the exhibit.

   Your task is to choose two significant events or transition periods. Then, select several photographs that represent each period and show two or more points of view. Because the exhibit's purpose is to inform the public, the photos need to be captioned and include an explanation of the historical situation being shown and the photographer's viewpoint.

Key Criteria

- The significance of the event/time period   • The subject and point of view represented   • The elements of design used by the photographer   • A four-part criticism of the photo (describe, interpret, analyze, evaluate)
- What you think the photographer thought about the subject   • Your personal connection to the photo

Other Evidence   **OE**

- Quiz on historical facts and sequence of events
- Series of journal entries   • Reflections on events and time periods from different perspectives
- Historical analysis sheet (stakeholders and perspectives)

Sample 2-Page Template, Page 2
History and Photography, Grade 4

Stage 3—Learning Plan

Learning Activities   **L**

A brief summary of the key learning activities is provided below.

- Distribute letter from Historical Society (task 1) and rubric. Present photo collection.
- Present students with an engaging photo of people in early 20th-century Virginia, depicting a certain event or time of social transition (i.e., segregated restaurant with white patrons).
- Ask them to create a caption that might accompany the photo in a magazine of the time period. Students share their captions.
- Lead a Socratic Seminar on the photo.
- In the middle of the seminar, present another photo showing the same "event" with a different perspective (i.e., segregated restaurant with African-American patrons).
- Continue seminar, comparing two photos.
- Post and discuss essential questions and understandings.
- Facilitate SQ3R of textbook section and other resource information regarding topic.
- Introduce a representative photo and one from another point of view. Lead students in four-part art criticism process (describe, interpret, analyze, evaluate), which will get them into the history depicted, the human subject, what the photographer wanted us to see. . . .
- Compare and contrast photo with text information (Venn diagram: primary and secondary sources).
- Continue these comparisons with most photos. Complete historical analysis sheet (looking at stakeholders' perspectives and outcomes of event).
- Begin daily journal entries. Prompt: Reflect on the event, considering different perspectives and your personal connection. Share in small groups.
- Repeat activities for other photos on other topics.
- Introduce Performance Task 2: Take a Walk in Someone Else's Shoes. Discuss rubric. Allow class time to complete.
- Present and discuss exemplar for Task 2. Discuss rubric.
- Engage students in self-evaluation.
- Exhibit displays using a "gallery walk."
- Analyze peer selections.
- Reflect on the unit.

Sample 2-Page Template, Page 1

Earth and Space Science, Grade 9

Title: ___Climate___ Subject/Course: ___Science—Earth Science___

Topic: ___Weather___ Grades: ___9___ Designers: ___Jim Dixon___

Stage 1—Desired Results

Established Goals: **G**

MA Strand 2.8 Earth and Space Science Strand 2, standard 8: Examine models and illustrate that global wind patterns within the atmosphere are determined by the unequal heating between the equator and poles, Earth's rotation, and the distribution of land and ocean.

Understandings: **U**

Students will understand that . . .

- The unequal heating between the equator and poles, Earth's rotation, and the distribution of land and ocean generate the global wind patterns that determine climate.
- Most of what goes on in the universe involves some form of energy being transformed into another. Transformations of energy usually produce some energy in the form of heat, which spreads around by radiation and conduction into cooler places.

Essential Questions: **Q**

- What causes weather and wind patterns?
- What factors affect climate?
- How do events in one geographical area affect another?
- How does climate affect agriculture?
- How can I apply these factors to locations on Earth to determine the climate?

Students will know . . . **K**

- Causes of wind and weather patterns.
- Factors affecting climate.
- Causes of the Coriolis effect.
- How events in one geographical area affect another.
- How climate affects agriculture.

Students will be able to . . . **S**

- Interpret data illustrating the relationship between air pressure and temperature.
- Interpret isobar maps of gradient pressure.
- Apply the concepts of Newton's First Law, the spherical geometry of the earth, and centripetal acceleration to the Coriolis effect.

Stage 2—Assessment Evidence

Performance Tasks: *Summary in GRASPS form* **T**

Comparing Climates

Students will be asked to research the climate in our area and two other areas. One will be at our latitude but in the interior of the continent. The other will be at our longitude but at a tropical location. The students will compare the climates of these locations in terms of climate-determining factors. They will do this in teams representing a climatological consulting firm seeking an account with a large agricultural business that has farms in each area.

Key Criteria

- Accuracy of predictions
- Thoroughness of explanation
- Quality of presentation

Other Evidence **OE**

- Open-book exam
- Quizzes on readings

Templates
Stage 1
Stage 2
Stage 3
Peer review
Exercises
Process sheets
Glossary

Sample 2-Page Template, Page 2
Earth and Space Science, Grade 9

Stage 3—Learning Plan

Learning Activities

1. Students will evaluate circulation cell diagrams by identifying directions of air movement under specific conditions and explain these movements in terms of differential heating.

2. Students will perform the "Let's Go Fly a Kite" activity. This is the hook!

   Let's Go Fly a Kite
   This is the introductory activity for the unit. After completing the first activity, in which students will learn about the relationship between air pressure and wind, they will make predictions about which campus location will have the best kite flying. Then the class will, kites in hand, travel around the campus looking for the best place to fly a kite. Will it be in the center of the football field? At the top of the hill behind the school? In the parking lot? We will then use our results to ask questions about what causes wind patterns, why wind patterns differ and what causes these differences. We may also ask students to travel around the area (go to the beach, etc.) and further compare kite flying. They may possibly videotape these experiments.

3. Students will read articles and perform a series of labs that illustrate Newton's First Law and centripetal acceleration. Then students will relate the the information they gather to the Coriolis effect.

4. Students will analyze maps showing isobars and label the wind directions (and explain their analysis and labeling).

5. Students will study why the angle of the sun's rays causes differential heating. This information will be applied to the different areas of Earth and seasons in our area.

6. Students will analyze an energy budget diagram showing the energy (heat) flow between the sun, Earth's surface and Earth's atmosphere.

7. Students will analyze diagrams showing high- and low-pressure centers and describe air flow around and between these centers.

8. Students will study cases (articles supplied by teacher) in which events such as El Niño and volcanoes in one part of the world are thought to affect weather in another part of the world. They will then propose mechanisms by which this is possible.

9. Students will complete the "Comparing Climates" proposal, including presentations and self-evaluation.

10. Students will take an open-book exam based on the unit understandings.

Templates · Stage 1 · Stage 2 · Stage 3 · Peer review · Exercises · Process sheets · Glossary

Templates

Stage 1

Stage 2

Stage 3

Peer review

Exercises

Process sheets

Glossary

Sample 2-Page Template, Page 1
Modern U.S. History, Grades 11–12

Title: ___A Society Erupts___   Subject/Course: ___Modern American History___

Topic: ___Civil Rights Movement___   Grades: ___11–12___   Designers: ___Mark Williams___

Stage 1—Desired Results

Established Goals: **G**

TEKS U.S. History, Standard No. 7—The student understands the effects of the civil rights movement.

Understandings: **U**
Students will understand that . . .

- Race was (and continues to be) a crucial element in U.S. life and politics.
- We have a difficult time honestly reconciling our beliefs with the record on civil rights.
- Racial, cultural, and socioeconomic differences can lead to misunderstanding, prejudice, oppression, and violence.

Essential Questions: **Q**

- Do our stated ideals cause progress or mask hypocrisy?
- What caused the race riots of the late 1960s?
- Could they happen again?
- Can the racial divisions that have plagued U.S. society be erased?

Students will know . . .   **K**
- History of the modern civil rights movement.
- Key leaders of the civil rights movement.
- Political strategies used to achieve civil rights.
- Government efforts to promote equality.
- Impact of changes in laws on opportunity.

Students will be able to . . .   **S**
- Interpret historical documents.
- Evaluate the effectiveness of government efforts to promote equality.
- Role-play historical figures.

Stage 2—Assessment Evidence

Performance Tasks: *Summary in GRASPS form*   **T**

Kerner Commission Role-Play   Students role-play being members of LBJ's Kerner Commission to determine the causes of urban rioting in the '60s. (Your goal is to determine why the urban riots happened. You must report to the president and the country on why the violence happened and what can be done about it. As a group, produce a collective report that must be thoughtful, thorough, and clearly presented. Your personal contribution will be judged through journal entries, observations of work and discussion, and sections of writing you produce.)

Key Criteria
- Historically accurate
- Clear and complete explanation
- Sound reasoning based on evidence
- Correct grammar and mechanics in writing

Other Evidence   **OE**
Quiz on readings: key events, leaders and strategies of the civil rights movement
Essay: Did the Kerner Commission reveal or sidestep the issue of race relations?

Sample 2-Page Template, Page 2
Modern U.S. History, Grades 11–12

Stage 3—Learning Plan

Learning Activities

L

Performance Task Overview: Using documentary sources and role-playing based on provided background information, students investigate, as though they were a government commission, the race riots of 1968. Their purpose is to discover what happened, why it happened, and what could be done to prevent it from happening again, as President Lyndon Johnson charged his own investigative commission to do. Some students play roles of participants in the events, others act as commission members. When the commission presents its report, all make comments for improvement. Finally, students study the aftermath to see if racial relations have improved since 1968.

1. After students have studied some information about the 1950s and early 1960s, they should understand that there was a strong consensus in the United States in the mid-1960s for social justice. At this point, students should do the background reading on the race riots in 1968. Ask the students what questions come to mind. They should be puzzled about how the nationwide consensus fell apart and violence broke out in the cities. They might be encouraged to wonder about relationships—to the Vietnam War, for example, or to more militant separatist African-American groups. Eventually they should define the questions President Johnson defined for the Kerner Commission: What happened? Why did it happen? What can be done to prevent it from happening again?

2. Divide the students into role-players (with role information sheets) and commission members. Send the commission members to the "archives" (your collection of documents on the history of racial relationships in the 20th century), and show the role-players the segments of "Eyes on the Prize" that deal with Elijah Mohammed, Malcolm X, the Black Power Movement, Martin Luther King's northern strategy (and his assassination), Chicago and Detroit. This helps them to visualize the environment in which their characters lived, and understand the tension that erupted. This enables students to convey the emotional side of their role, which is so important for the commission to experience. The commission members need to be coached to develop questions on the basis of the documents they read, to test hypotheses they might have, given what they learned about patterns of discrimination, racism, or any changes for the better. Give them a list of the people who will come to "testify" (with their occupations or positions) so that they can prepare appropriate questions.

3. Appoint a chair and have the commission begin hearings. It may take a few days to get through 10 "witnesses," but if the questioning is good and the witnesses are able to develop good answers on the spot, the exercise will be well worth the time.

4. Allow the commission time to discuss its findings and to develop a report. Perhaps members could make an outline of the report for duplication, and then present the report orally. While they are doing this, the role-players could do some journal writing and begin to develop their own ideas about what caused the riots.

5. Discuss the commission's preliminary report. Be sure to have the commission members identify the sources of their information for the benefit of the role-players. The role-players should note that some historical perspective is helpful in analyzing this situation. Then have the students read the excerpts from an actual preliminary report, or some excerpts from the Kerner Commission report.

6. Assign the students the paper on what happened and why. Have them exchange and comment on their papers, develop a rubric for excellence, and revise and rewrite their papers.

Templates · Stage 1 · Stage 2 · Stage 3 · Peer review · Exercises · Process sheets · Glossary

6-Page Template, Page 1

Templates

Stage 1

Stage 2

Stage 3

Peer review

Exercises

Process sheets

Glossary

Unit Cover Page

Unit Title: _____ Grade Levels: _____

Subject/Topic Areas: _____

Key Words: _____

Designed by: _____ Time Frame: _____

School District: _____ School: _____

Brief Summary of Unit (including curricular context and unit goals):

Unit design status: ❐ Completed template pages—Stages 1, 2, and 3

❐ Completed blueprint for each performance task ❐ Completed rubrics

❐ Directions to students *and* teachers ❐ Materials and resources listed

❐ Suggested accommodations ❐ Suggested extensions

Status: ○ Initial draft (date _____) ○ Revised draft (date _____)

○ Peer reviewed ○ Content reviewed ○ Field tested ○ Validated ○ Anchored

6-Page Template, Page 2

Stage 1—Identify Desired Results

Established Goals:

> **G**

What understandings are desired?

> *Students will understand that . . .*　　**U**

What essential questions will be considered?

> **Q**

What key knowledge and skills will students acquire as a result of this unit?

> *Students will know . . .*　　**K**　　*Students will be able to . . .*　　**S**

6-Page Template, Page 3

Templates

Stage 1

Stage 2

Stage 3

Peer review

Exercises

Process sheets

Glossary

Stage 2—Determine Acceptable Evidence

What evidence will show that students understand?

Performance Tasks* (summary in GRASPS form): **T**

Complete a Performance Task Blueprint for each task (next page).

Other Evidence (quizzes, tests, prompts, observations, dialogues, work samples): **OE**

Student Self-Assessment and Reflection: **SA**

6-Page Template, Page 4

Performance Task Blueprint

What understandings and goals will be assessed through this task? **G**

What criteria are implied in the standards and understandings *regardless* of the task specifics? What qualities must student work demonstrate to signify that standards were met?

Through what authentic performance task will students demonstrate understanding? **T**

What student products and performances will provide evidence of desired understandings?

By what criteria will student products and performances be evaluated?

Templates

Stage 1

Stage 2

Stage 3

Peer review

Exercises

Process sheets

Glossary

6-Page Template, Page 5

Templates

Stage 1

Stage 2

Stage 3

Peer review

Exercises

Process sheets

Glossary

Stage 3—Plan Learning Experiences and Instruction
Consider the WHERETO elements.   **L**

_____

_____

_____

_____

_____

_____

_____

_____

_____

_____

_____

_____

_____

_____

6-Page Template, Page 6

Stage 3—Plan Learning Experiences and Instruction

Consider the WHERETO elements.

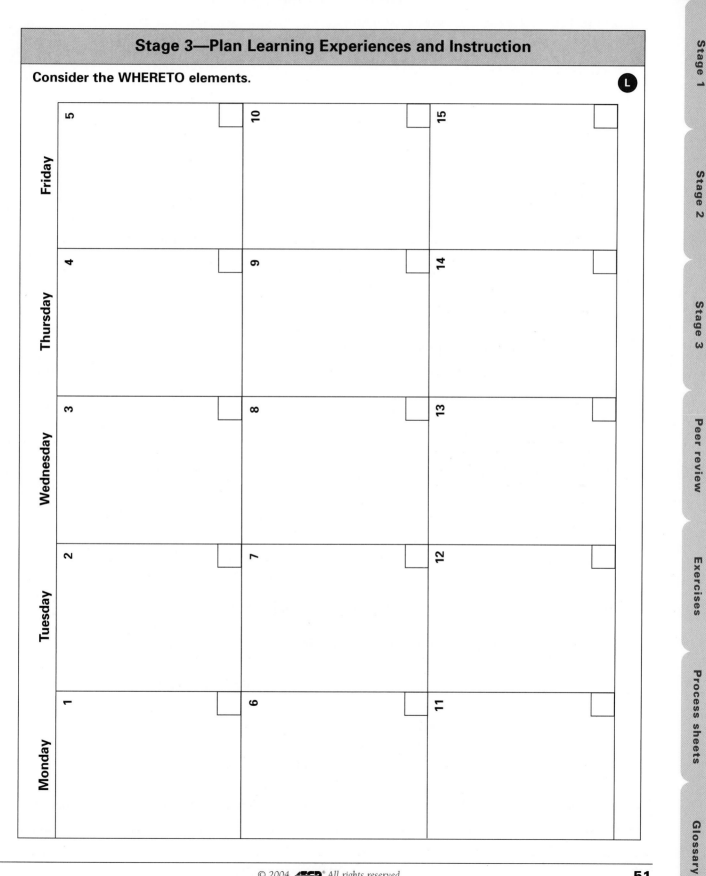

	Monday	Tuesday	Wednesday	Thursday	Friday
	1	2	3	4	5
	6	7	8	9	10
	11	12	13	14	15

Templates

Stage 1

Stage 2

Stage 3

Peer review

Exercises

Process sheets

Glossary

Sample 6-Page Template, Page 1
Nutrition, Grades 5–7

Unit Cover Page

Unit Title: _You Are What You Eat_   Grade Levels: _5th_

Subject/Topic Areas: _Health and Nutrition_

Key Words: _nutrition, health, wellness, balanced diet, food pyramid_

Designed by: _Bob James_   Time Frame: _3 weeks_

School District: _Montgomery Knolls P.S._   School: _Cheshire Cat Elem._

Brief Summary of Unit (including curricular context and unit goals):

In this introductory unit of the health education course, students will learn about human nutritional needs, the food groups, the nutritional benefits of various foods, the USDA Food Pyramid guidelines, and health problems associated with poor nutrition. They will design an illustrated nutrition brochure to teach younger children about the importance of good nutrition for healthy living, work in cooperative groups to analyze a hypothetical family's diet and recommend ways to improve their nutritional value, and conduct research on health problems resulting from poor eating habits.

In the culminating performance task, students develop and present a proposed menu for an upcoming three-day outdoor education program. Their menu for meals and snacks should meet the USDA Food Pyramid recommendations. The unit concludes with students evaluating their personal eating habits and the extent to which they eat healthy.

Unit design status: ❐ Completed template pages—Stages 1, 2, and 3

☑ Completed blueprint for each performance task   ❐ Completed rubrics

❐ Directions to students _and_ teachers   ❐ Materials and resources listed

❐ Suggested accommodations   ❐ Suggested extensions

Status: ○ Initial draft (date _3/12/98_)   ○ Revised draft (date _7/14/02_)

☑ Peer reviewed   ○ Content reviewed   ☑ Field tested   ○ Validated   ○ Anchored

---

Sample 6-Page Template, Page 2
Nutrition, Grades 5–7

Stage 1—Identify Desired Results

Established Goals:

Standard 6—Students will understand essential concepts about nutrition and diet. **G**

   6, a—Students will use an understanding of nutrition to plan appropriate diets for themselves and others.

   6, c —Students will understand their own individual eating patterns and ways these patterns may be improved.

What understandings are desired?

Students will understand that . . . **U**

- A balanced diet contributes to physical and mental health.
- The USDA Food Pyramid presents relative guidelines for nutrition.
- Dietary requirements vary for individuals based on age, gender, activity level, weight, and overall health.
- Healthful living requires an individual to act on available information about good nutrition even if it means breaking comfortable habits.

What essential questions will be considered?

- What is healthful eating? **Q**
- How does what I eat affect my health?
- Are you a healthful eater? How would you know?
- How could a healthy diet for one person be unhealthy for another?
- Why are there so many health problems in the United States caused by poor eating despite all of the available information?

What key knowledge and skills will students acquire as a result of this unit?

Students will know . . . **K**	*Students will be able to . . .* **S**
• Key terms—protein, fat, calorie, carbohydrate, cholesterol.	• Read and interpret nutrition information on food labels.
• Types of foods in each food group and their nutritional values.	• Analyze diets for nutritional value.
• The USDA Food Pyramid guidelines.	• Plan balanced diets for themselves and others.
• Variables influencing nutritional needs.	
• Specific health problems caused by poor nutrition.	

Templates

Stage 1

Stage 2

Stage 3

Peer review

Exercises

Process sheets

Glossary

Sample 6-Page Template, Page 3
Nutrition, Grades 5–7

Stage 2: Determine Acceptable Evidence

What evidence will show that students understand?

Performance Tasks* (summary in GRASPS form): **T**

You Are What You Eat—Students create an illustrated brochure to teach younger children about the importance of good nutrition for healthful living. Offer younger students ideas for breaking bad eating habits.

Chow Down—Students develop a three-day menu for meals and snacks for an upcoming outdoor education camp experience. They write a letter to the camp director to explain why their menu should be selected (by showing that it meets the USDA Food Pyramid recommendations, yet is tasty enough for the students). Include at least one modification for a specific dietary condition (e.g., diabetic or vegetarian) or religious consideration.

*Complete a Performance Task Blueprint for each task (next page).

OE

Other Evidence (quizzes, tests, prompts, observations, dialogues, work samples):

Quiz: Food groups and the USDA Food Pyramid

Prompt: Describe two health problems that could arise as a result of poor nutrition and explain how they could be avoided.

Skill Check: Interpret nutrition information on food labels.

SA

Student Self-Assessment and Reflection:

1. Self-assess the brochure, *You Are What You Eat.*
2. Self-assess the camp menu, *Chow Down.*
3. Reflect: To what extent are you a healthy eater at the end of unit (compared to the beginning)?

Sample 6-Page Template, Page 4

Nutrition, Grades 5–7

Performance Task Blueprint

What understandings and goals will be assessed through this task? **G**

Students will plan appropriate diets for themselves and others.

What criteria are implied in the standards and understandings *regardless* of the task specifics? What qualities must student work demonstrate to signify that standards were met?

- Nutritionally sound
- Comparison of taste vs. nutrition
- Feasible

Through what authentic performance task will students demonstrate understanding?

Task Overview:

Since we have been learning about nutrition, the camp director at the Outdoor Ed. Center has asked us **T** to propose a nutritionally balanced menu for our three-day trip to the center later this year. Using the USDA Food Pyramid guidelines and the nutrition facts on food labels, design a plan for three days, including the three main meals and three snacks (a.m., p.m., and campfire). Your goal is a tasty and nutritionally balanced menu. Include at least one modification for a specific dietary condition (e.g., diabetic or vegetarian) or religious consideration. In addition to your menu, prepare a letter to the camp director explaining how your menu meets the USDA nutritional guidelines. Include a chart showing a breakdown of the fat, protein, carbohydrates, vitamins, minerals, and calories.

What student products and performances will provide evidence of desired understandings?

Menu with chart of nutritional values and at least one dietary modification

Letter to camp director

By what criteria will student products and performances be evaluated?

- Menu meets USDA guidelines
- Nutritional values chart is accurate and complete
- Menu includes at least one dietary modification

- Effective explanation of nutritional value and taste appeal of proposed menu
- Proper letter form
- Correct spelling and grammar conventions

Templates · Stage 1 · Stage 2 · Stage 3 · Peer review · Exercises · Process sheets · Glossary

Templates

Stage 1

Stage 2

Stage 3

Peer review

Exercises

Process sheets

Glossary

Sample 6-Page Template, Page 5
Nutrition, Grades 5–7

Stage 3—Plan Learning Experiences and Instruction

Consider the WHERETO elements.   **L**

1. Begin with an entry question (Can the foods you eat cause zits?) to hook students into considering the effects of nutrition on their lives.   **H**

2. Introduce the essential questions and discuss the culminating unit performance tasks (Chow Down and personal eating action plan).   **W**

3. Note: Key vocabulary terms are introduced as needed by the various learning activities and performance tasks. Students read and discuss relevant selections from the Health textbook to support the learning activities and tasks. As an ongoing activity, students keep a chart of their daily eating and drinking for later review and evaluation.   **E**

4. Present concept attainment lesson on the food groups. Then, have students practice categorizing pictures of foods accordingly.   **E**

5. Introduce the Food Pyramid and identify foods in each group. Students work in groups to develop a poster of the Food Pyramid containing cut-out pictures of foods in each group. Display the posters in the classroom or hallway.   **E**

6. Give quiz on the food groups and Food Pyramid (matching format).   **E**

7. Review and discuss the nutrition brochure from the USDA. Discussion question: Must everyone follow the same diet in order to be healthy?   **R**

8. Working in cooperative groups, students analyze a hypothetical family's diet (deliberately unbalanced) and make recommendations for improved nutrition. Teacher observes and coaches students as they work.   **E-2**

9. Have groups share their diet analyses and discuss as a class.   **E, E-2**
   (Note: Collect and review the diet analyses to look for misunderstandings needing instructional attention.)

10. Each student designs an illustrated nutrition brochure to teach younger children about the importance of good nutrition for healthy living and the problems associated with poor eating. This activity is completed outside of class.   **E, T**

11. Students share brochures with members of their group for a peer assessment based on criteria. Allow students to make revisions based on feedback.   **R, E-2**

12. Show and discuss the video, "Nutrition and You." Discuss the health problems linked to poor eating.   **E**

13. Students listen to, and question, a guest speaker (nutritionist from the local hospital) about health problems caused by poor nutrition.   **E**

14. Students respond to written prompt: Describe two health problems that could arise as a result of poor nutrition and explain what changes in eating could help to avoid them. (These are collected and graded by teacher.)   **E-2**

15. Teacher models how to read and interpret food label information on nutritional values. Then, have students practice using donated boxes, cans, and bottles (empty!).   **E**

16. Students work independently to develop the three-day camp menu. Evaluate and give feedback on the camp menu project. Students self- and peer-assess their projects using rubrics.   **E-2, T**

17. At the conclusion of the unit, students review their completed daily eating chart and self-assess the healthfulness of their eating. Have they noticed changes? Improvements? Do they notice changes in how they feel or their appearance?   **E-2**

18. Students develop a personal "eating action plan" for healthful eating. These are saved and presented at upcoming student-involved parent conferences.   **E-2, T**

19. Conclude the unit with student self-evaluation regarding their personal eating habits. Have each student develop a personal action plan for their healthful-eating goal.   **E-2, T**

Sample 6-Page Template, Page 6
Nutrition, Grades 5–7

Stage 3—Plan Learning Experiences and Instruction

Consider the WHERETO elements. (L)

Monday	Tuesday	Wednesday	Thursday	Friday
1 (HW) 1. Hook students with a discussion of eating habits and "zits." 2. Introduce essential questions and key vocabulary. 3. Have students begin a food diary to record their daily eating patterns.	**2** (E) 4. Present concept attainment lesson on food groups, then categorize foods. 5. Have students read and discuss the nutrition brochure from the USDA.	**3** (ET) 6. Present lesson on the Food Pyramid and identify foods in each group. 7. Read and discuss relevant selections from the Health textbook. Provide illustrated pamphlet for lower-level readers.	**4** (ET) 8. Present and discuss the video, "Nutrition and You." 9. Have students design an illustrated nutrition brochure to teach younger children about the importance of good nutrition for healthy living.	**5** (ET) 10. Assess and give feedback on the brochures. Allow students to self- and peer-assess the brochures using a list of criteria.
6 (E) 11. Working in cooperative groups, have students analyze a diet for a hypothetical family and make recommendations for improved nutrition.	**7** (R) 12. Conduct a group review and give feedback regarding the diet analyses. Allow revisions.	**8** (E) 13. Have students listen to and question guest speaker (nutritionist from local hospital) about health problems caused by poor nutrition.	**9** (ET) 14. Have students conduct research on health problems resulting from poor eating. Provide students with options for how they share their findings.	**10** (E) 15. Model how to interpret food label information for nutritional values. Have students practice interpreting food labels.
11 (E) 16. Review the camp menu rubric so that students understand the criteria. Have them work independently to develop a three-day camp menu.	**12** (R) 17. Observe and coach students as they work on their menus.	**13** (E) 18. Evaluate and give feedback on the camp menu project. Have students self- and peer-assess their projects using the rubric.	**14** (ET) 19. Have students review their food diaries to look for changing patterns in their eating. Have each student set a personal goal for improved nutrition.	**15** (ET) 20. Conclude the unit with student self-evaluation regarding their personal eating habits. Have each student develop a personal action plan for their healthful eating goal.

Side tabs: Templates · Stage 1 · Stage 2 · Stage 3 · Peer review · Exercises · Process sheets · Glossary

Stage 1— Desired Results

Design Tools and Samples

Templates

Stage 1

Stage 2

Stage 3

Peer review

Exercises

Process sheets

Glossary

Backward Design: Stage 1

Stage 1—Desired Results

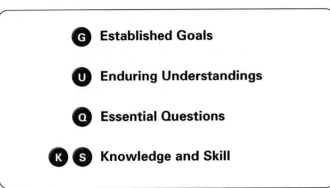

G Established Goals

U Enduring Understandings

Q Essential Questions

K **S** Knowledge and Skill

In Stage 1, we consider the desired results of the design according to the following four categories:

1. **Established Goals—** **G** These typically include national, state, local or professional standards; course or program objectives; and district learner outcomes.

2. **Enduring Understandings—** **U** Stated as full-sentence statements, the understandings specify what we want students to come to understand about the big ideas.

3. **Essential Questions—** **Q** These open-ended provocative questions are designed to guide student inquiry and focus instruction for "uncovering" the important ideas of the content.

4. **Knowledge and Skills—** **K** **S** These are the more discrete objectives that we want students to know and be able to do.

Design Standards for Stage 1—To what extent does the design focus on the big ideas of targeted content?

Consider: Are . . .

○ The targeted understandings enduring, based on transferable big ideas at the heart of the discipline, and in need of "uncovering"?

○ The targeted understandings framed by questions that spark meaningful connections, provoke genuine inquiry and deep thought, and encourage transfer?

○ The essential questions provocative, arguable, and likely to generate inquiry around central ideas (rather than a "pat" answer)?

○ Appropriate goals (e.g., content standards, benchmarks, curriculum objectives) identified?

○ Valid and unit-relevant knowledge and skills identified?

Stage 1—Key Design Elements with Prompts

Templates

Stage 1

Stage 2

Stage 3

Peer review

Exercises

Process sheets

Glossary

Stage 1—Identify Desired Results

Established Goals:

In Box **G**, we identify one or more Goals (e.g., content standards, course or program objectives, and learning outcomes) that the design targets. **G**

What understandings are desired?

Students will understand that . . . **U**

In Box **U**, we identify the Enduring Understandings, based on the transferable big ideas that give the content meaning and connect the facts and skills.

What essential questions will be considered?

In Box **Q**, we frame the Essential Questions to guide student inquiry and focus instruction for uncovering the important ideas of the content. **Q**

What key knowledge and skills will students acquire as a result of this unit?

Students will know . . . **K**   *Students will be able to . . .* **S**

In Box **K** and **S**, we identify the key Knowledge **K** and Skills **S** we want students to know and be able to do. The targeted knowledge and skills **K** can be of three different kinds: (1) They can refer to the building blocks for the desired understandings **U**; (2) They can refer to the knowledge and skills stated or implied in the goals **G**; and (3) They can refer to the "enabling" knowledge and skills needed to perform the complex assessment tasks identified in Stage 2.

Stage 1—Key Design Elements

(Web)

In Stage 1, designers consider the following elements. A variety of examples and design tools are provided to assist you. **Note:** *There is no required sequence to the design process. Designers can enter at any point. However, all of the design elements should be considered.*

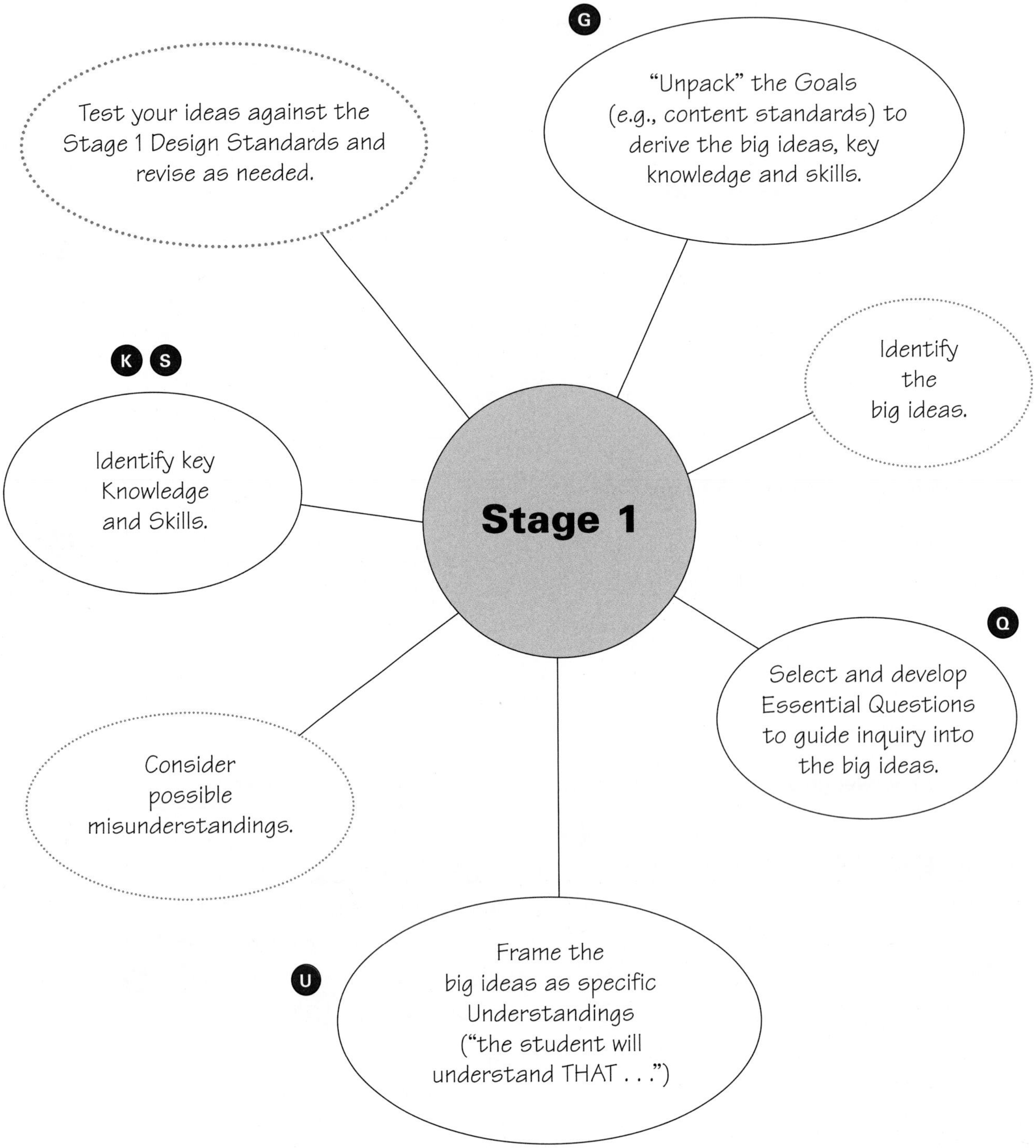

Stage 1—Key Design Elements

Nutrition, Grades 5–7

Stage 1—Identify Desired Results

Established Goals:

Standard 6—Students will understand essential concepts about nutrition and diet.   **G**
   6, a—Students will use an understanding of nutrition to plan appropriate diets for themselves and others.
   6, c—Students will understand their own individual eating patterns and ways that those patterns may be improved.

What understandings are desired?

Students will understand that . . .   **U**

- A balanced diet contributes to physical and mental health.
- The USDA Food Pyramid presents relative guidelines for nutrition.
- Dietary requirements vary for individuals based on age, activity level, weight, and overall health.
- Healthful living requires an individual to act on available information about good nutrition even if it means breaking comfortable habits.

What essential questions will be considered?

- What is healthful eating?   **Q**
- How does what I eat affect my health?
- Are you a heathful eater? How would you know?
- How could a healthy diet for one person be unhealthy for another?
- Why are there so many health problems in the United States caused by poor nutrition despite all of the available information?

What key knowledge and skills will students acquire as a result of this unit?

Students will know . . .   **K**

- Key terms—protein, fat, calorie, carbohydrate, cholesterol.
- Types of foods in each food group and their nutritional values.
- The USDA Food Pyramid guidelines.
- Variables influencing nutritional needs.
- General health problems caused by poor nutrition.

Students will be able to . . .   **S**

- Read and interpret nutrition information on food labels.
- Analyze diets for nutritional value.
- Plan balanced diets for themselves and others.

Templates
Stage 1
Stage 2
Stage 3
Peer review
Exercises
Process sheets
Glossary

Stage 1—Key Design Elements
English, High School

Stage 1—Identify Desired Results

Established Goals:

MA Standard 8—Understanding a Text: *Students will identify the basic facts and main ideas in a text and use them as the basis for interpretation.*
MA Standard 19—Writing: *Students will write with a clear focus, coherent organization, and sufficient detail.*
MA Standard 20—Writing: *Students will write for different audiences and purposes.*

(G)

What understandings are desired?

Students will understand that . . .

- Novelists often provide insights about human experience and inner life through fictional means.
- Writers use a variety of stylistic techniques to engage and persuade their readers.
- Holden Caulfield reflects common adolescent experiences but masks deep-seated personal problems about growing up and relating to others.

(U)

What essential questions will be considered?

- What is the relationship between fiction and truth? What truths can best be rendered fictionally?
- Does Holden represent adolescence? Is he abnormal, or are all adolescents "abnormal"? Who is genuine and who is "phony"? Why do people act phony?
- How do authors hook and hold readers? How does J. D. Salinger engage you?
- How do writers persuade their readers?

(Q)

What key knowledge and skills will students acquire as a result of this unit?

Students will know . . . **(K)**

- The plot and characters of *Catcher in the Rye.*
- Various stylistic techniques that J. D. Salinger employed.
- The steps in the writing process.
- Persuasive writing techniques.

Students will be able to . . . **(S)**

- Apply strategies for interpretive reading.
- Develop a well-reasoned hypothesis through a close reading of a text.
- Apply the writing process to produce a draft and a revision of a persuasive written product.
- Reflect on their comprehension of a text, and consider their own misunderstandings.

Templates · Stage 1 · Stage 2 · Stage 3 · Peer review · Exercises · Process sheets · Glossary

Structure of Knowledge— Definitions of the Elements

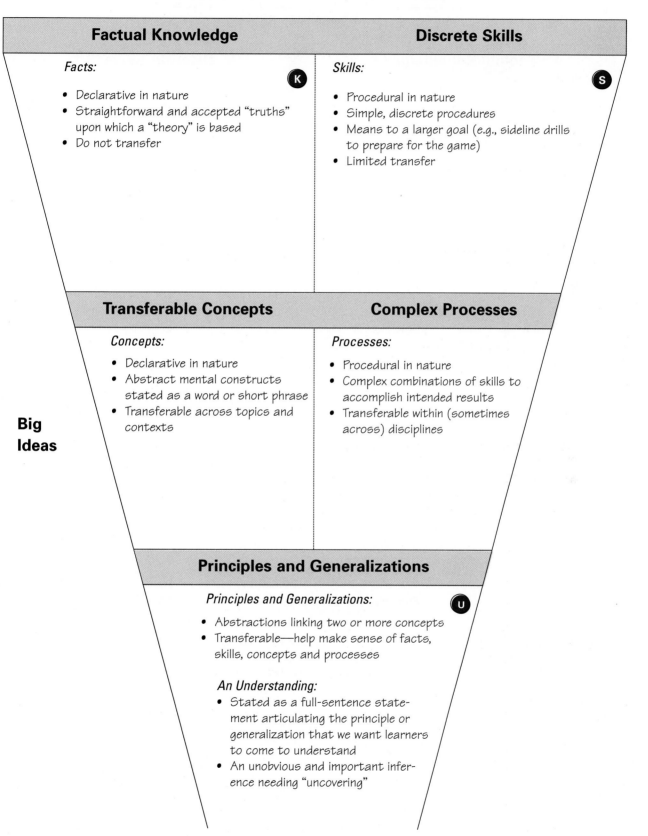

Factual Knowledge

Facts: **K**

- Declarative in nature
- Straightforward and accepted "truths" upon which a "theory" is based
- Do not transfer

Discrete Skills

Skills: **S**

- Procedural in nature
- Simple, discrete procedures
- Means to a larger goal (e.g., sideline drills to prepare for the game)
- Limited transfer

Transferable Concepts

Concepts:

- Declarative in nature
- Abstract mental constructs stated as a word or short phrase
- Transferable across topics and contexts

Complex Processes

Processes:

- Procedural in nature
- Complex combinations of skills to accomplish intended results
- Transferable within (sometimes across) disciplines

Big Ideas

Principles and Generalizations

Principles and Generalizations: **U**

- Abstractions linking two or more concepts
- Transferable—help make sense of facts, skills, concepts and processes

An Understanding:
- Stated as a full-sentence statement articulating the principle or generalization that we want learners to come to understand
- An unobvious and important inference needing "uncovering"

Templates | Stage 1 | Stage 2 | Stage 3 | Peer review | Exercises | Process sheets | Glossary

Structure of Knowledge
U.S. History

Topic: World War II

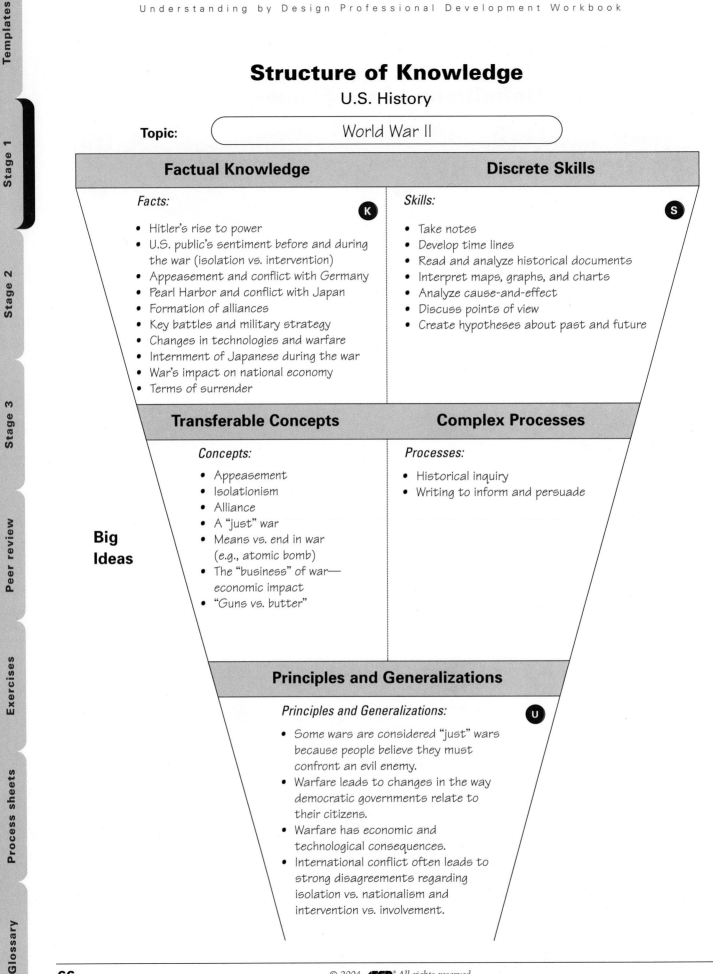

Factual Knowledge

Facts: **K**

- Hitler's rise to power
- U.S. public's sentiment before and during the war (isolation vs. intervention)
- Appeasement and conflict with Germany
- Pearl Harbor and conflict with Japan
- Formation of alliances
- Key battles and military strategy
- Changes in technologies and warfare
- Internment of Japanese during the war
- War's impact on national economy
- Terms of surrender

Discrete Skills

Skills: **S**

- Take notes
- Develop time lines
- Read and analyze historical documents
- Interpret maps, graphs, and charts
- Analyze cause-and-effect
- Discuss points of view
- Create hypotheses about past and future

Transferable Concepts

Concepts:

- Appeasement
- Isolationism
- Alliance
- A "just" war
- Means vs. end in war (e.g., atomic bomb)
- The "business" of war—economic impact
- "Guns vs. butter"

Complex Processes

Processes:

- Historical inquiry
- Writing to inform and persuade

Big Ideas

Principles and Generalizations

Principles and Generalizations: **U**

- Some wars are considered "just" wars because people believe they must confront an evil enemy.
- Warfare leads to changes in the way democratic governments relate to their citizens.
- Warfare has economic and technological consequences.
- International conflict often leads to strong disagreements regarding isolation vs. nationalism and intervention vs. involvement.

Sidebar labels: Templates | Stage 1 | Stage 2 | Stage 3 | Peer review | Exercises | Process sheets | Glossary

Structure of Knowledge
Reading

Topic: Reading

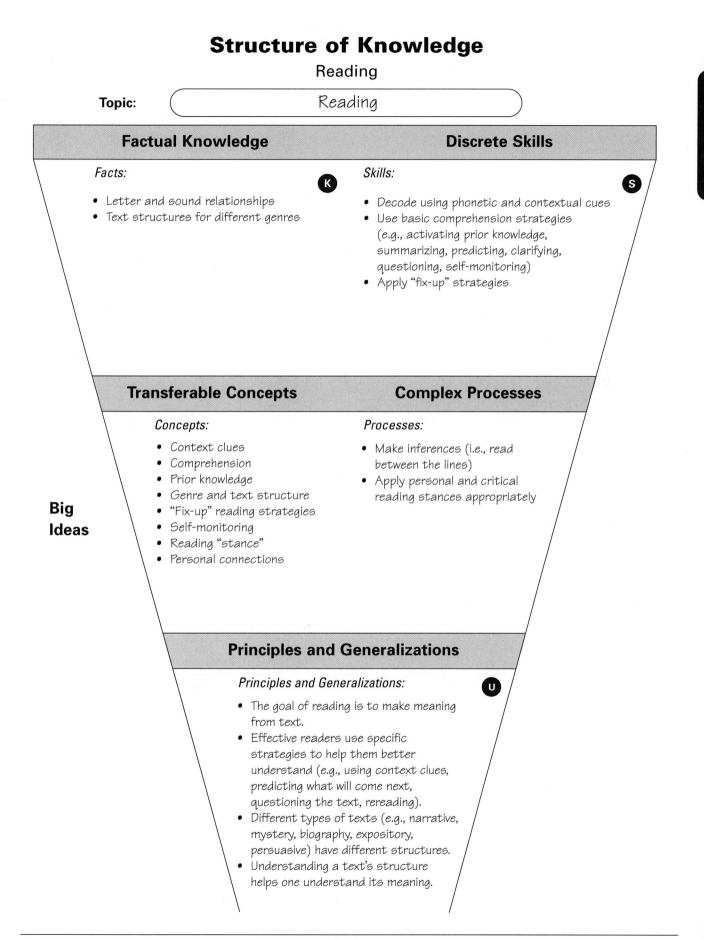

Factual Knowledge	**Discrete Skills**

Facts: **K**

- Letter and sound relationships
- Text structures for different genres

Skills: **S**

- Decode using phonetic and contextual cues
- Use basic comprehension strategies (e.g., activating prior knowledge, summarizing, predicting, clarifying, questioning, self-monitoring)
- Apply "fix-up" strategies

Transferable Concepts	**Complex Processes**

Concepts:

- Context clues
- Comprehension
- Prior knowledge
- Genre and text structure
- "Fix-up" reading strategies
- Self-monitoring
- Reading "stance"
- Personal connections

Processes:

- Make inferences (i.e., read between the lines)
- Apply personal and critical reading stances appropriately

Big Ideas

Principles and Generalizations

Principles and Generalizations: **U**

- The goal of reading is to make meaning from text.
- Effective readers use specific strategies to help them better understand (e.g., using context clues, predicting what will come next, questioning the text, rereading).
- Different types of texts (e.g., narrative, mystery, biography, expository, persuasive) have different structures.
- Understanding a text's structure helps one understand its meaning.

Templates   Stage 1   Stage 2   Stage 3   Peer review   Exercises   Process sheets   Glossary

Structure of Knowledge

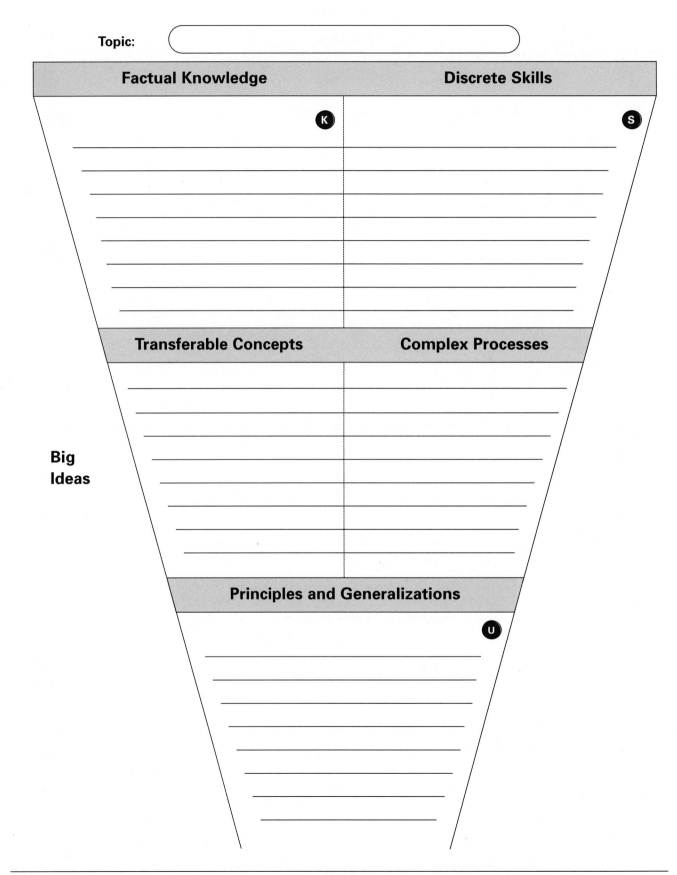

Topic:

Factual Knowledge ⬤K | **Discrete Skills** ⬤S

Transferable Concepts | **Complex Processes**

Big Ideas

Principles and Generalizations ⬤U

A Big Idea . . .

(description)

Provides a "conceptual lens" for prioritizing content.

A Big Idea refers to core concepts, principles, theories, and processes that should serve as the focal point of curricula, instruction, and assessment. Big Ideas reflect expert understanding and anchor the discourse, inquiries, discoveries, and arguments in a field of study. They provide a basis for setting curriculum priorities to focus on the most meaningful content.

Serves as an organizer for connecting important facts, skills, and actions.

Big Ideas function as the "conceptual Velcro" for a topic of study. They connect discrete knowledge and skills to a larger intellectual frame and provide a bridge for linking specific facts and skills. A focus on these larger ideas helps students to see the purpose and relevance of content.

Transfers to other contexts.

Discrete facts do not transfer. Big Ideas are powerful because they embody transferable ideas, applicable to other topics, inquiries, contexts, issues and problems. Because we can never cover all the knowledge on a given topic, a focus on the Big Ideas helps to manage information overload. Big Ideas provide the conceptual throughlines that anchor a coherent curriculum.

\Manifests itself in various ways within disciplines.

Big Ideas are typically revealed through one or more of the following forms: a core concept (e.g., adaptation), a focusing theme (e.g., man's inhumanity to man), an ongoing issue or debate (e.g., conservative vs. liberal), a puzzling paradox (e.g., poverty amidst plenty), an important process (e.g., writing process), an authentic problem or persistent challenge (e.g., illiteracy, voter apathy), an illuminating theory (e.g., Manifest Destiny), an underlying assumption (e.g., the markets are rational) or differing perspectives (e.g., terrorist vs. freedom fighter). Additional examples of these Big-Idea categories are provided on the next several pages.

Requires uncoverage because it is an abstraction.

A Big Idea is inherently abstract. Its meaning is not always obvious to students, and simply covering it (i.e., the teacher or textbook defining it) will not ensure student understanding. "Coverage" is unlikely to cause genuine insight; understanding must be earned. Thus, the idea must be uncovered—its meaning discovered, constructed or inferred by the learners, with the aid of the teacher and well-designed learning experiences.

Templates

Stage 1

Stage 2

Stage 3

Peer review

Exercises

Process sheets

Glossary

Templates

Stage 1

Stage 2

Stage 3

Peer review

Exercises

Process sheets

Glossary

Big Ideas Reflected Throughout Design

Stage 1—Desired Results

Established Goals: (G)

Big Ideas are often implied and sometimes stated in goals or content standards. Look for key concepts, consider the ideas in key nouns.

Understandings: (U) *Students will understand that . . .*	**Essential Questions:** (Q)

Big Ideas are explicitly highlighted here.

Students will know . . . (K)	*Students will be able to . . .* (S)

Big Ideas are implied here. Consider the larger ideas that connect the facts and the larger purposes for mastering the skill.

Stage 2—Assessment Evidence

Performance Tasks: (T)	**Other Evidence:** (OE)
A constant focus on and effective use of Big Ideas should be at the heart of performance tasks (as reflected in task guidelines and rubrics).	Quizzes, tests, and prompts should relate to the Big Ideas (e.g., oral or written questions on one or more of the Essential Questions).

Stage 3—Learning Plan

Learning Activities: (L)

The learning plan should ensure that Big Ideas are uncovered through inquiry activities and explicit instruction. The overall goal is to help learners make sense of the content, connect discrete facts and skills to larger ideas, apply this knowledge in meaningful ways, and see the purpose of learning activities.

Big Ideas Manifested

Big Ideas typically manifest themselves in one or more of the following forms.

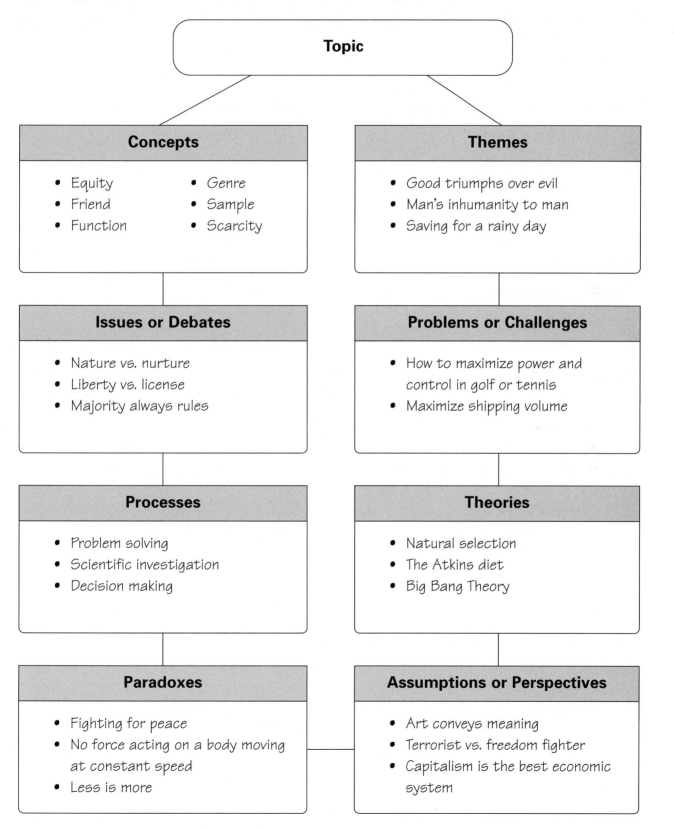

Topic

Concepts

- Equity
- Friend
- Function
- Genre
- Sample
- Scarcity

Themes

- Good triumphs over evil
- Man's inhumanity to man
- Saving for a rainy day

Issues or Debates

- Nature vs. nurture
- Liberty vs. license
- Majority always rules

Problems or Challenges

- How to maximize power and control in golf or tennis
- Maximize shipping volume

Processes

- Problem solving
- Scientific investigation
- Decision making

Theories

- Natural selection
- The Atkins diet
- Big Bang Theory

Paradoxes

- Fighting for peace
- No force acting on a body moving at constant speed
- Less is more

Assumptions or Perspectives

- Art conveys meaning
- Terrorist vs. freedom fighter
- Capitalism is the best economic system

Templates

Stage 1

Stage 2

Stage 3

Peer review

Exercises

Process sheets

Glossary

Concepts—Transferable Big Ideas

Samples	
❏ abundance or scarcity	❏ fairness
❏ acceptance or rejection	❏ friendship
❏ adaptation	❏ harmony
❏ aging or maturity	❏ honor
❏ balance	❏ interactions
❏ challenge	❏ interdependence
❏ change or continuity	❏ invention
❏ character	❏ justice
❏ communities	❏ liberty
❏ conflict	❏ loyalty
❏ connections	❏ migration
❏ cooperation	❏ mood
❏ correlation	❏ order
❏ courage	❏ patterns
❏ creativity	❏ perspective
❏ culture	❏ production or consumption
❏ cycles	❏ proof
❏ defense or protection	❏ survival
❏ democracy	❏ repetition
❏ discovery	❏ rhythm
❏ diversity	❏ symbol
❏ environments	❏ systems
❏ equilibrium	❏ technology
❏ evolution	❏ tyranny
❏ exploration	❏ wealth
❏ other _____	
❏ other _____	

From Topics to Big Ideas

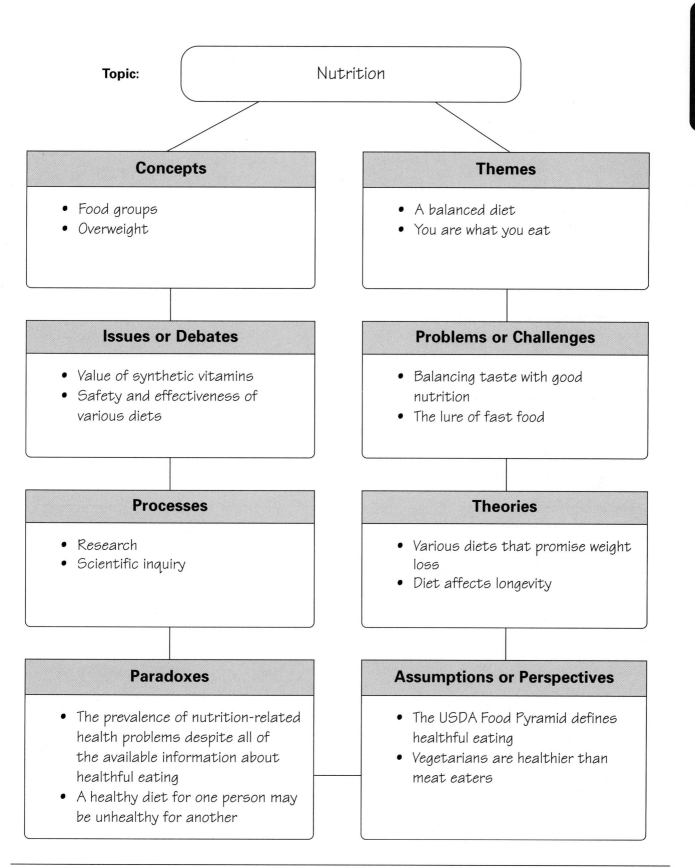

Topic: Nutrition

Concepts
- Food groups
- Overweight

Themes
- A balanced diet
- You are what you eat

Issues or Debates
- Value of synthetic vitamins
- Safety and effectiveness of various diets

Problems or Challenges
- Balancing taste with good nutrition
- The lure of fast food

Processes
- Research
- Scientific inquiry

Theories
- Various diets that promise weight loss
- Diet affects longevity

Paradoxes
- The prevalence of nutrition-related health problems despite all of the available information about healthful eating
- A healthy diet for one person may be unhealthy for another

Assumptions or Perspectives
- The USDA Food Pyramid defines healthful eating
- Vegetarians are healthier than meat eaters

Templates · Stage 1 · Stage 2 · Stage 3 · Peer review · Exercises · Process sheets · Glossary

Templates

Stage 1

Stage 2

Stage 3

Peer review

Exercises

Process sheets

Glossary

From Topics to Big Ideas

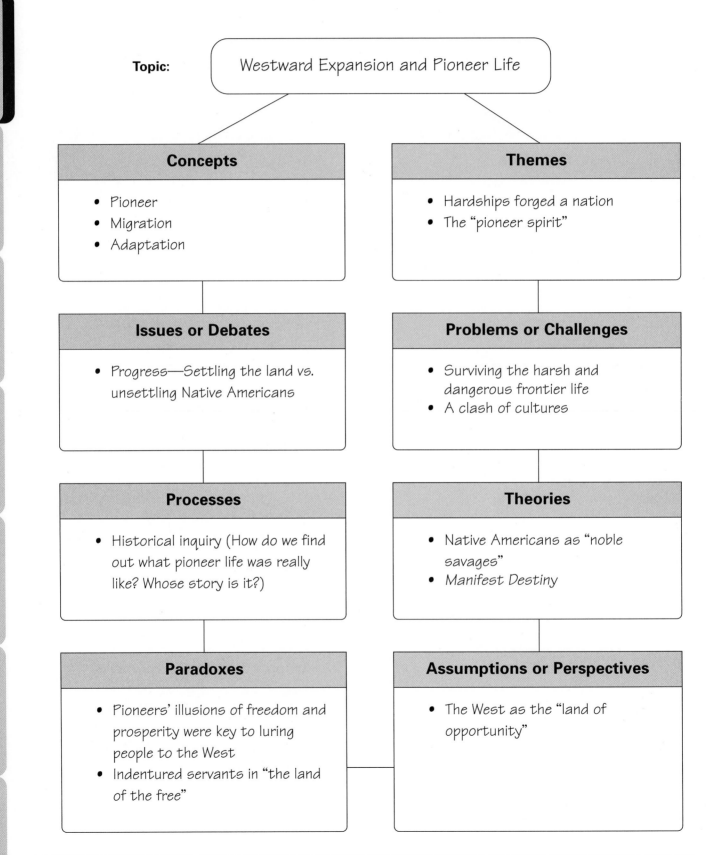

Topic: Westward Expansion and Pioneer Life

Concepts

- Pioneer
- Migration
- Adaptation

Themes

- Hardships forged a nation
- The "pioneer spirit"

Issues or Debates

- Progress—Settling the land vs. unsettling Native Americans

Problems or Challenges

- Surviving the harsh and dangerous frontier life
- A clash of cultures

Processes

- Historical inquiry (How do we find out what pioneer life was really like? Whose story is it?)

Theories

- Native Americans as "noble savages"
- Manifest Destiny

Paradoxes

- Pioneers' illusions of freedom and prosperity were key to luring people to the West
- Indentured servants in "the land of the free"

Assumptions or Perspectives

- The West as the "land of opportunity"

From Topics to Big Ideas

Given the topic of your unit, brainstorm possible Big Ideas using the following categories.

Topic:

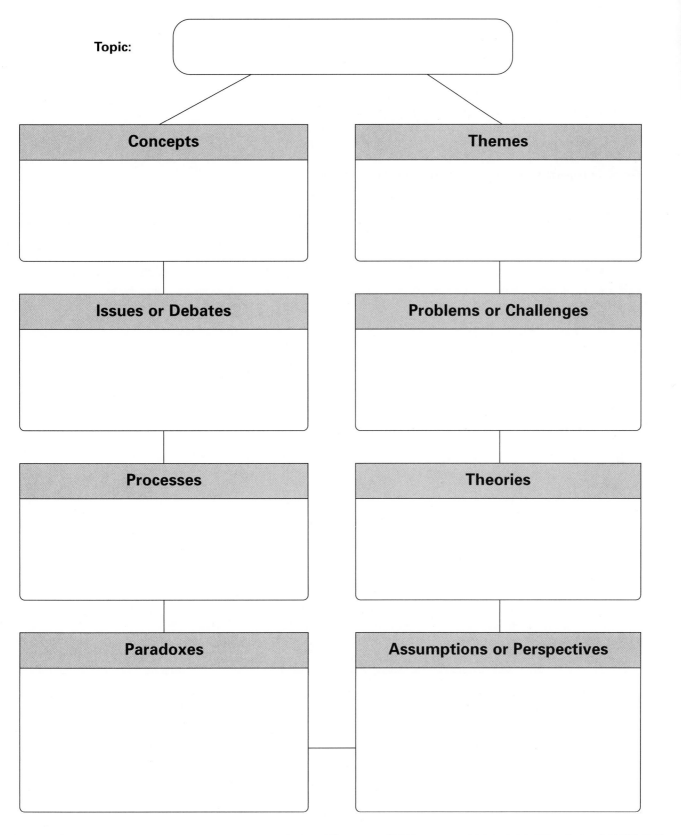

Concepts	Themes

Issues or Debates	Problems or Challenges

Processes	Theories

Paradoxes	Assumptions or Perspectives

Templates Stage 1 Stage 2 Stage 3 Peer review Exercises Process sheets Glossary

Finding the Big Ideas in Skills
Persuasive Writing

A Big Idea is a central and organizing notion. It gives meaning and connection to discrete facts and skills. It is a core idea in a subject, has lasting value and transfers to other inquiries and requires uncovering because it is not obvious.

A Big Idea in a skill area may be considered in terms of
- **Key concepts**—"persuasion" in persuasive writing
- **Purpose, value**—persuasion attempts to influence beliefs and behavior.
- **Strategy, tactics**—effective persuaders make an effort to know their audience.
- **Context**—when to use logic and when to appeal to emotion

Given an important skill, use the space below to brainstorm Big Ideas.

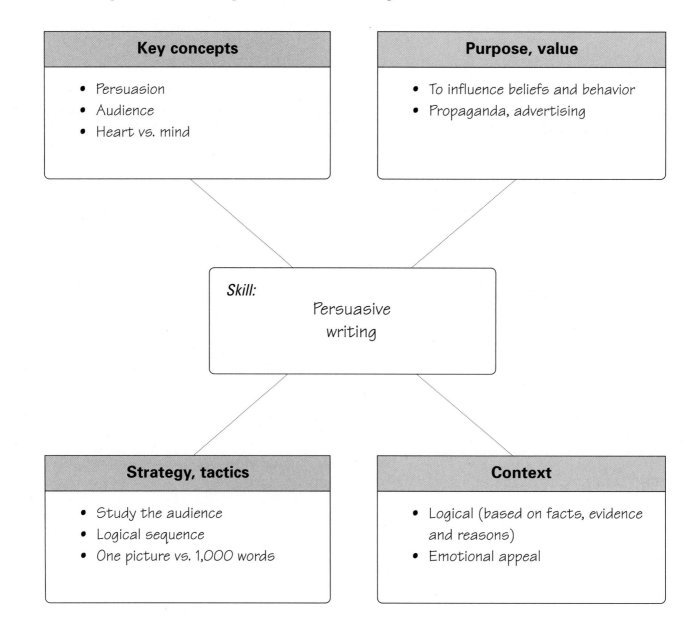

Key concepts
- Persuasion
- Audience
- Heart vs. mind

Purpose, value
- To influence beliefs and behavior
- Propaganda, advertising

Skill: Persuasive writing

Strategy, tactics
- Study the audience
- Logical sequence
- One picture vs. 1,000 words

Context
- Logical (based on facts, evidence and reasons)
- Emotional appeal

Templates

Stage 1

Stage 2

Stage 3

Peer review

Exercises

Process sheets

Glossary

Finding the Big Ideas in Skills

A Big Idea is a central and organizing notion. It gives meaning and connection to discrete facts and skills. It is a core idea in a subject, has lasting value and transfers to other inquiries and requires uncovering because it is not obvious.

A Big Idea in a skill area may be considered in terms of
- **Key concepts**—the Big Ideas underlying skill performance
- **Purpose, value**—what the skill accomplishes
- **Strategy, tactics**—what enhances effectiveness
- **Context**—when to use the skill or strategy

Given an important skill, use the space below to brainstorm Big Ideas.

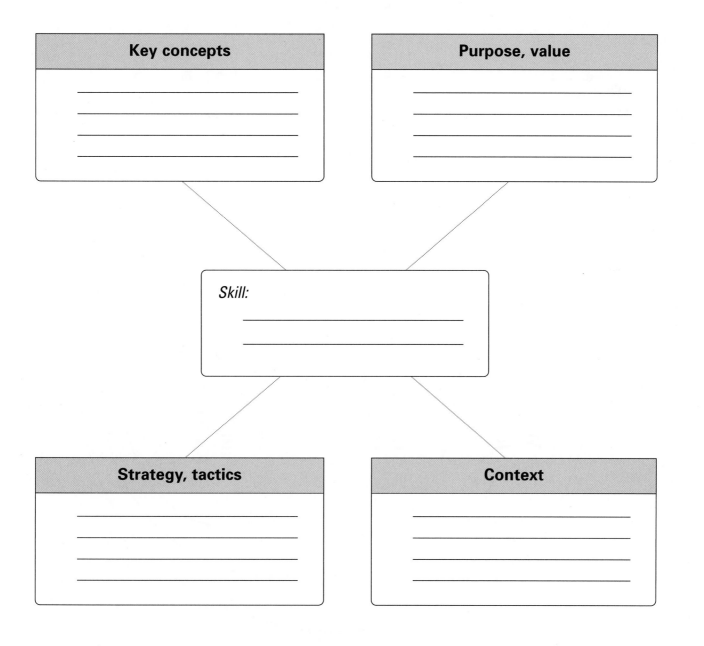

77

Templates Stage 1 Stage 2 Stage 3 Peer review Exercises Process sheets Glossary

Clarifying Content Priorities
Nutrition, Grades 5–7

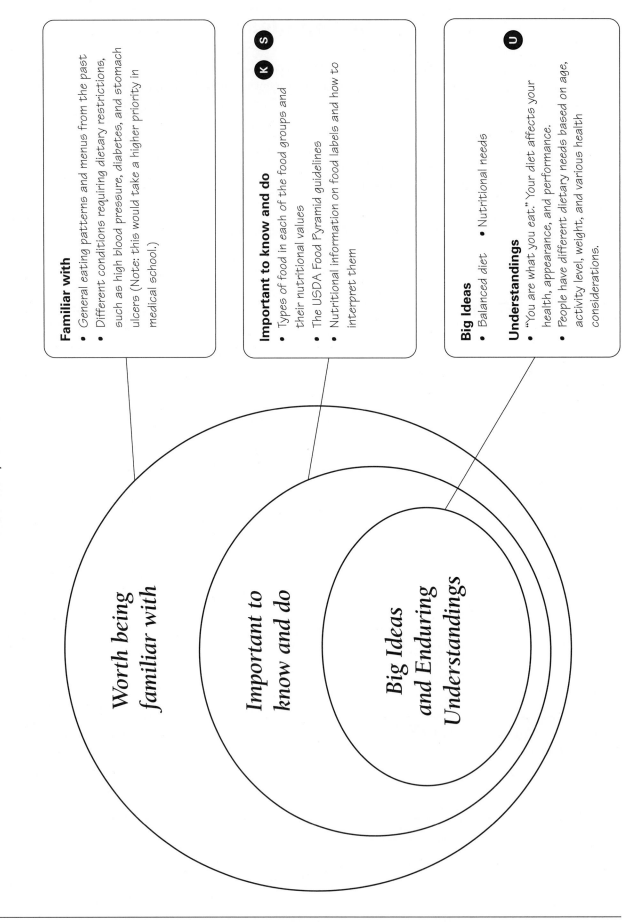

Familiar with
- General eating patterns and menus from the past
- Different conditions requiring dietary restrictions, such as high blood pressure, diabetes, and stomach ulcers (Note: this would take a higher priority in medical school.)

Important to know and do **K** **S**
- Types of food in each of the food groups and their nutritional values
- The USDA Food Pyramid guidelines
- Nutritional information on food labels and how to interpret them

Big Ideas **U**
- Balanced diet • Nutritional needs

Understandings
- "You are what you eat." Your diet affects your health, appearance, and performance.
- People have different dietary needs based on age, activity level, weight, and various health considerations.

Worth being familiar with

Important to know and do

Big Ideas and Enduring Understandings

Clarifying Content Priorities
Statistics, High School or College

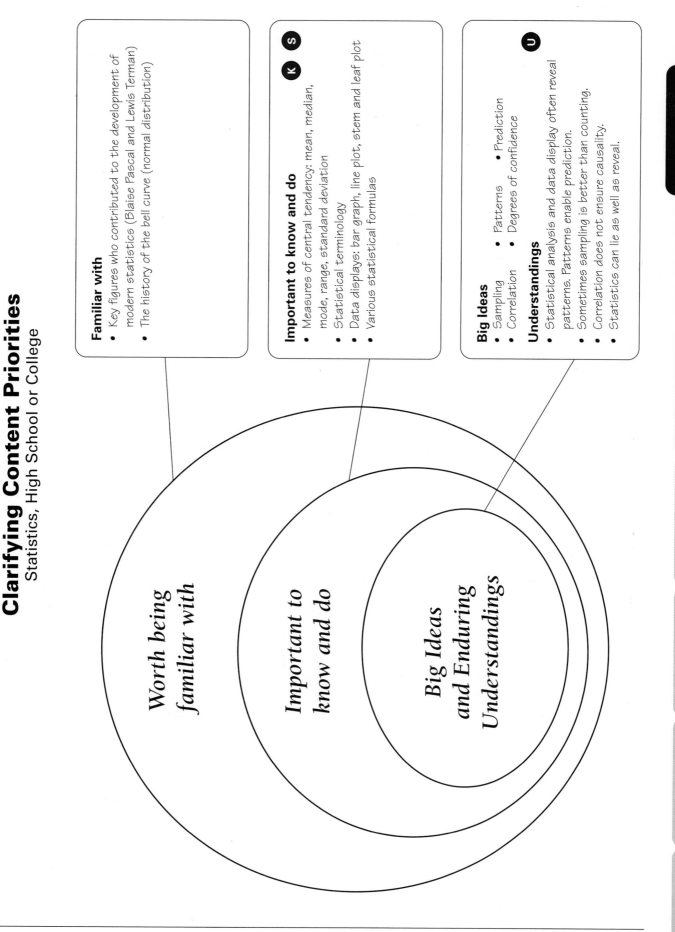

Familiar with
- Key figures who contributed to the development of modern statistics (Blaise Pascal and Lewis Terman)
- The history of the bell curve (normal distribution)

K **S**

Important to know and do
- Measures of central tendency: mean, median, mode, range, standard deviation
- Statistical terminology
- Data displays: bar graph, line plot, stem and leaf plot
- Various statistical formulas

U

Big Ideas
- Sampling • Patterns • Prediction
- Correlation • Degrees of confidence

Understandings
- Statistical analysis and data display often reveal patterns. Patterns enable prediction.
- Sometimes sampling is better than counting.
- Correlation does not ensure causality.
- Statistics can lie as well as reveal.

Worth being familiar with

Important to know and do

Big Ideas and Enduring Understandings

Templates · Stage 1 · Stage 2 · Stage 3 · Peer review · Exercises · Process sheets · Glossary

Clarifying Content Priorities

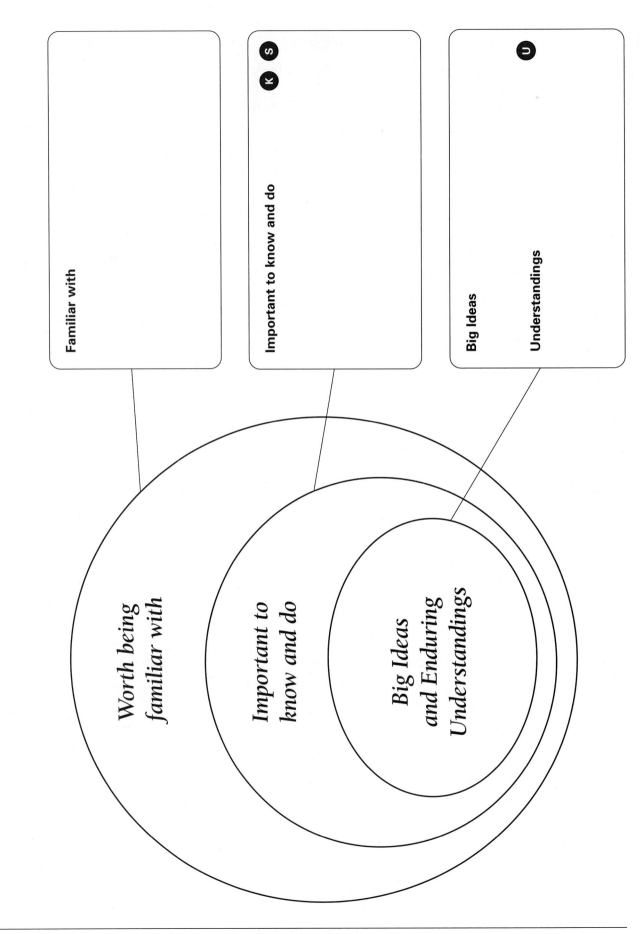

Familiar with

Important to know and do

Big Ideas

Understandings

Worth being familiar with

Important to know and do

Big Ideas and Enduring Understandings

Identifying Essential Questions and Understandings
Scientific Method

Use one or more of the following questions to filter topics or big ideas to identify possible essential questions and desired understandings.

Topics and Big Ideas:

> The Scientific Method

What essential questions are raised by this idea or topic? What, *specifically*, about the idea or topic do you want students to come to understand?

Why study the Scientific Method? So what?

What makes the study of the Scientific Method universal?

If the unit on the Scientific Method is a story, what's the moral of the story?

What's the Big Idea implied in the skill or process of the Scientific Method?

What larger concept, issue, or problem underlies the Scientific Method?

What couldn't we do if we didn't understand the Scientific Method?

How is the Scientific Method used and applied in the larger world?

What is a real-world insight about the Scientific Method?

What is the value of studying the Scientific Method?

Essential Questions: **Q**
- How is scientific knowledge generated and vaildated?
- What is science? How do we know what to believe in science?

Understandings: **U**
- Science involves the systematic isolation and control of relevant variables. (It is not simply a process of trial and error.)
- A scientific theory is validated through replication.

Templates | Stage 1 | Stage 2 | Stage 3 | Peer review | Exercises | Process sheets | Glossary

Identifying Essential Questions and Understandings
Music

Use one or more of the following questions to filter topics or big ideas to identify possible essential questions and desired understandings.

Topics and Big Ideas:

> Music Theory

What essential questions are raised by this idea or topic? What, *specifically*, about the idea or topic do you want students to come to understand?

Why study music theory? So what?

What makes the study of music theory universal?

If the unit on music theory is a story, what's the moral of the story?

What's the Big Idea implied in the skill or process of music theory?

What larger concept, issue, or problem underlies music theory?

What couldn't we do if we didn't understand music theory?

How is music theory used and applied in the larger world?

What is a real-world insight about music theory?

What is the value of studying music theory?

Essential Questions: **Q**
- What makes music engaging?
- How does music convey feeling and evoke emotion?

Understandings: **U**
- Carefully placed intervals of silence make music more dramatic.
- Surprises within familiar melodies, harmonies, rhythms, and progressions are at the heart of creativity in music.

Identifying Essential Questions and Understandings
Design Tool with Prompts

Use one or more of the following questions to filter topics or big ideas to identify possible essential questions and desired understandings.

Topics and Big Ideas:

What essential questions are raised by this idea or topic?
What, *specifically*, about the idea or topic do you
want students to come to understand?

Why study _____? So what?

What makes the study of _____ universal?

If the unit on _____ is a story, what's the moral of the story?

What's the Big Idea implied in the skill or process of _____?

What larger concept, issue, or problem underlies _____?

What couldn't we do if we didn't understand _____?

How is _____ used and applied in the larger world?

What is a real-world insight about _____?

What is the value of studying _____?

Essential Questions: Q

Understandings: U

Templates

Stage 1

Stage 2

Stage 3

Peer review

Exercises

Process sheets

Glossary

Drafting a Design from Big Ideas
Statistics

Established Goals: **G**

All students will connect mathematics to other learning by understanding the interrelationships of mathematical ideas and the roles that mathematics and mathematical modeling play in other disciplines and in life.

—NJ Mathematics Standard 3

Understandings: **U**

- Statistics can represent or model complex phenomena.
- Statistics can be manipulated to obscure the truth.
- There are various mathematical means for reaching "fair" decisions.

Essential Questions: **Q**

- What are the limits of mathematical representation and modeling?
- What mathematical methods provide the "fairest" rankings?
- What is "average"?
- How can mathematics help us decide (e.g., in grading, voting, ranking)?

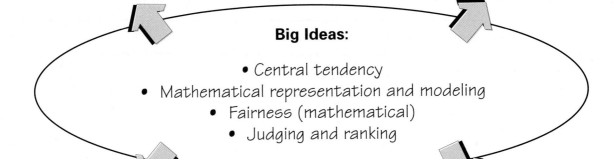

Big Ideas:

- Central tendency
- Mathematical representation and modeling
- Fairness (mathematical)
- Judging and ranking

Predictable Misunderstandings and Errors:

- Computing the "average" or determining the majority is the only fair method.

- Statistics never lie.

- Mathematics cannot help us resolve differences of opinion about fairness.

Goals or Rationale:

I want students to understand the varied uses, and pros and cons, of each measure of central tendency. I want them to recognize the value of math in everyday situations, including matters of opinion. These understandings will give them greater power in making sense of statistics and overcoming common misconceptions about probability and fairness.

Drafting a Design from Big Ideas
Reading

Established Goals: (G)

Students will read and respond in individual, literal, critical, and evaluative ways to literary, informational, and persuasive texts; describe the text by giving an initial reaction to the text and explaining its general content and purpose; and generate questions before, during, and after reading, writing, listening, and viewing.

—CT Language Arts Standard 1—Reading and Responding

Understandings: (U)

- Reading involves making sense of the text, not just decoding the words.
- Sometimes authors convey their ideas indirectly and the reader must infer their meanings.
- Friends are trusted people who look out for our interests.
- True friendship is often revealed in times of trouble.

Essential Questions: (Q)

- What do good readers do?
- Why do writers and speakers sometimes mean something other than what they write or say?
- How do we read between the lines?
- Who are my true friends, and how do I know?

Big Ideas:

- Reading for meaning
- Indirect expression
- True friends vs. acquaintances
- Fair-weather friends

Predictable Misunderstandings and Errors:

- Reading is decoding the words.
- If it's in a book, it must be true.
- Authors always write exactly what they mean.
- A friend is someone you like to play with.
- Friends never argue.

Goals or Rationale:

I have two simultaneous goals:
(1) develop greater skill in reading for meaning, and (2) gain a greater understanding of the qualities of true friendship. Through *Frog and Toad Are Friends* and other stories, I want students to learn that careful reading and thinking can help us explore difficult questions.

Templates | Stage 1 | Stage 2 | Stage 3 | Peer review | Exercises | Process sheets | Glossary

Drafting a Design from Big Ideas
History

Established Goals: (G)

The student will understand the causes and effects of the Civil War with emphasis on slavery, states' rights, leadership, settlement of the West, secession, and military events.

—*Virginia Standards of Learning—History 5.7*

Understandings: (U)

- There is rarely a single, obvious cause to a complex historical event.
- History is "story," and who tells the story affects how it is presented.
- States' rights disagreements, differences in the cultures and economies of North and South, and disputes over slavery were key causes of the Civil War.
- The legacy of the Civil War is still felt in regional differences, in national and regional politics, and matters of cultural values.

Essential Questions: (Q)

- What were the obvious (and unobvious) causes of the Civil War?
- Whose "story" is it?
- Is there ever a "just" war?
- Why would a brother kill a brother?
- In what ways are the effects of the Civil War still with us?

Big Ideas:

- Slavery (as economic, political, and moral issue)
- Federal control vs. states' rights
- "Just" cause

Predictable Misunderstandings and Errors:

- The war was fought over the morality of slavery, and the "good guys" won.
- If it is in a history book, it must be true.
- Most events have a single, obvious cause and obvious effects.

Goals or Rationale:

I want students to learn that the Civil War was complex, and that its meaning has changed over time, varies by place and still affects us and our views. I also want them to be aware of the horror of war and to empathize with the effects on families and sense of self (as conveyed so well in Ken Burns's *Civil War* video series).

Drafting a Design from Big Ideas

Established Goals: **G**

Understandings: **U**

Essential Questions: **Q**

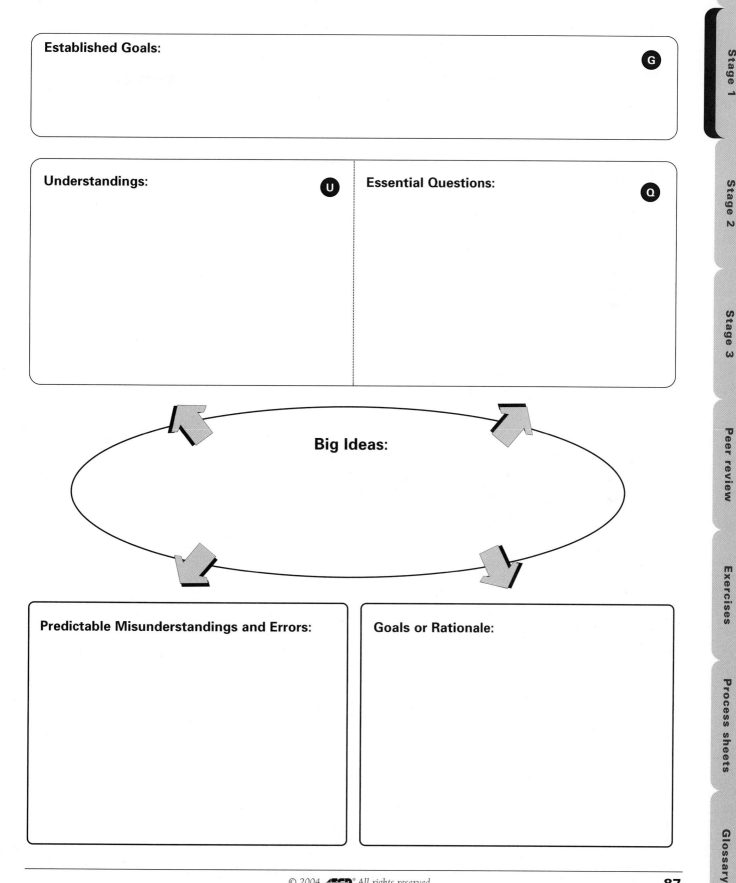

Big Ideas:

Predictable Misunderstandings and Errors:

Goals or Rationale:

Templates

Stage 1

Stage 2

Stage 3

Peer review

Exercises

Process sheets

Glossary

Concept Attainment for Essential Questions

Part 1—Examine the following examples and nonexamples to determine the common characteristics of Essential Questions. List these in the box below.

Essential Questions

1. How are "form" and "function" related in biology?
2. How do effective writers hook and hold their readers?
3. Who "wins" and who "loses" when technologies change?
4. Should it be an axiom if it is not obvious?
5. What distinguishes fluent foreigners from native speakers?
6. How would life be different if we couldn't measure time?

Nonessential Questions

7. How many legs does a spider have? How does an elephant use its trunk?
8. What is "foreshadowing"? Can you find an example of foreshadowing in the story?
9. What is the original meaning of the term, "technology" (from its Greek root, *techne*)?
10. By what axioms are we able to prove the Pythagorean theorem?
11. What are some French colloquialisms?
12. How many minutes are in an hour? How many hours are in a day?

List common characteristics of Essential Questions:

Part 2—Use your list of characteristics as criteria to determine which of the following are Essential Questions. Check "yes" or "no" after each example.

	YES	NO
13. What is the relationship between popularity and greatness in literature?	❏	❏
14. When was the Magna Carta signed?	❏	❏
15. Crustaceans—what's up with that?	❏	❏
16. Which president of the United States has the most disappointing legacy?	❏	❏
17. When is an equation linear?	❏	❏
18. To what extent are common sense and science related?	❏	❏

Refine your list of key characteristics of Essential Questions:

Essential Questions—Samples

Ｑ

Arithmetic (numeration)
- What is a number? Why do we have numbers? What if we didn't have numbers?
- Can everything be quantified?

Arts (visual and performing)
- Where do artists get their ideas?
- How does art reflect, as well as shape, culture?

Culinary Arts
- When is it ok to deviate from the recipe?
- What makes a safe kitchen?

Dance
- How and what can we communicate through the language of dance?
- In what ways can motion evoke emotion?

Economics
- What determines value?
- Can macroeconomics inform microeconomics (and vice versa)?

Foreign Language
- What distinguishes a fluent foreigner from a native speaker?
- What can we learn about our own language and culture from studying another?

Geography
- What makes places unique and different?
- How does where we live influence *how* we live?

Government
- Who should decide?
- How should we balance the rights of individuals with the common good?

Health
- What is healthful living?
- How can a diet be healthy for one person and not another?

Templates

Stage 1

Stage 2

Stage 3

Peer review

Exercises

Process sheets

Glossary

Templates

Stage 1

Stage 2

Stage 3

Peer review

Exercises

Process sheets

Glossary

Essential Questions—Samples (continued)

Q

History
- Whose story is it? Is history the story told by the winners?
- What can we learn from the past?

Literature
- What makes a great book?
- Can fiction reveal truth? Should a story teach you something?

Mathematics
- When is the "correct" answer not the best solution?
- What are the limits of mathematical representation and modeling?

Music
- How are sounds and silence organized in various musical forms?
- What roles does music play in the world?

Physical Education and Athletics
- Who is a winner?
- Is pain necessary for progress in athletics? ("No pain, no gain")

Reading and Language Arts
- What makes a great story?
- How do you read between the lines?
- Why do we punctuate? What if we didn't have punctuation marks?

Science
- To what extent are science and common sense related?
- How are "form" and "function" related in biology?

Technology
- In what ways can technology enhance expression and communication? In what ways might technology hinder it?
- What are the pros and cons of technological progress?

Writing
- Why write?
- How do effective writers hook and hold their readers?
- What is a complete thought?

Essential Questions

(description)

Ⓠ

Have no simple "right" answer; they are meant to be argued.

Essential Questions yield inquiry and argument—a variety of plausible (and arguable) responses, not straight-forward facts that end the matter. They serve as doorways into focused yet lively inquiry and research. They should *uncover* rather than cover the subject's controversies, puzzles, and perspectives. They are intended to result in conclusions drawn by the learner, not recited facts. For example, Does art reflect culture or help shape it? Can we look but not see? Why do "seers" see what the rest of us don't? Does the artist see more clearly or look elsewhere?

Are designed to provoke and sustain student inquiry, while focusing learning and final performances.

Essential Questions work best when they are designed and edited to be thought provoking to students, engaging them in sustained, focused inquiries that culminate in important performance. Such questions often involve the counterintuitive, the visceral, the whimsical, the controversial, the provocative. For example, Is the Internet dangerous for kids? Are censorship and democracy compatible? Does food that is good for you have to taste bad? Why write? Students develop and deepen their understanding of important ideas as they explore these questions.

Often address the conceptual or philosophical foundations of a discipline.

Essential Questions reflect the most historically important issues, problems, and debates in a field of study. For example, Is history inevitably biased? What is a proof? Nature or nurture? By examining such questions, students are engaged in thinking like an expert.

Raise other important questions.

Thought-provoking Essential Questions are naturally generative. They lead to other important questions within, and sometimes across, subject boundaries. For example, In nature, do only the strong survive? leads to What do we mean by "strong"? Are insects strong (since they are survivors)? What does it mean to be psychologically strong? Inquiries into human biology and the physics of physiology also follow.

Naturally and appropriately recur.

The same important questions are asked and asked again throughout one's learning and in the history of the field. For example, What makes a great book great? Are the Harry Potter novels great books? These questions can be productively examined and reexamined by 1st graders as well as college students. Over time, student responses become more sophisticated, nuanced, well-reasoned and supported as their understandings deepen.

Stimulate vital, ongoing rethinking of big ideas, assumptions, and prior lessons.

Essential questions challenge our unexamined assumptions, the inevitable simplification of our earlier learning, and the arguments we may unthinkingly take for granted. They force us to ask deep questions about the nature, origin, and extent of our understanding. For example, In light of fractions, place value, irrationals, and negative square roots—what is a number? Is it "democratic" to have an electoral college? What IS a friend? Can the enemy of my enemy be my friend? What is a story, if a story has no clear plot or moral? Is history more of a story than a science? What are the implications for studying history, if so?

Types of Questions

Q

Overarching Questions

These questions point beyond the particulars of a unit to the larger, transferable Big Ideas and enduring understandings. Practically speaking, the specific topics, events, or texts of the unit are typically not mentioned in the framing of overarching questions. For example, Is science fiction great literature? is an overarching question for any unit on a specific text such as *Stranger in a Strange Land.*

Topical Questions

These questions are subject- and topic-specific. Topical questions frame a unit of study. They guide the exploration of Big Ideas and processes within particular subjects. For example, What aspects of *Stranger in a Strange Land* are plausible? guides inquiry within a specific literature unit. This unit question links to the overarching question, How "true" is a fictional story? This question is addressed within other English and Language Arts units.

Samples

Art
- In what ways does art reflect culture as well as shape it?
- How do artists choose tools, techniques, and materials to express their ideas?

Unit on masks
- What do masks and their use reveal about the culture?
- What tools, techniques, and materials are used in creating masks from different cultures?

Literature
- What makes a great story?
- How do effective writers hook and hold their readers?

Unit on mysteries
- What is unique about the mystery genre?
- How do great mystery writers hook and hold their readers?

Science
- How does an organism's structure enable it to survive in its environment?
- How do organisms survive in harsh or changing environments?

Unit on insects
- How do the structure and behavior of insects enable them to survive?
- How do insects survive when their environment changes?

Mathematics
- If axioms are like the rules of the game, when should we change the rules?

Unit on the parallel postulate
- Why is this an axiom if it's so complex?
- What no longer holds true if we deny it?

History and Government
- How do governments balance the rights of individuals with the common good?
- How and why do we provide checks and balances on government power?

Unit on the U.S. Constitution
- In what ways does the Constitution attempt to limit abuse of government powers?
- Does separation of powers (three branches of government) create a deadlock?

Drafting Essential Questions
Reading and Literature

Q

Overarching Essential Questions	Adapt these questions or generate new ones
What makes a great book or story great? What is the relationship between popularity and greatness in literature? Is a "good read" always a great book?	
Why read fiction? Can a fictional story be "true"? What is the relationship between "fiction" and "truth"? Is historical fiction a contradiction?	
What is a story? How are stories from other places and times about me? Must a story have a moral? Must a story have heroes and villains? Should a story or fairy tale teach you something?	
Why read? What can we learn from print? Can all of our experiences be put into words? Does literature primarily reflect culture or shape it? To what extent is written text conservative and to what extent dangerous?	
What do good readers do? What do they do when they don't understand? How do texts differ? How should I read different types of texts?	
What is the author saying? How do I know? What is the gist? What is the main idea? How do I read between the lines? How do I know I am getting the point and not merely imposing my views and experience?	
From whose viewpoint are we reading? What is the author's angle or perspective? What should we do when texts or authors disagree?	
What's new and what's old here? Have we run across this idea before? So what? Why does it matter?	

Templates

Stage 1

Stage 2

Stage 3

Peer review

Exercises

Process sheets

Glossary

Drafting Essential Questions

Writing, Listening, and Speaking

Q

Overarching Essential Questions	Adapt these questions or generate new ones
Writing Why write? What if writing didn't exist? Why share personal experiences in writing? To what extent is the pen mightier than the sword? How is written language different from spoken language? What makes writing worth reading?	
How do writers express their thoughts and feelings? Where do ideas for writing come from? What makes writing flow?	
How do effective writers hook and hold their readers? What makes writing easy to follow? What is the best beginning? ending? What is the best order (sequence)? What is a complete thought?	
Why am I writing? For whom? What am I trying to achieve through my writing? Who will read my writing? What will work best for my audience?	
Speaking and Listening Why speak? What do good speakers sound like? How do good speakers express their thoughts and feelings? What makes a speaker easy to follow? How is spoken language different from written language? What is body language? Why use it?	
Why am I speaking? What am I trying to say? To whom am I speaking? Who will listen? How can I help them understand me?	
What does a good listener listen for? Can one hear but not listen?	

Drafting Essential Questions
History and Geography

Q

Overarching Essential Questions	Adapt these questions or generate new ones
Historical Analysis and Interpretation Why study history? What can we learn from the past? How am I connected to people in the past? To what extent is history different from the past?	
How do we know what happened in the past? What can we legitimately infer from artifacts? What should we do when primary sources disagree? Who do we believe and why? Whose "story" is it? Is history inevitably biased? Is history the story told by the "winners"? Who were the "winners" and who were the "losers" in any historical event?	
What causes change? What remains the same? How do patterns of cause and effect manifest themselves in the chronology of history? How has the world changed, and how might it change in the future? Is it always true that those who do not learn from history are doomed to repeat it?	
Geography Why is "where" important? Why is/was _____ located there? What makes places unique and different? What defines a region? How do a region's geography, climate, and natural resources affect the way people live and work? How does where I live influence how I live? Why do people move?	
What story do maps and globes tell? How and why do maps and globes change? How do maps and globes reflect history?	

Templates · Stage 1 · Stage 2 · Stage 3 · Peer review · Exercises · Process sheets · Glossary

Drafting Essential Questions

Government and Politics

Overarching Essential Questions	Adapt these questions or generate new ones
Who should govern or rule? Should the majority always rule? Why do we have rules and laws? Who should make the rules and laws? Is it ever OK to break the law? To what extent should society control individuals? How do governments balance the rights of individuals with the common good? What are "inalienable rights"? Should _____ be restricted or regulated? (e.g., immigration, alcohol/drugs, media) When? Who decides?	
How do the structures and functions of government interrelate? How do different political systems vary in their toleration and encouragement of change? How do politics and economics interrelate?	
How do personal responsibilities and civic responsibilities differ? Can an individual really make a difference? What are the roles and responsibilities of citizens in a democracy? What is a good citizen? How do citizens (both individually and collectively) influence government policy?	
What is power? What forms does it take? How is power gained, used, and justified? How can abuse of power be avoided? Is a two-party system best?	
What constitutes a great leader? Are great leaders made or born (nature or nurture)?	

Government and Politics

Templates

Stage 1

Stage 2

Stage 3

Peer review

Exercises

Process sheets

Glossary

Drafting Essential Questions
Economics and Culture

(Q)

Overarching Essential Questions	Adapt these questions or generate new ones
Economics Why do we have money? What is the difference between needs and wants? How does something acquire value? How much should things cost? Who decides? Who should produce goods and services? How does the free market system affect my life? our community? our society? the world? Should government regulate business and economy? What goods and services should government provide? Who should pay? Who should benefit? Should everyone be expected to work? What does it mean to "make a living"?	
How does technological change influence people's lives? society? What social, political, and economic opportunities and problems arise from changes in technology?	
Culture What does it mean to be "civilized"? Are modern civilizations more civilized than ancient ones? Why should we study other cultures? Who are the "heroes" in a culture and what do they reveal about the culture? How and why do we celebrate holidays? What are the significant symbols and icons of civilizations and cultures? Who and what do we memorialize?	
What happens when cultures collide? How are all religions the same? How and why do beliefs change? Why do people fight? Is conflict inevitable? What is worth fighting for? Is there a "just" war? What is revolution? Are revolutions inevitable?	

Templates · Stage 1 · Stage 2 · Stage 3 · Peer review · Exercises · Process sheets · Glossary

Drafting Essential Questions
Mathematics

Q

Overarching Essential Questions	Adapt these questions or generate new ones
What kind of problem is it? What do the best problem solvers do? What should we do when we're stuck? What does it mean to reason mathematically? When is the "correct" mathematical answer not the best solution?	
What is a number? Can everything be quantified? What couldn't we do if we didn't have or couldn't use numbers? Why do we have negative numbers? irrational numbers? imaginary numbers?	
What is a pattern? How do we find patterns? What can patterns reveal?	
How might we show _____? In what other ways (how else)? How do we best represent the part and whole relationship? the pattern? the sequence?	
What are the limits of mathematical modeling? In what ways does a model illuminate and in what ways does it distort? How can numbers (data) lie or mislead?	
How does what we measure influence how we measure? How does how we measure influence what we conclude?	
When is estimation better than counting and when not? When is simplification helpful? harmful? When should we sample? When shouldn't we? How much or many (of a sample) is enough?	
How sure are you? What's the likely margin of error? How accurate (precise) is it? How accurate (precise) does this need to be? What is proof? Do I have one?	

Drafting Essential Questions
Science and Chemistry

Q

Overarching Essential Questions	Adapt these questions or generate new ones
Nature of Science What is science? How does it differ from other disciplines? How is scientific knowledge generated and validated? How are scientific questions answered? How do we decide which scientific claims to believe? What's the evidence? How are science and common sense related? How does opinion affect inquiry? What is the role of serendipity in scientific advances? How do you study the unobservable? How do you measure the unquantifiable? What drives scientific and technological advancement? In what ways do technological advances influence scientific inquiry? How might advances in science and technology affect society?	
Chemistry How is the periodic table organized? How can materials with the same chemical composition be so different (e.g., graphite, diamonds)? How is energy conserved? How is matter conserved? How are materials recycled or disposed of? How do the unique chemical and physical properties of water make life on earth possible? What is the role of carbon in the molecular diversity of life? How do structures of biologically important molecules (e.g., carbohydrates, lipids, proteins, nucleic acids) account for their functions? How do enzymes regulate the rate of chemical reactions? Why do you gasp for breath during exercise? Why and how does the ozone hole form? What happens to acid rain?	

Templates

Stage 1

Stage 2

Stage 3

Peer review

Exercises

Process sheets

Glossary

Templates

Stage 1

Stage 2

Stage 3

Peer review

Exercises

Process sheets

Glossary

Drafting Essential Questions
Science

Q

Overarching Essential Questions	Adapt these questions or generate new ones
Life Science How do we come to know the natural world and our place in it? How do we classify the things around us? What is the basis of life? How can we prove cells make up living things? How are characteristics of living things passed on through generations? How are form and function related in biology? How do the structure and behavior patterns of organisms enable them to survive? How do organisms survive in harsh or changing environments? How do species change through time? How are new populations developed through natural selection? What are the life cycles of living things? How do living things obtain and use energy? How does energy move? Where does it go? What is a system? How do systems interact? How does an ecosystem respond to change? Is this a healthy place? What's the evidence?	
Physical Science How are force and motion connected? How do forces affect the motion of an object? How do we measure matter? How and why does matter change? How is energy conserved? How is matter conserved? How do matter and energy relate? What natural phenomena are generated by heat? How and why do machines make work easier? How are energy transformations applied in today's world? What relationships, if any, exist among different kinds of atoms? How are molecules arranged in different states of matter?	

100

Drafting Essential Questions
Visual and Performing Arts

Q

Overarching Essential Questions	Adapt these questions or generate new ones
What is art? Where can we find art? Why and how do people create art? What makes art "great"? How does art communicate?	
How does art reflect as well as shape culture? What can artworks tell us about a society? What can we learn from studying the art of others? How do artists from different eras explore and express similar themes?	
What is the artistic process? What factors influence artistic expression? How and where do artists get their ideas? How do artists express their ideas? What does the design of art say about its creator? How do you know when the creative process is complete?	
How can we "read" and understand a work of art? Who determines the meaning of art? Does art have a message? How would we know? Should art have a message? Is one picture worth 1,000 words?	
How is feeling or mood conveyed musically? visually? through movement? In what ways have technological changes influenced artistic expression? Is the medium the message? Are some media better than others (e.g., for communicating particular ideas or emotions)?	
Do artists have a responsibility to their audiences? to society? Should we ever censor artistic expression? Should aesthetics supersede function? Is art more important than utility? What if we didn't have the arts in our world?	

Templates

Stage 1

Stage 2

Stage 3

Peer review

Exercises

Process sheets

Glossary

Drafting Essential Questions
World Languages

Overarching Essential Questions	Adapt these questions or generate new ones
Why learn another language? Why study another culture? How does language shape culture? How does culture shape language? How do native speakers differ from fluent foreigners? Why isn't a dictionary enough? What do I do when my ideas are more complex than my ability to communicate them? How can one express complex ideas using simple terms?	

Drafting Essential Questions
Physical Education and Health

Overarching Essential Questions	Adapt these questions or generate new ones
What is healthful living? What is wellness? Who is a winner? How does physical fitness relate to health? What constitutes a lifelong sport? When is physical activity good and not so good for your body?	
What strategies do the top performers and teams use? Is pain necessary for progress in athletics? How do you achieve greater power without losing control? What type of feedback is best? How can you best use feedback to improve performance?	

Templates

Stage 1

Stage 2

Stage 3

Peer review

Exercises

Process sheets

Glossary

Drafting Essential Questions
Media and Technology

Overarching Essential Questions	Adapt these questions or generate new ones
How can technology enhance understanding? In what ways can technology enhance expression and communication? In what ways might technology hinder it? What are the pros and cons of technological progress? Should technology be controlled? by whom? How can we find out things we want to know? What is the best source of information? What do you have to remember vs. what can you just look up? What makes information "true"? Is some information better than other information on the same topic? How do we judge? How do we know what to believe (from what we hear, read, see on the Internet)?	

Drafting Essential Questions
Education

Overarching Essential Questions	Adapt these questions or generate new ones
What educational beliefs about teaching and learning do we share? To what extent do our policies, priorities, and actions reflect our educational beliefs? How would people know that we are a standards-based school and district? What content is worth uncovering? How will we know that students *really* understand the Big Ideas? Are we assessing everything we value? Is anything important falling through the cracks because we are not assessing it? To what extent is instruction engaging and effective? How might we walk the talk and apply standards to our own work? How might we work smarter and more effectively? Would you want your child to attend school?	

Templates

Stage 1

Stage 2

Stage 3

Peer review

Exercises

Process sheets

Glossary

Essential Questions in Skill Areas

Statistics, Reading, and Athletics

A common misunderstanding among many educators is that teaching for understanding of Big Ideas is not really central to the teaching of skill-focused areas, such as beginning literacy, physical education, and mathematics. On the contrary, everything we know about learning tells us that teaching for conceptual understanding is essential to more accurate and efficient skill performance. Essential questions in skill areas may be considered in terms of the following categories:

- **Key concepts**—*What are the Big Ideas underlying effective skill performance?*
- **Purpose, value**—*Why is the skill important?*
- **Strategy, tactics**—*What strategies do skilled performers employ? How can skill performance become more efficient and effective?*
- **Context**—*When should you use the skill or strategy?*

Use the space below to brainstorm possible Essential Questions for important skills.

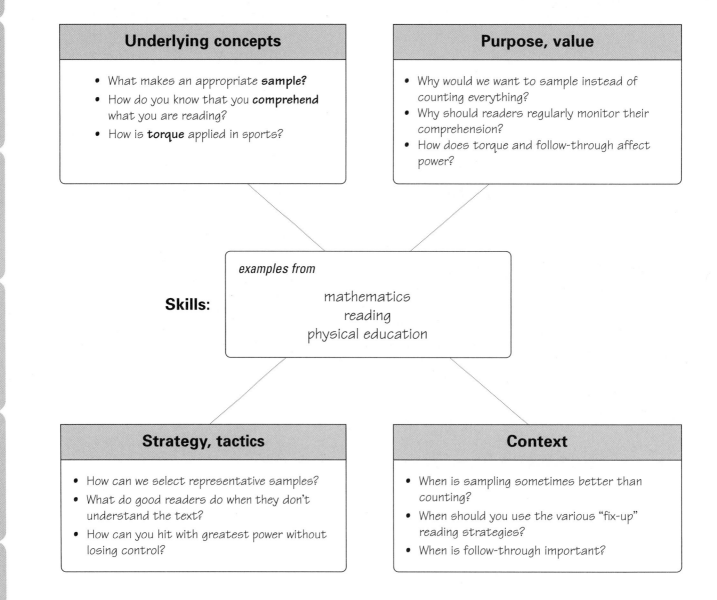

Underlying concepts

- What makes an appropriate **sample?**
- How do you know that you **comprehend** what you are reading?
- How is **torque** applied in sports?

Purpose, value

- Why would we want to sample instead of counting everything?
- Why should readers regularly monitor their comprehension?
- How does torque and follow-through affect power?

Skills:

examples from

mathematics
reading
physical education

Strategy, tactics

- How can we select representative samples?
- What do good readers do when they don't understand the text?
- How can you hit with greatest power without losing control?

Context

- When is sampling sometimes better than counting?
- When should you use the various "fix-up" reading strategies?
- When is follow-through important?

Essential Questions in Skill Areas

A common misunderstanding among many educators is that teaching for understanding of Big Ideas is not really central to the teaching of skill-focused areas, such as beginning literacy, physical education, and mathematics. On the contrary, everything we know about learning tells us that teaching for conceptual understanding is essential to more accurate and efficient skill performance. Essential questions in skill areas may be considered in terms of the following categories:

Essential questions in skill areas may be considered in terms of the following categories:

- **Key concepts**—*What are the Big Ideas underlying effective skill performance?*
- **Purpose, value**—*Why is the skill important?*
- **Strategy, tactics**—*What strategies do skilled performers employ? How can skill performance become more efficient and effective?*
- **Context**—*When should you use the skill?*

Use the space below to brainstorm possible Essential Questions for important skills.

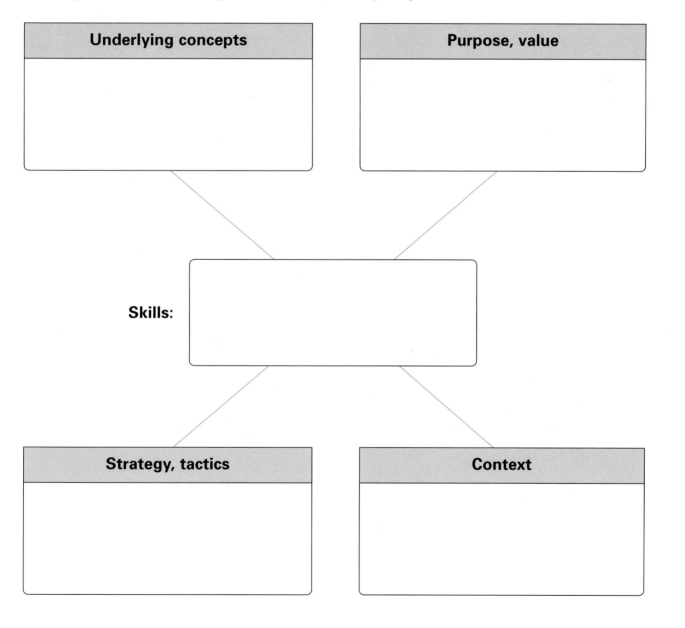

Underlying concepts	Purpose, value

Skills:

Strategy, tactics	Context

Templates

Stage 1

Stage 2

Stage 3

Peer review

Exercises

Process sheets

Glossary

Tips for Using Essential Questions

1. Organize programs, courses, units of study, and lessons around the questions. Make the "content" answer the questions.

2. Select or design assessment tasks (up front) that are explicitly linked to the questions. The tasks and performance standards should clarify what acceptable pursuit of, and answers to, the questions actually looks like.

3. Use a reasonable number of questions per unit (two to five). Make less be more. Prioritize content for students to make the work clearly focus on a few key questions.

4. Frame the questions in "kid language" as needed to make them more accessible. Edit the questions to make them as engaging and provocative as possible for the age group.

5. Ensure that every student understands the questions and sees their value. Conduct a survey or informal check, as necessary, to ensure this understanding and recognition.

6. Derive and design specific concrete exploratory activities and inquiries for each question.

7. Sequence the questions so that they naturally lead from one to another.

8. Post the essential questions in the classroom and encourage students to organize notebooks around them to make clear their importance for study and note taking.

9. Help students to personalize the questions. Have them share examples, personal stories, and hunches. Encourage them to bring in clippings and artifacts to help make the questions come alive.

10. Allot sufficient time for "unpacking" the questions—examining subquestions and probing implications—mindful of student age, experience, and other instructional obligations. Use question and concept maps to show relatedness of questions.

11. Share your questions with other faculty to make planning and teaching for cross-subject matter coherence more likely. Encourage ideas to promote overarching questions schoolwide—ask teachers to post their questions in the faculty room and in department meeting and planning areas. Type and circulate questions in the faculty bulletin. Present and discuss questions at faculty and P.T.S.A. meetings.

Other tips:

_____

_____

_____

_____

_____

Concept Attainment for Framing Enduring Understandings

U

Part 1—Examine the following examples to determine the common characteristics of effectively framed enduring understandings.

Properly Framed	**Improperly Framed**
The student will understand that . . .	*The student will understand . . .*
1. In a free-market economy, price is a function of supply and demand.	6. That the price of long-distance phone calls has declined during the past decade.
2. True friendship is revealed during difficult times, not happy times.	7. True friendship.
3. Statistical analysis and data display often reveal patterns that may not be obvious.	8. How to calculate mean, median, and mode.
4. The most efficient and effective stroke mechanics in swimming involve pushing the maximum amount of water directly backward.	9. That they should not cup their hands when swimming the freestyle.
5. The interaction of heredity and experience influences behavior.	10. DNA.

List common characteristics of the properly framed examples:

Part 2—Use your list of characteristics as criteria to determine which of the following examples are effectively framed as Enduring Understandings. Check "yes" or "no" after each example.

	YES	NO
11. The concept of estivation.	☐	☐
12. The USDA Food Pyramid presents relative, not absolute, guidelines for a balanced diet.	☐	☐
13. Mathematical models simplify reality to enable useful solutions.	☐	☐
14. How to tell time.	☐	☐
15. The causes and effects of the Civil War.	☐	☐
16. That the *Magna Carta* was signed on June 15, 1215.	☐	☐

Templates
Stage 1
Stage 2
Stage 3
Peer review
Exercises
Process sheets
Glossary

Enduring Understandings
Samples Arranged by Subject

U

Arithmetic (numeration)
- Numbers are concepts that enable people to represent quantities, sequences, and rates.
- Different number systems can represent the same quantities (e.g., bases).

Art
- The greatest artists often break with established traditions and techniques to better express what they see and feel.
- Available tools, techniques, and resources influence artistic expression.
- Great art addresses universal themes of human existence.

Business and Marketing
- No business can successfully satisfy all consumers with the same product, so it must identify its target market.
- Patterns of consumption inform production and marketing decisions.

Dance
- Dance is a language of shape, space, timing, and energy.
- Movement can communicate ideas and feelings.

Economics
- In a free-market economy, price is a function of supply and demand.
- Relative scarcity may lead to trade and economic interdependence or to conflict.

Foreign Language
- Studying other languages and cultures offers insights into our own.
- Meaning is conveyed through phrasing, intonation, and syntax. (Just because you can translate all the words doesn't mean you understand the speaker.)

Geography
- The topography, climate, and natural resources of a region influence the culture, economy, and lifestyle of its inhabitants.
- All maps distort Earth's representation of area, shape, distance, and direction.

Government
- Democratic governments must balance the rights of individuals with the common good.
- A written constitution sets forth the terms and limits of a government's power.
- Different political systems vary in their tolerance and encouragement of innovation.

Templates
Stage 1
Stage 2
Stage 3
Peer review
Exercises
Process sheets
Glossary

Enduring Understandings (continued)
Samples Arranged by Subject

Health
- Dietary requirements vary for individuals based on age, activity level, weight, metabolism, and health.
- Participation in lifelong sports promotes physical and mental health.

History
- History involves interpretation; historians can and do disagree.
- Historical interpretation is influenced by one's perspective (e.g., freedom fighters vs. terrorists).

Media and Technology
- Technological progress presents new possibilities and problems.
- Just because information is on the Internet or in a book doesn't make it true.

Literature
- Novelists often provide insights about human experience through fiction.
- An effective story engages the reader by setting up questions—tensions, mystery, dilemmas, or uncertainty.
- Everybody is entitled to an opinion about what a text means, but the text supports some interpretations more than others.

Mathematics
- Sometimes the "correct" mathematical answer is not the best solution to real-world problems.
- Heuristics are strategies that can aid problem solving (e.g., breaking a complex problem into chunks, creating a visual representation, working backward from the desired result, guess and check).
- Statistical analysis and data display often reveal patterns that may not be obvious.

Music
- The silence is as important as the notes.
- Popular music has shifted from emphasizing melody and lyrics to emphasizing multilayered rhythms.

Philosophy and Religion
- Ethicists disagree on whether the results of an action or a person's intentions matter most in judging the morality of actions.
- One gains insight into a culture by studying its religious traditions.

Templates | Stage 1 | Stage 2 | Stage 3 | Peer review | Exercises | Process sheets | Glossary

Enduring Understandings (continued)
Samples Arranged by Subject

U

Physical Education and Athletics
- Creating space away from the ball or puck spreads the defense and increases scoring opportunities (e.g., in basketball, soccer, football, hockey, water polo, and lacrosse).
- The most efficient and effective swimming strokes involve pulling and pushing the water directly backward.
- Proper follow-through increases accuracy when throwing (e.g., baseball, basketball) and swinging (e.g., golf, tennis).

Reading/Language Arts
- Effective readers use specific strategies to help them better understand the text (e.g., using context clues, questioning the author, predicting what will come next, rereading, summarizing).
- Different types of texts (e.g., narrative, mystery, biography, expository, persuasive) have different structures.
- Understanding a text's structure helps a reader better understand its meaning.

Science
- Scientific claims must be verified by independent investigations.
- Standardized measures allow people to more accurately describe the physical world.
- Correlation does not ensure causality.

Teaching
- Effective teaching results from careful and thoughtful planning.
- The need for behavior management is reduced when teaching is engaging and meaningful to the learners.
- A teacher's job is not to cover a textbook. The textbook should serve as a resource, not the syllabus.

Writing
- Audience and purpose (e.g., to inform, persuade, entertain) influence the use of literary techniques (e.g., style, tone, word choice).
- Writers do not always say what they mean. Indirect forms of expression (e.g., satire, irony) require readers to read between the lines to find the intended meaning.
- Punctuation marks and grammar rules are like highway signs and traffic signals. They guide readers through the text to help avoid confusion.

From Goals or Topics to Enduring Understandings

Westward Expansion and Pioneer Life

Given the goals or topics of your unit, use the web organizer below to brainstorm possible understandings.

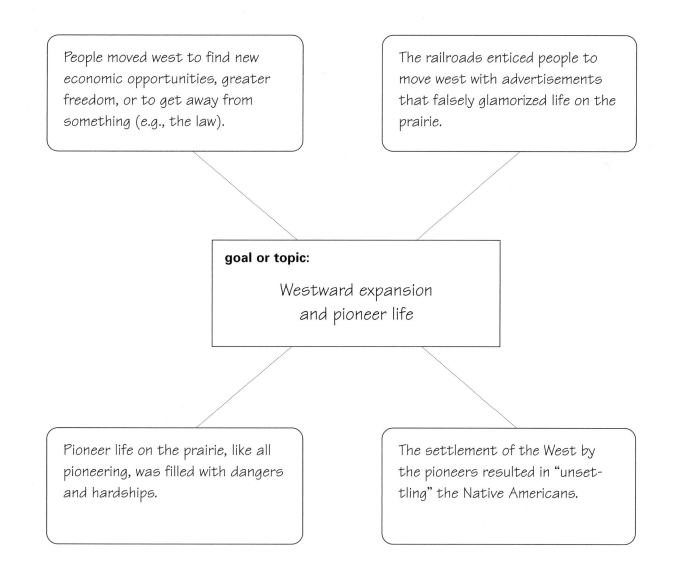

People moved west to find new economic opportunities, greater freedom, or to get away from something (e.g., the law).

The railroads enticed people to move west with advertisements that falsely glamorized life on the prairie.

goal or topic:

Westward expansion and pioneer life

Pioneer life on the prairie, like all pioneering, was filled with dangers and hardships.

The settlement of the West by the pioneers resulted in "unsettling" the Native Americans.

Templates

Stage 1

Stage 2

Stage 3

Peer review

Exercises

Process sheets

Glossary

From Goals or Topics to Enduring Understandings

Templates

Stage 1

Stage 2

Stage 3

Peer review

Exercises

Process sheets

Glossary

Given the goals or topics of your unit, use the web organizer below to brainstorm possible understandings.

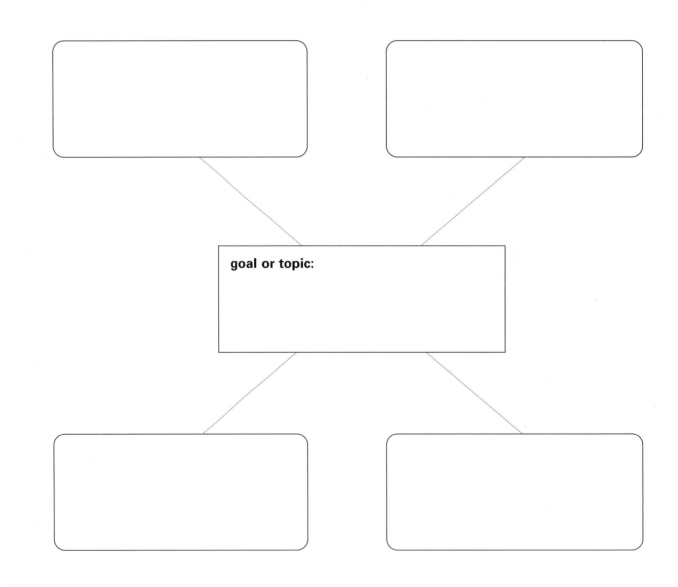

goal or topic:

Linking Big Ideas to Construct Enduring Understandings

Combine two or more Big Ideas to form generalizations. Use linking verbs or verb phrases to connect the ideas.

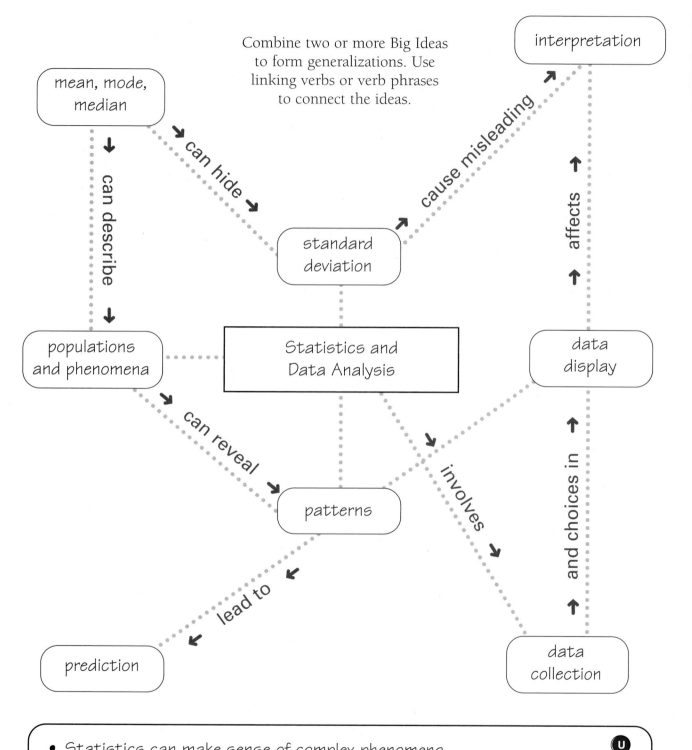

- Statistics can make sense of complex phenomena.
- Data analysis often reveals patterns and enables prediction.
- Choices in data collection and representation affect interpretation.
- Statistics can mislead as well as reveal.

Templates · Stage 1 · Stage 2 · Stage 3 · Peer review · Exercises · Process sheets · Glossary

Two Types of Enduring Understandings

Ⓤ

Overarching Understandings	**Topical Understandings**
These understandings point beyond the specifics of a unit to the larger, transferable insights we want students to acquire. They often reflect year-long course or K–12 program understandings. The specific topics, events, or texts of the unit are typically not mentioned in the overarching understandings.	Topical understandings are subject- and topic-specific. They focus on the *particular* insights we want students to acquire about the topic within a unit of study. Topical understandings are less likely to transfer to other topics.

Examples

Art
- The greatest artists often break with established traditions and techniques to better express what they see and feel.

Unit on impressionism
- Impressionist artists departed from traditional painting forms by using color, light, and shadow to convey the *impression* of reflected light, at a particular moment.

Economics
- Price is a function of supply and demand.

Unit on money (elementary)
- The cost of a Beanie Baby depends on demand and availability at any given time.

Literature
- The modern novel overturns many traditional story elements and norms to provide a more authentic and engaging narrative.

Unit on Catcher in the Rye
- Holden Caulfield is an alienated antihero, not simply a weird kid who mistrusts adults.

History and Government
- Democracy requires a free and courageous press, willing to question authority.

Unit on the U.S. Constitution
- The Watergate incident, exposed by the press, represented a major constitutional crisis.

Mathematics
- Mathematics allows us to see patterns that might have remained unseen.

Unit on statistics
- Statistical analysis and graphic displays often reveal patterns in seemingly random data or populations, enabling predictions.

Physical Education
- A muscle that contracts through its full range of motion will generate more force.

Unit on golf
- A full stroke with follow-through will increase your distance on a drive.

Science
- Gravity is not a physical thing but a term describing the constant rate of acceleration of all falling objects.

Unit on gravitational force
- Vertical height, not the angle and distance of descent, determines the eventual speed of a falling object.

Left margin tabs: Templates | Stage 1 | Stage 2 | Stage 3 | Peer review | Exercises | Process sheets | Glossary

An Enduring Understanding . . . Ⓤ

(description)

Involves the Big Ideas that give meaning and importance to facts.

Enduring understandings are made up of the concepts, principles, and theories that weave many facts into revealing and useful patterns. They involve the (few) organizing priority ideas that enable us to make sense of past lessons, conduct current inquiry, and create new knowledge.

Can transfer to other topics, fields, and adult life.

Such understandings endure in that they enable us to make vital and informative connections in our learning—as students and as adults. For example, the idea that "might does not make right" applies to both playground disputes and international diplomacy.

Is usually not obvious, often counterintuitive, and easily misunderstood.

An understanding is an inference, not a fact. It is an insight derived from inquiry. Key understandings in intellectual fields (e.g., in physics: *Objects remain in motion at a constant velocity if no force acts on them*) often violate common sense and conventional wisdom. They are thus often prone to misunderstanding by students. These understandings therefore cannot be covered; they must be uncovered.

May provide a conceptual foundation for basic skills.

Though skill-based teaching in mathematics, foreign language, and physical education does not seem to deal with "understandings" in most units, all skills derive their value from the strategic principles that help us know when and how to use the skill. The understandings also justify the use of a skill (e.g., the student who can explain why you should use a bent-arm pull in swimming freestyle) and enable the student to extend the use of the skill to new situations (e.g., the use of bent-arm pull in backstroke).

Is deliberately framed as a generalization—the "moral of the story."

An understanding is a generalization derived from inquiry. It is the specific insight that should be inferred from study of the topic (not just the stating of the topic)—what we want the student leaving the study to realize. Note: The enduring understanding of a unit might be that there is no single agreed-upon understanding, or that people disagree about how the issues, facts, text should be understood.

Templates · Stage 1 · Stage 2 · Stage 3 · Peer review · Exercises · Process sheets · Glossary

Tips on Framing Understandings

> ## Frame the desired understanding as a full-sentence generalization in response to the phrase, "Students will understand that . . ."

State *specifically* what about the topic students are expected to grasp. Many curricular frameworks, content standards documents, and teacher objectives make the mistake of framing understandings as a topic (e.g., *students will understand the water cycle*) or skill (e.g., *students will understand how to multiply*).

We recommend that you summarize the *particular* understandings you are after, being as specific as possible about the insights that should result from exploring the topic (e.g., *data analysis and graphic displays often reveal helpful patterns and enable prediction*).

A practical way to accomplish this is to frame the understandings in response to the stem: "students will understand that . . ." (e.g., *the Civil War was fought initially over states' rights issues and regional economic politics, not just the morality of slavery*). This approach helps to clarify the desired generalizations that we want students to come to understand, while avoiding the problems of stating the understanding in terms of a topic or skill.

Another way to think about it: If your unit topic is a "story," then what is the moral of your story? By stating the understanding as a "moral of the story," designers move beyond topics to clarify the complete understanding they seek. For example, a moral in a unit on animal adaptation is *Living organisms have developed adaptive mechanisms to enable them to survive harsh or changing environments.*

> ## Beware of stating an understanding as a truism or vague generality.

Avoid truisms. Truisms are statements that are true by definition (e.g., *triangles have three sides*) or state the obvious (e.g., *musicians work with sounds to create music*). Likewise, vague generalities (e.g., *the United States is a complex country* or *writing involves many different elements*) are too global to provide useful and transferable insights into important ideas. A practical tip: Check to see that your stated understandings do not end in an adjective (e.g., *fractions are important*).

> ## Avoid the phrase, "Students will understand how to . . ."

Such a statement is ambiguous. One meaning is that the student will develop certain skills. This kind of objective is best placed in Box **S** (Skill) on the design template. Another meaning of "understand how" implies that there are insights essential to wise use of the skill—e.g., knowing *why* something works or is useful. Those desired insights should be made explicit and framed as understand-ings in Box **U** of the template.

A practical way to accomplish this is to specify "why?" "how?" "when?" and "so what?" when identifying desired understandings in skill areas.

Anticipating Misunderstandings

Desired Understanding	Possible Misunderstanding
Friendship is often revealed more through challenging times than during happy times.	People with whom you hang are your friends. Once a friend, always a friend.
Gravitational force is the only significant force acting on a ball once it has been thrown.	When a ball is thrown by the pitcher, there are two forces acting on it as it travels toward the catcher.
States' rights issues, linked to regional economies, were a chief cause of the Civil War.	The Civil War was fought over the evil of slavery, and the good guys won.
. . . for a skill area	Possible Error or Misunderstanding
Listening is not passive. Effective listeners actively monitor their understanding of the speaker's message by summarizing, clarifying, and questioning.	All I need to do is sit still, keep my eyes on the speaker, and hear all of the words.

Use the spaces below to identify possible misunderstandings for your identified understandings or skills.

Templates

Stage 1

Stage 2

Stage 3

Peer review

Exercises

Process sheets

Glossary

From Skills and Ideas to Understandings

It is commonly believed that teaching in the "skill" areas does not involve Big Ideas. But Big Ideas manifest themselves as key **concepts** underlying the skill, the **purpose** or intent of using the skill, **strategies or tactics** and the **context of use** (i.e., when to apply the skill).

Stated as a skill:	Underlying Big Ideas:	Specific generalizations to be understood: (U)
swimming: mechanics of arm strokes (freestyle, backstroke, breaststroke, butterfly, side stroke)	• Efficient • Maximum power • "Backward" push • Surface area	• The most efficient and effective stroke mechanics push the maximum amount of water directly backward. • A flat (vs. cupped) palm offers the maximum surface area. • A bent-arm pull enables a swimmer to push water directly backward with greatest power.
adding fractions	• Part to whole • Relating "likes" to "likes"	• When "parts" are combined, they have to be framed in terms of the same "whole."

Sidebar tabs: Templates, Stage 1, Stage 2, Stage 3, Peer review, Exercises, Process sheets, Glossary

Knowledge and Skills
(Samples)

Knowledge	Skills

What we want students to know:

- Vocabulary
- Terminology
- Definitions
- Key factual information
- Formulas
- Critical details
- Important events and people
- Sequence and timelines

What we want students to be able to do:

- Basic skills—decoding, arithmetic computation
- Communication skills—listening, speaking, writing
- Thinking skills—compare, infer, analyze, interpret
- Research, inquiry, investigation skills
- Study skills—notetaking
- Interpersonal, group skills

Students will know . . . **K**

☐ _____
_____

☐ _____
_____

☐ _____
_____

☐ _____
_____

☐ _____
_____

☐ _____
_____

Students will be able to . . . **S**

☐ _____
_____

☐ _____
_____

☐ _____
_____

☐ _____
_____

☐ _____
_____

☐ _____
_____

Templates | Stage 1 | Stage 2 | Stage 3 | Peer review | Exercises | Process sheets | Glossary

Unpacking Goals—Method 1
Language Arts

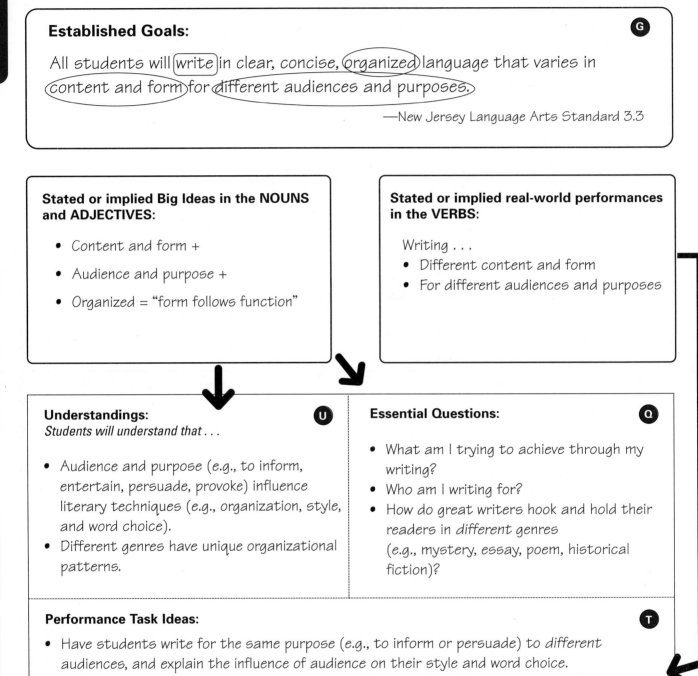

Established Goals: Ⓖ

All students will write in clear, concise, organized language that varies in content and form for different audiences and purposes.

—New Jersey Language Arts Standard 3.3

Stated or implied Big Ideas in the NOUNS and ADJECTIVES:

- Content and form +
- Audience and purpose +
- Organized = "form follows function"

Stated or implied real-world performances in the VERBS:

Writing . . .
- Different content and form
- For different audiences and purposes

Understandings: Ⓤ
Students will understand that . . .

- Audience and purpose (e.g., to inform, entertain, persuade, provoke) influence literary techniques (e.g., organization, style, and word choice).
- Different genres have unique organizational patterns.

Essential Questions: Ⓠ

- What am I trying to achieve through my writing?
- Who am I writing for?
- How do great writers hook and hold their readers in *different genres* (e.g., mystery, essay, poem, historical fiction)?

Performance Task Ideas: Ⓣ

- Have students write for the same purpose (e.g., to inform or persuade) to *different audiences,* and explain the influence of audience on their style and word choice.
- Have students write on the same content in *different genres* (e.g., essay, poem, letter to the editor, etc.), and explain the genre's influence on organization, style, and word choice.

Templates   Stage 1   Stage 2   Stage 3   Peer review   Exercises   Process sheets   Glossary

Unpacking Goals—Method 1
Math

Established Goals: Ⓖ

All students will [connect] mathematics to other learning by understanding the interrelationships of mathematical ideas <u>and the</u> roles that mathematics and (mathematical modeling) play in (other disciplines and in life.)

—New Jersey Mathematics Standard 4.3

Stated or implied Big Ideas in the NOUNS and ADJECTIVES:

- Mathematical modeling in various disciplines and life

Stated or implied real-world performances in the VERBS:

- Examples of effective mathematical modeling of real-life data or phenomena
- Critically review a mathematical model for its appropriateness to a given real-life situation

Understandings: Ⓤ
Students will understand that . . .

- Mathematical models simplify and connect phenomena so that we might better understand them.
- Mathematical models must be viewed critically so that they do not distort or mislead.

Essential Questions: Ⓠ

- In what ways is mathematical modeling useful?
- How do you know if your model is a good one (for a particular situation)?
- What are the limits of mathematical modeling?

Performance Task Ideas: Ⓣ

- Have students create a mathematical model for a selected real-world situation (e.g., seasonal temperatures).
- Have students critically review a mathematical model for its appropriateness to a given situation (e.g., the Mercator Projection for representing the globe in two-dimensions).

Unpacking Goals—Method 1

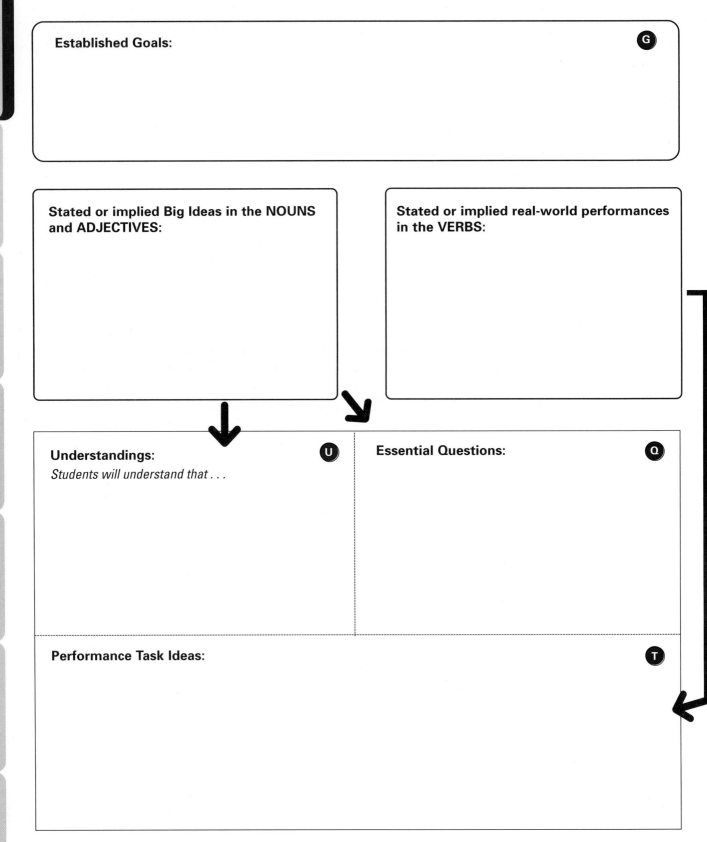

Established Goals: **G**

Stated or implied Big Ideas in the NOUNS and ADJECTIVES:

Stated or implied real-world performances in the VERBS:

Understandings: **U**
Students will understand that . . .

Essential Questions: **Q**

Performance Task Ideas: **T**

Templates

Stage 1

Stage 2

Stage 3

Peer review

Exercises

Process sheets

Glossary

Unpacking Goals—Method 2
Visual Arts

Established Goals: **G**

Visual Arts, Goal 2—The student will recognize the visual arts as a basic aspect of history and human experience.

Source: Baltimore County, MD, Public Schools

To meet the standards, students will need to understand that

U

- Artistic expression is influenced by time, place, and culture.
- One gains insights into a culture by analyzing and interpreting its visual arts.
- Available tools, techniques, and resources influence the ways in which artists and artisans express themselves.

To understand, students will need to consider such questions as

Q

- To what extent is art shaped by time, place, and culture?
- In what ways does art shape culture?
- Are artists cultural visionaries, reporters, or reactionaries?
- Who determines the meaning of art?
- How does technology influence artistic expression?

To understand, students will need to

know . . . **K**

- Visual art design elements (concepts and terminology)—line, color, form, texture, pattern, space.
- Visual art design principles—balance, rhythm, perspective, emphasis, unity.
- Ways artists employ various technologies.
- Relevant historical and cultural information about various periods.

be able to . . . **S**

- Analyze and interpret works of art.
- Compare works of art from different periods and cultures to determine the distinguishing visual characteristics (e.g., Medieval, Renaissance).
- Communicate their analyses and interpretations verbally and visually.

Templates · Stage 1 · Stage 2 · Stage 3 · Peer review · Exercises · Process sheets · Glossary

Templates

Stage 1

Stage 2

Stage 3

Peer review

Exercises

Process sheets

Glossary

Unpacking Goals—Method 2
Scientific Progress

Established Goals: **G**

STANDARD 4 (elementary): Scientific progress is made by asking meaningful questions and conducting careful investigations.

Source: California Science Standards

To meet the standards, students will need to understand that **U**

- Scientific knowledge develops as a result of carefully controlled investigations.
- The scientific method deliberately isolates and controls key variables. (It is not just "trial and error.")
- Scientific knowledge must be verified through replication.

To understand, students will need to consider such questions as **Q**

- How do we know what to believe in science?
- To what extent is science "trial and error"?
- What's the difference between scientific theory, common sense, and strong belief?
- Does accurate prediction mean we understand "how" and "why"?

To understand, students will need to

know . . . **K**

- Key terms related to scientific investigation—attribute, conclusion, data, observation, classification, comparison, hypothesis, measure, prediction, variable.

be able to . . . **S**

- Make predictions based on patterns of observation (rather than guessing).
- Measure length, weight, temperature, and liquid volume with appropriate tools and express measurements in standard and nonstandard units.
- Compare and sort common objects based on two or more physical attributes.
- Write or draw descriptions of a sequence of steps, events, or observations.

Unpacking Goals—Method 2

Established Goals: **G**

To meet the standards, students will need to understand that

U

To understand, students will need to consider such questions as

Q

To understand, students will need to

know . . .   **K**   be able to . . .   **S**

125

Templates

Stage 1

Stage 2

Stage 3

Peer review

Exercises

Process sheets

Glossary

Design Checklist—Stage 1

Established Goals **G**

1. _____ Only those goals or content standards that are directly relevant to the unit *and* assessed in Stage 2 are listed.

Understandings **U**

2. _____ The understandings derive from or are aligned with appropriate goals (e.g., content standards or curriculum objectives).

3. _____ The understandings are both overarching (to promote transfer of Big Ideas) and topical (specific enough to focus teaching, learning, and assessment).

4. _____ The understandings are framed as full-sentence generalizations in response to the stem: "The students will understand that . . ."

5. _____ The understandings are not obvious or true by definition (i.e., factual knowledge). They need to be uncovered (rather than merely stated) in order for students to come to understand them.

Essential Questions **Q**

6. _____ Overarching essential questions clarify the Big Ideas and connect to other topics and contexts, while topical essential questions frame and guide inquiry into the topic.

7. _____ The essential questions are thought provoking and arguable, rather than "leading" questions that point to the facts.

8. _____ As needed, the essential questions are framed in appropriate "kid language" to make them accessible to students.

Knowledge and Skill **K** **S**

9. _____ Key knowledge and skills, needed to meet the standards and enable the desired understandings, are identified.

Templates

Stage 1

Stage 2

Stage 3

Peer review

Exercises

Process sheets

Glossary

Stage 1 Draft Design for Review

Topic: Immigration—4th grade

Review Comments:

Established Goals: **G**

Students will use a variety of intellectual skills to demonstrate their understanding of major ideas, eras, themes, developments, and turning points in the history of the United States and New York.

Source: N.Y. Social Studies Standards

Students will understand that **U**

- Global and world history has greatly affected immigration to the United States.
- Ellis Island was a U.S. immigration processing center until 1954.
- The United States is a "melting pot," as reflected by the diverse ethnicity of today's students.
- The United States had an open-door policy, which contributed to the country's growth.

Q

- What specific events in the world influenced immigration to the United States?
- What type of procedure did immigrants follow when entering the United States between 1892 and 1952?
- Why was the United States nicknamed a "melting pot"?
- Who are some important immigrants who came to the United States, and what are their contributions to the culture?
- Why do nations set immigration quotas?

Students will know **K**

- Relevant vocabulary words.
- Specific historical events that have affected U.S. immigration (e.g., California Gold Rush).
- Specific historical world events that affected U.S. immigration (e.g., Irish Potato Famine).
- Obstacles and risks faced by immigrants to the United States.

Students will be able to **S**

- Create and interpret charts based on immigration statistics.
- Conduct an interview (e.g., with an immigrant as a primary source of information)
- Debate the controversial issue of immigration (e.g., quotas versus open-door policy).
- Write a research report relating to the unit.

Templates

Stage 1

Stage 2

Stage 3

Peer review

Exercises

Process sheets

Glossary

Templates

Stage 1

Stage 2

Stage 3

Peer review

Exercises

Process sheets

Glossary

Stage 1 Draft Design with Comments

Topic: Immigration—4th grade

Review Comments:

Established Goals: **G**

Students will use a variety of intellectual skills to demonstrate their understanding of major ideas, eras, themes, developments, and turning points in the history of the United States and New York.

Source: N.Y. Social Studies Standards

The identified content standard is appropriate for the topic. However, it is very broad and needs to be "unpacked" (below) to provide greater specificity to focus the unit.

Students will understand that **U**

1. Global and world history has greatly affected immigration to the United States.
2. Ellis Island was a U.S. immigration processing center until 1954.
3. The United States is a "melting pot," as reflected by the diverse ethnicity of today's students.
4. The United States had an open-door policy, which contributed to the country's growth.

Item 1 is a "truism" and needs to be framed as a specific generalization or omitted.
Item 2 is a straightforward fact.
Items 3 and 4 are closer to understandings, but need refinement.
For example, Item 4 could be stated, "The United States continues to debate the benefits and risks of immigration."

---

1. What specific events in the world influenced immigration to the United States? **Q**
2. What type of procedure did immigrants follow when entering the United States between 1892 and 1952?
3. Why was the United States nicknamed a "melting pot"?
4. Who are some important immigrants who came to the United States, and what are their contributions to the culture?
5. Why do nations set immigration quotas?

Questions 1, 2, and 4 are factual, not essential.
Questions 3 and 5 are promising.
For 3, consider a more open, provocative question, such as, "Who is an American?"
For 5, consider a more debatable question, such as, "Who should be allowed into the country?"

Students will know **K**

1. Relevant vocabulary words.
2. Specific historical events that have affected U.S. immigration (e.g., California Gold Rush).
3. Specific historical world events that affected U.S. immigration (e.g., Irish Potato Famine).
4. Obstacles and risks faced by immigrants to the United States.

The identified knowledge seems appropriate for the topic. However, Question 4 does not reflect any questions or understandings. Perhaps add an essential question, such as, "What makes immigrating difficult?"
Add "the changes in immigration policies over the years" to Question 4.

Students will be able to **S**

1. Create and interpret charts based on immigration statistics.
2. Conduct an interview (e.g., with an immigrant as a primary source of information)
3. Debate the controversial issue of immigration (e.g., quotas versus open-door policy).
4. Write a research report relating to the unit.

The identified skills seem appropriate and reflect an inquiry approach to exploring the topic.

Stage 1 Draft Design for Review

Topic: Strength Training, High School

Established Goals: **G**

Standard 2.20—Demonstrate exercises in strength training, cardiovascular activities, and flexibility training
Standard 2.20—Conduct a personally developed physical activity program.

Source: MA—Physical Activity and Fitness

Students will understand that **U**

- Strength training will enhance or make easier physical tasks that are performed in daily activities such as work or play.
- Strength training can be adapted to the needs and lifestyle of anyone.
- Safety when strength training should never be compromised.

Q
- What are the benefits of strength training?
- Can strength training include exercises or activities other than weight lifting?
- What effect do strength-training exercises have on my body?
- If I lift weights will I look like a body builder?
- Would it be possible to strength train to tone my body?

Students will know **K**

- Strength training includes both power (high weight, low repetition) and endurance (lower weight with high reps).
- Muscle groups work in antagonistic pairs so that two-way movement can be accomplished (e.g., biceps—arm flexion or triceps—arm extension).
- Basic physiology concepts concerning muscle and bones.

Students will be able to **S**

- Demonstrate proper techniques for performing various strength training exercises.
- Safety spot for a partner during the preparation and execution phase of the various exercises.
- Design a personal strength training program.

Review Comments:

129

Stage 1 Draft Design for Review

Topic: Measurement—Elementary

Established Goals: **G**

2., 7. Select the most appropriate standard unit to measure length and area.

4., 5. Estimate, measure, record, compare, and order objects by length, height, perimeter, area and circumference using standard units.

Source: Alberta, CN Mathematics Curriculum Standards

Students will understand that   **U**

- Measuring is a common, everyday practice.
- Units are standard and relate to each other.
- We use different units to measure different things.

   Q

- How do we use measurement every day?
- Why do we use standard units?
- Why do we need to measure things?

Students will know   **K**

- How to demonstrate an understanding of standard units and how they relate to each other.
- How to describe and compare common items through the language of measurement.

Students will be able to   **S**

- Select appropriate units for specific tasks and justify their choice.
- Estimate, measure, and compare items of specific length, area, circumference, perimeter, and height.
- Create shapes of different areas.

Review Comments:

Templates   Stage 1   Stage 2   Stage 3   Peer review   Exercises   Process sheets   Glossary

Frequently Asked Questions About Stage 1

1. What is the relationship between Big Ideas, Understandings and Essential Questions?

The illustration on p. 133 defines these terms and depicts their interrelationship.

2. Is there a specific sequence for completing Stage 1?

No. We have observed a variety of successful approaches. Some people begin with Established Goals **G** then develop the Understandings **U** and Essential Questions **Q**, and finish by listing the Knowledge **K** and Skills **S** objectives. Others prefer to start with Goals, move to Knowledge and Skills, and then consider the Understandings and Questions. Another option is to begin by developing Essential Questions linked to the topic and then completing the other sections.

The most important thing is the outcome—a coherent Stage 1 design with all of the elements aligned. The process for getting there is flexible.

3. It is important that our teaching be directed toward our state content standards and benchmarks. How do content standards fit into the UbD framework?

We encourage teachers to "unpack" content standards, especially those that focus on discrete facts and skills, to identify the related Big Ideas and Essential Questions. Of course, we are not suggesting that teachers ignore the specifics of the content standards. The specific facts and skills identified in the content standards and benchmarks (and assessed on state tests) are listed under **K** and **S**. The Big Ideas and Essential Questions serve as "conceptual Velcro" to help connect the specific facts and skills to transferable concepts and principles.

4. Should there be an Essential Question for each identified Understanding?

Although there is not a need for a one-to-one correspondence, there should be a clear connection between the Questions and Understandings. Think of the Essential Questions

Templates

Stage 1

Stage 2

Stage 3

Peer review

Exercises

Process sheets

Glossary

Templates
Stage 1
Stage 2
Stage 3
Peer review
Exercises
Process sheets
Glossary

as doorways for exploring the Big Ideas, leading to the desired Understandings. We would expect to see one (or more) doorways (Essential Questions) tied to the identified Understandings.

5. Why do teachers in some subjects and grade levels struggle in Stage 1?

Teachers who focus on skills (e.g., in primary grades, beginning levels of world languages, mathematics, and physical education) tend to find Stage 1 especially challenging. Often there is the belief that UbD doesn't apply to skills teaching. However, we propose that Big Ideas often underlie skill areas, and skill performance is enhanced when the learner understands them. We encourage teachers to help learners come to understand four aspects of a skill: underlying *concepts* (what makes this skill or strategy work?), the *purpose* (what larger goal will this skill help you accomplish?), use of *strategies* (what strategies or tactics will help you learn and use the skill more efficiently and effectively?), and *context* (when should this skill or strategy be used?).

Research confirms that when skills are taught based on such understandings, not just through drill and practice, learners are better equipped to apply the skill flexibly in various situations.

Big Ideas, Understandings, and Essential Questions

The following visual represents the interrelationship among Big Ideas, Understandings and Essential Questions.

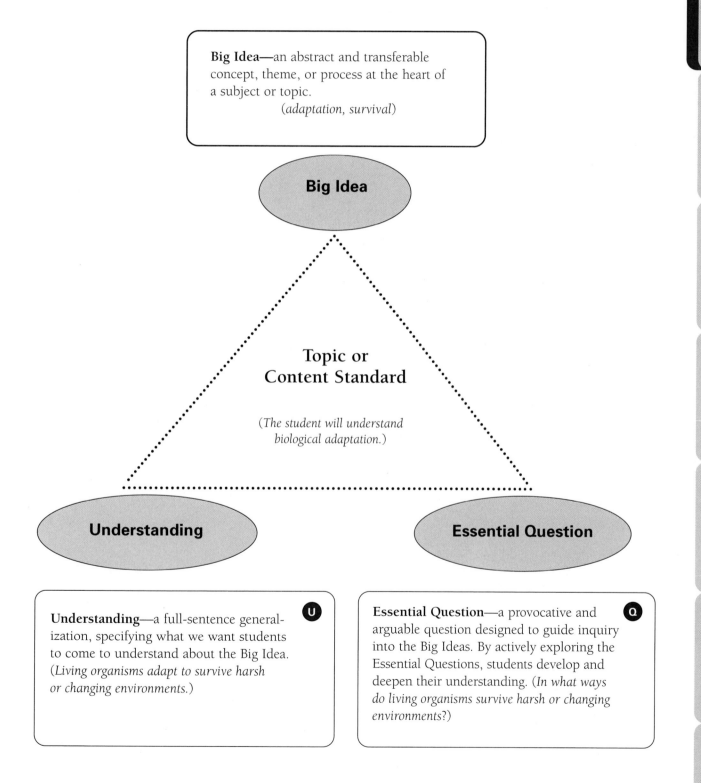

Big Idea—an abstract and transferable concept, theme, or process at the heart of a subject or topic. (*adaptation, survival*)

Big Idea

Topic or Content Standard

(*The student will understand biological adaptation.*)

Understanding

Essential Question

Understanding—a full-sentence generalization, specifying what we want students to come to understand about the Big Idea. (*Living organisms adapt to survive harsh or changing environments.*)

Essential Question—a provocative and arguable question designed to guide inquiry into the Big Ideas. By actively exploring the Essential Questions, students develop and deepen their understanding. (*In what ways do living organisms survive harsh or changing environments?*)

Templates

Stage 1

Stage 2

Stage 3

Peer review

Exercises

Process sheets

Glossary

Stage 2—Evidence

Design Tools and Samples

Backward Design: Stage 2

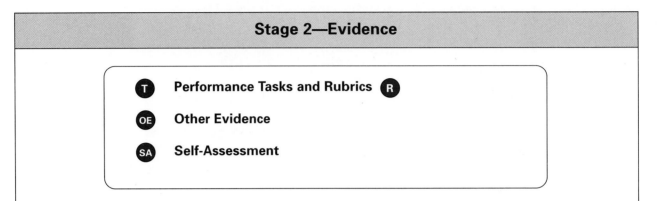

Stage 2—Evidence

T Performance Tasks and Rubrics **R**

OE Other Evidence

SA Self-Assessment

In Stage 2 we consider the assessment evidence needed to determine the extent to which students have achieved the desired results in Stage 1. In **T** we identify the **Performance Tasks** and **Rubrics** **R** that anchor the unit by providing evidence of student understanding. All Other Evidence (e.g., diagnostic and formative assessments, quizzes, tests, observations, prompted writing and speaking) goes in **OE** . In **SA** we specify any student **Self-Assessments** that will be included.

The goal in Stage 2 is to obtain valid, reliable, credible, and useful evidence. The key mantra is to Think like an assessor, not an activity designer. There should be a tight alignment between the desired results we seek and the evidence we plan to collect.

STAGE 2—*To what* extent do the assessments provide valid, reliable and sufficient measures of the desired results?

Consider: Are . . .

○ Students asked to exhibit their understanding through authentic performance tasks?

○ Appropriate criterion-based rubrics used to judge student products and performances?

○ A variety of appropriate assessment formats provided as additional evidence of learning?

○ Students encouraged to self-assess?

Templates

Stage 1

Stage 2

Stage 3

Peer review

Exercises

Process sheets

Glossary

Stage 2—Key Design Elements
(Web with Prompts)

Consider the following elements as you identify the evidence needed to determine the extent to which the desired results (Stage 1) have been achieved. Examples and design tools are provided to assist you.

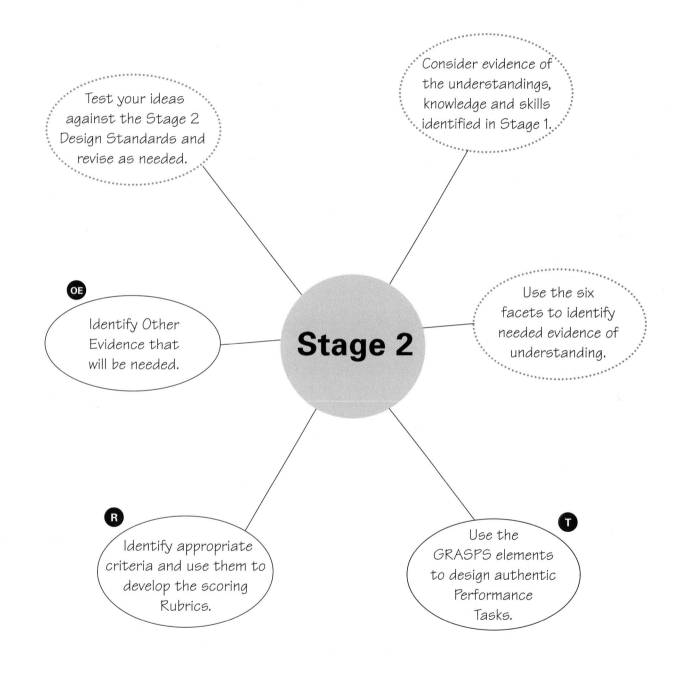

Templates

Stage 1

Stage 2

Stage 3

Peer review

Exercises

Process sheets

Glossary

Alignment: The Logic of Backward Design
(What do the understandings imply for assessment?)
Friendship—Elementary School

Stage 1	Stage 2	
If the desired result is for learners to . . .	*Then, you need evidence of the student's ability to . . .*	*So, the assessments need to include some things like . . .*
Understand that (U) • Friendship demands honesty and openness. • True friendship is often revealed during hard times, not happy times. • It is sometimes hard to know who your true friends really are. **And thoughtfully consider the questions . . .** (Q) • Who is a true friend? • What makes a friendship last?	APPLY: What applications would enable us to infer students' understanding of what they have learned? What kinds of performances and products, if done well, would provide valid ways of distinguishing between understanding and mere recall? EXPLAIN: What must students be able to explain, justify, support, or answer about their work for us to infer genuine understanding? How can we test their ideas and applications to find out if they really understand what they have said and done?	(T) (OE) • Order a friend: Order a "true" friend over the phone from a friendship catalog. What qualities should your friend have? • Dear Abby: Give advice in a case where a child told a white lie to avoid embarrassing his friend. • Develop an informative brochure for younger students to help them know who their true friends are. • Create a comic strip or book to illustrate friendship actions. • Tell or draw a story showing what happens when two friends don't see eye-to-eye. • Explain your choices to the salesperson (for the order-a-friend task) • Explain who your friends are and why they are your friends. • Describe the qualities of a true friend. Justify the qualities you selected. • Respond to quotes about friendship, e.g., "A friend in need is a friend indeed." "The enemy of my enemy is my friend."

Alignment: The Logic of Backward Design
(What do the understandings imply for assessment?)

Statistics

Stage 1	Stage 2	
If the desired result is for learners to . . .	**Then, you need evidence of the student's ability to . . .**	**So, the assessments need to include some things like . . .**
Understand that **(U)** • Statistical analysis and graphic display often reveal patterns in data. • Pattern recognition enables prediction. • Inferences from data patterns can be plausible but invalid (as well as implausible but valid). • Correlation does not ensure causality. **(Q)** **And thoughtfully consider the questions . . .** • What's the trend? • What will happen next? • In what ways can data and statistics "lie" as well as reveal?	APPLY: What applications would enable us to infer student understanding of what they have learned? What kinds of performances and products, if done well, would provide valid ways of distinguishing between understanding and mere recall? EXPLAIN: What must students be able to explain, justify, support, or answer about their work for us to infer genuine understanding? How can we test their ideas and applications to find out if they really understand what they have said and done?	**(T)** **(OE)** • Using past performances in the men's and women's marathon, predict the men's and women's marathon times for 2020. • Chart various scenarios for a savings program (e.g., for college, retirement). Give financial advice. Explain the implausibility of compound interest. • Analyze the past 15 years of AIDS cases to determine the trend. (Note: The data start out looking linear but become exponential.) • Write an article or a letter to the editor about why the marathon analysis is plausible but incorrect. • Develop a brochure to would-be investors on why early saving with small amounts is better than later with large amounts. • Create a graphic display with accompanying written explanation to illustrate the exponential nature of AIDS cases.

139

Templates

Stage 1

Stage 2

Stage 3

Peer review

Exercises

Process sheets

Glossary

Alignment: The Logic of Backward Design
(What do the understandings imply for assessment?)

_____

_____

_____

Stage 1	Stage 2	
If the desired result is for learners to . . . ⟹	**Then, you need evidence of the student's ability to . . .** ⟹	**So, the assessments need to include some things like . . .**
Understand that: (U)	APPLY: What applications would enable us to infer student understanding of what they have learned? What kinds of performances and products, if done well, would provide valid ways of distinguishing between understanding and mere recall?	(T) (OE)
And thoughtfully consider the questions . . . (Q)	EXPLAIN: What must students be able to explain, justify, support, or answer about their work for us to infer genuine understanding? How can we test their ideas and applications to find out if they really understand what they have said and done?	

Curricular Priorities and Assessment Methods

In effective assessments, we see a match between the type or format of the assessment and the needed evidence of achieving the desired results. If the goal is for students to learn basic facts and skills, then paper-and-pencil tests and quizzes generally provide adequate and efficient measures. However, when the goal is deep understanding, we rely on more complex performances to determine whether our goal has been reached. The graphic below reveals the general relationship between assessment types and the evidence they provide for different curriculum targets.

Assessment Methods

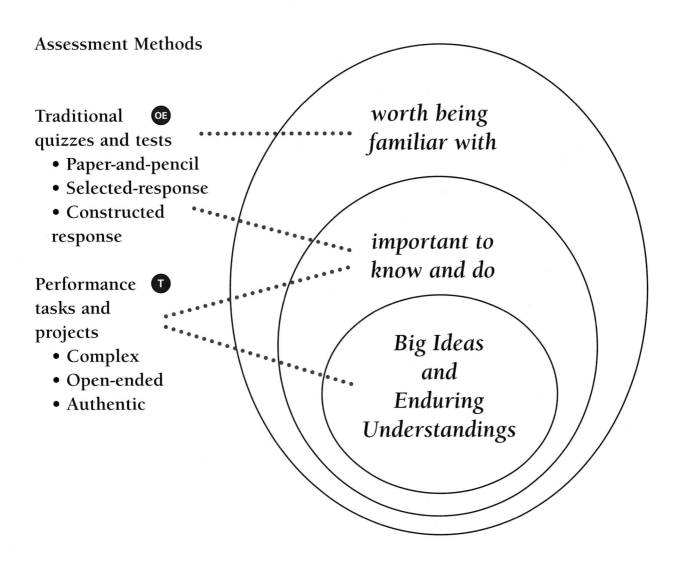

Collecting Diverse Evidence from Assessments

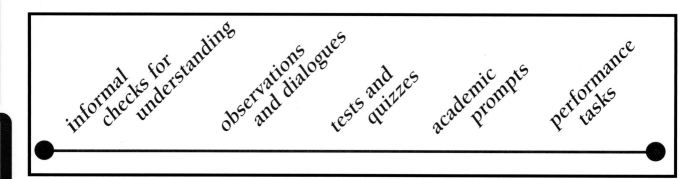

Performance Tasks

Complex challenges that mirror the issues and problems faced by adults. Ranging in length from short-term tasks to long-term, multistaged projects, they yield one or more tangible products and performances. They differ from academic prompts in the following ways:

- The setting is real or simulated and involves the kind of constraints, background "noise," incentives, and opportunities an adult would find in a similar situation (i.e., they are authentic)
- Typically require the student to address an identified audience (real or simulated)
- Are based on a specific purpose that relates to the audience
- Allow students greater opportunity to personalize the task
- Are not secure: the task, evaluative criteria, and performance standards are known in advance and guide student work

Academic Prompts

Open-ended questions or problems that require the student to think critically, not just recall knowledge, and to prepare a specific academic response, product, or performance. Such questions or problems

- Require constructed responses to specific prompts under school and exam conditions
- Are "open," with no single best answer or strategy expected for solving them
- Are often "ill structured," requiring the development of a strategy
- Involve analysis, synthesis, and evaluation
- Typically require an explanation or defense of the answer given and methods used
- Require judgment-based scoring based on criteria and performance standards
- May or may not be secure
- Involve questions typically only asked of students in school

Quiz and Test Items

Familiar assessment formats consisting of simple, content-focused items that

- Assess for factual information, concepts, and discrete skill
- Use selected-response (e.g., multiple-choice, true-false, matching) or short-answer formats
- Are convergent, typically having a single, best answer
- May be easily scored using an answer key or machine
- Are typically secure (i.e., items are not known in advance)

Informal Checks for Understanding

Ongoing assessments used as part of the instructional process. Examples include teacher questioning, observations, examining student work, and think alouds. These assessments provide feedback to the teacher and the student. They are not typically scored or graded.

Sources of Assessment Evidence: Self-Assessment

Directions: Use the following scale to rate your level of use of each of the following assessment tools (at the classroom, school, or district level). What do the survey results suggest? What patterns do you notice? Are you collecting appropriate evidence for *all* the desired results, or only those that are easiest to test and grade? Is an important learning goal falling through the cracks because it is not being assessed?

> 5 = Extensive Use
> 4 = Frequent Use
> 3 = General Use
> 2 = Sporadic Use
> 1 = Infrequent Use
> 0 = No Evidence of Use

1. _____ Selected-response-format (e.g., multiple-choice, true-false) quizzes and tests

2. _____ Written responses to academic prompts (short-answer format)

3. _____ Extended written products (e.g., essays, lab reports)

4. _____ Visual products (e.g., PowerPoint show, mural)

5. _____ Oral performances (e.g., oral report, foreign language dialogues)

6. _____ Student demonstrations (e.g., skill performance in physical education)

7. _____ Long-term, authentic assessment projects (e.g., senior exhibit)

8. _____ Portfolios—collections of student work over time

9. _____ Reflective journals or learning logs

10. _____ Informal, ongoing observations of students

11. _____ Formal observations of students using observable indicators or criteria list

12. _____ Student self-assessments

13. _____ Peer reviews and peer response groups

14. _____ Other: _____

Collecting Evidence from Various Assessment Types
Nutrition, Grades 5–7

Templates
Stage 1
Stage 2
Stage 3
Peer review
Exercises
Process sheets
Glossary

Stage 1—Desired Results

Established Goals: **G**

Standard 1 Intermediate—Students will use an understanding of the elements of good nutrition to plan appropriate diets.

Understandings: **U**
Students will understand that . . .

- A balanced diet contributes to physical and mental health.
- The USDA Food Pyramid presents relative guidelines for nutrition.
- Dietary requirements vary for individuals based on age, activity level, weight, and overall health.

Essential Questions: **Q**

- What is healthful eating?
- Could a healthy diet for one person be unhealthy for another?
- Why are there so many health problems in the United States caused by poor nutrition despite all the available information?

Students will know . . .   **K**

- Key terms—protein, fat, calorie, carbohydrate, cholesterol.
- Types of foods in each food group and their nutritional values.
- USDA Food Pyramid guidelines and variables influencing nutritional needs.
- Health problems caused by poor diet.
- How to interpret nutritional information on food labels.

Stage 2—Assessment Evidence

☑ ☐ ☐ ☐   **Performance tasks**   (camp menu, menu plan)   **T**

☑ ☑ ☐ ☐   **Quizzes**   (food groups and Food Pyramid guidelines)   **OE**

(interpreting food labels)

☑ ☐ ☐ ☐   **Tests**   (health problems caused by poor diet)

☑ ☐ ☐ ☐   **Student work samples**   (nutrition brochure)

☑ ☐ ☐ ☐   **Observations**   (during lunch in cafeteria)

☑ ☐ ☐ ☐   **Other**   (self-assessment on personal eating habits)

Collecting Evidence from Various Assessment Types

Stage 1—Desired Results

Established Goals: **G**

Understandings: **U**
Students will understand that . . .

Essential Questions: **Q**

Students will know . . . **K**

Stage 2—Assessment Evidence

☐ ☐ ☐ ☐ **Performance tasks** **T**

☐ ☐ ☐ ☐ **Quizzes** **OE**

☐ ☐ ☐ ☐ **Tests**

☐ ☐ ☐ ☐ **Student work samples**

☐ ☐ ☐ ☐ **Observations**

☐ ☐ ☐ ☐ **Other** _____

Templates　Stage 1　Stage 2　Stage 3　Peer review　Exercises　Process sheets　Glossary

Collecting Sufficient Evidence
Mathematics, Elementary School

Effective assessment requires multiple sources of evidence—a photo album, not a single snapshot. Use the following worksheet to brainstorm possible sources of evidence of understanding a Big Idea or meeting an established goal such as a designated content standard.

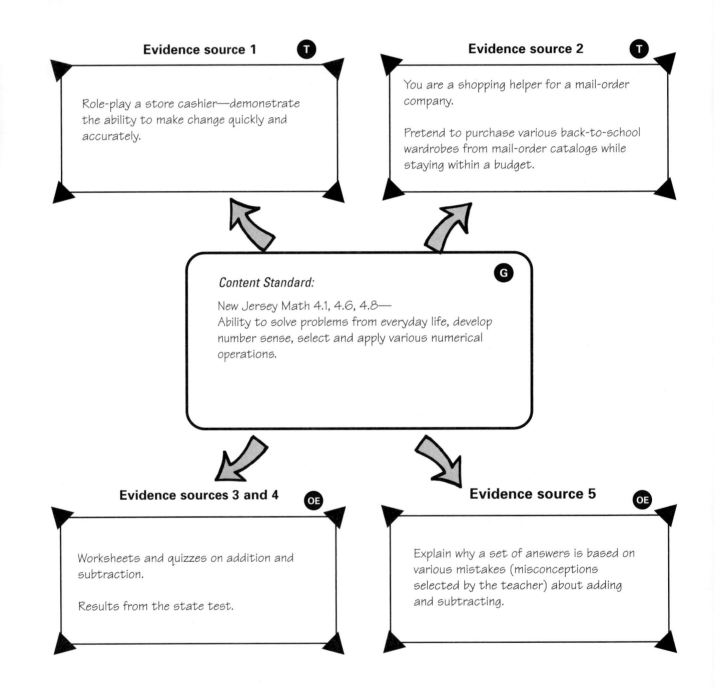

Evidence source 1 **T**

Role-play a store cashier—demonstrate the ability to make change quickly and accurately.

Evidence source 2 **T**

You are a shopping helper for a mail-order company.

Pretend to purchase various back-to-school wardrobes from mail-order catalogs while staying within a budget.

G

Content Standard:

New Jersey Math 4.1, 4.6, 4.8—
Ability to solve problems from everyday life, develop number sense, select and apply various numerical operations.

Evidence sources 3 and 4 **OE**

Worksheets and quizzes on addition and subtraction.

Results from the state test.

Evidence source 5 **OE**

Explain why a set of answers is based on various mistakes (misconceptions selected by the teacher) about adding and subtracting.

Templates · Stage 1 · Stage 2 · Stage 3 · Peer review · Exercises · Process sheets · Glossary

Collecting Sufficient Evidence
Teacher Supervision

Effective assessment requires multiple sources of evidence—a photo album, not a single snapshot. Use the following worksheet to brainstorm possible sources of evidence of understanding a Big Idea or meeting an established goal such as a designated content standard.

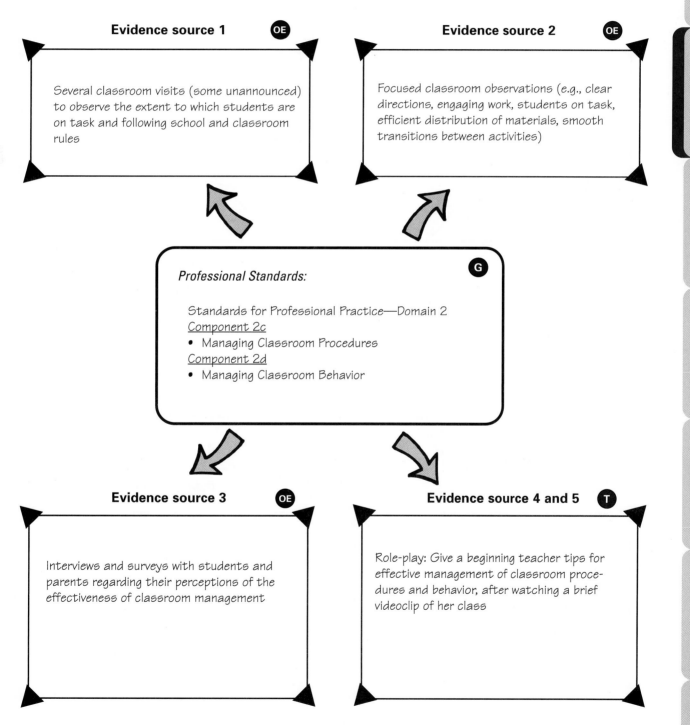

Evidence source 1 OE

Several classroom visits (some unannounced) to observe the extent to which students are on task and following school and classroom rules

Evidence source 2 OE

Focused classroom observations (e.g., clear directions, engaging work, students on task, efficient distribution of materials, smooth transitions between activities)

Professional Standards: G

Standards for Professional Practice—Domain 2
Component 2c
• Managing Classroom Procedures
Component 2d
• Managing Classroom Behavior

Evidence source 3 OE

Interviews and surveys with students and parents regarding their perceptions of the effectiveness of classroom management

Evidence source 4 and 5 T

Role-play: Give a beginning teacher tips for effective management of classroom procedures and behavior, after watching a brief videoclip of her class

Templates

Stage 1

Stage 2

Stage 3

Peer review

Exercises

Process sheets

Glossary

Collecting Acceptable and Sufficient Evidence

Effective assessment requires multiple sources of evidence—a photo album, not a single snapshot. Use the following worksheet to brainstorm possible sources of evidence of understanding a Big Idea or meeting an established goal such as a designated content standard.

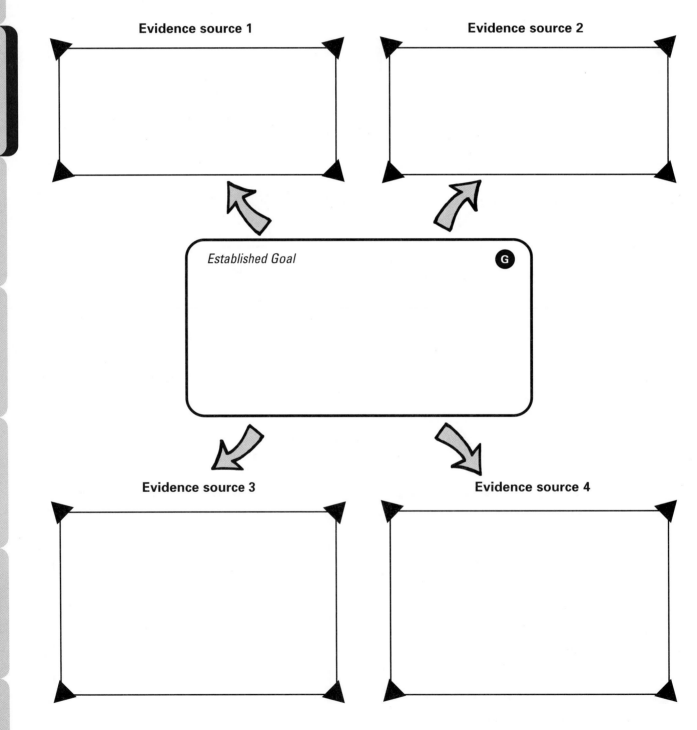

Evidence source 1

Evidence source 2

Established Goal **G**

Evidence source 3

Evidence source 4

A Collection of Assessment Evidence
Nutrition, Grades 5–6

Performance Tasks:

You Are What You Eat—Students create an illustrated brochure to teach younger children about the importance of good nutrition for healthful living. Offer younger students ideas for breaking bad eating habits.

T

Chow Down—Students develop a three-day menu for meals and snacks for an upcoming Outdoor Education camp experience. They write a letter to the camp director to explain why their menu should be selected (by showing that it meets the USDA Food Pyramid recommendations, yet it is tasty enough for the students). Include at least one modification for a specific dietary condition (diabetic or vegetarian) or religious consideration.

Other Evidence:
(e.g., tests, quizzes, prompts, work samples, observations)

Quiz—The food groups and the USDA Food Pyramid

OE

Prompt—Describe two health problems that could arise as a result of poor nutrition and explain how these could be avoided.

Skill Check—Interpret nutritional information on food labels.

Student Self-Assessment and Reflection:

1. Self-assess the brochure, *You Are What You Eat.*
2. Self-assess the camp menu, *Chow Down.*
3. Reflect on the extent to which you eat healthy at the end of unit (compared to the beginning).

SA

Templates · Stage 1 · Stage 2 · Stage 3 · Peer review · Exercises · Process sheets · Glossary

Templates

Stage 1

Stage 2

Stage 3

Peer review

Exercises

Process sheets

Glossary

A Collection of Assessment Evidence
English, High School

Performance Tasks:

T

What's Wrong with Holden?—You are a member of an advisory committee for the hospital where Holden Caulfield is telling his story. After a close reading and discussion of Holden's account of the events of the preceding December, your task is to write (1) a summary report for the hospital; and (2) a letter to Holden's parents explaining what is wrong with Holden. You should prepare for a meeting with the parents to explain and justify your analysis of Holden's behavior.

Other Evidence:
(e.g., tests, quizzes, prompts, work samples, observations)

OE

1. Essay—"He was the kind of phony who has to give himself room when he answers someone's question. . . . " Students will write to explain Holden's concern for authenticity.

2. Letter—Each student will write a one-page letter describing Holden from the point of view of another character in the novel.

3. Quizzes—Three quizzes on plot details.

4. Journal—Students respond in their journals at the end of each reading assignment to these questions: (a) What is the most important thing you learn about Holden in this section of the novel? (b) What is the most important unanswered question about Holden at this point in the novel?

Student Self-Assessment and Reflection:

SA

The final journal entry is a reflection guided by three questions:
1. What changed for you in the way you saw Holden as this book went along?
2. If, as some people claim, "misunderstanding is inevitable," what were your misunderstandings before and during this unit?
3. If you were to teach this novel to next year's students, what would you do to ensure that they really understand the novel (rather than simply read it)?

A Collection of Assessment Evidence

Topic: _____

Performance Tasks:

[T]

Other Evidence:
(e.g., tests, quizzes, prompts, work samples, observations)

[OE]

Student Self-Assessment and Reflection:

[SA]

Templates   Stage 1   Stage 2   Stage 3   Peer review   Exercises   Process sheets   Glossary

What Does the Goal Imply for Assessment?
Visual Arts

Established Goals: **G**

The student will recognize the visual arts as a basic aspect of history and human experience.

—Visual Arts, Goal 2

Content (nouns)

- Artistic expression
- Culture
- Visual design elements

Process (verbs)

- Compare
- Analyze
- Interpret

Understandings **U**

- Artistic expression is influenced by time, place, and culture.
- One gains insights into a culture by analyzing and interpreting its visual arts.
- Available tools, techniques, and resources influence the ways in which artists and artisans express themselves.

Task and prompt ideas **T** **OE**

- Task: Prepare a graphic organizer for comparing three works of art from different periods and cultures. Explain the distinguishing visual characteristics and techniques of each.
- Task: Create imagery using the visual characteristics, tools and techniques from a given period (e.g., Romantic era) to reflect some aspect of contemporary culture.
- Prompt: How do today's digital media enable contemporary artists to express themselves?

Templates

Stage 1

Stage 2

Stage 3

Peer review

Exercises

Process sheets

Glossary

What Does the Goal Imply for Assessment?
Civil War, High School

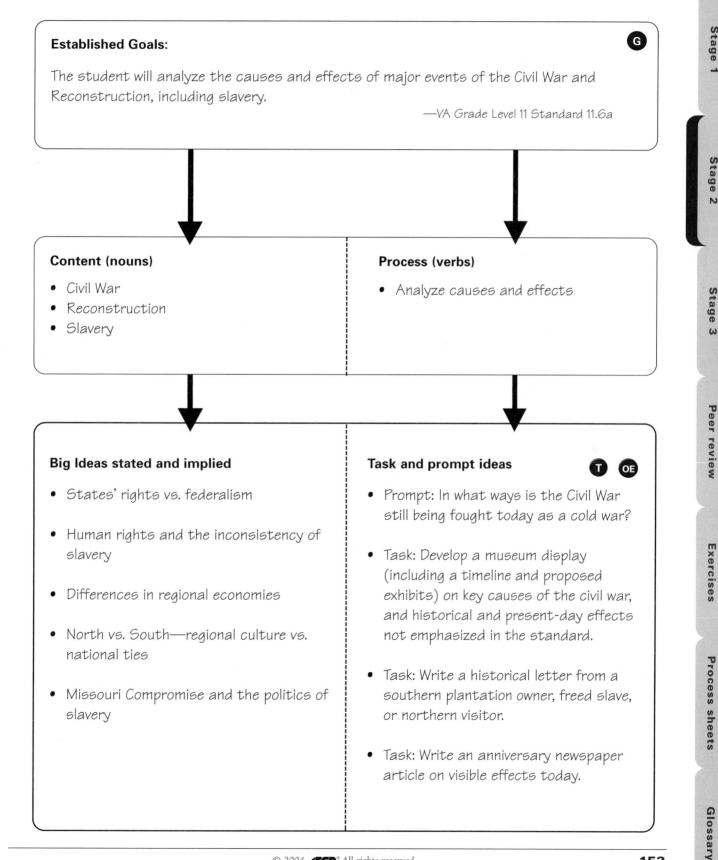

Established Goals: **G**

The student will analyze the causes and effects of major events of the Civil War and Reconstruction, including slavery.

—VA Grade Level 11 Standard 11.6a

Content (nouns)

- Civil War
- Reconstruction
- Slavery

Process (verbs)

- Analyze causes and effects

Big Ideas stated and implied

- States' rights vs. federalism

- Human rights and the inconsistency of slavery

- Differences in regional economies

- North vs. South—regional culture vs. national ties

- Missouri Compromise and the politics of slavery

Task and prompt ideas **T** **OE**

- Prompt: In what ways is the Civil War still being fought today as a cold war?

- Task: Develop a museum display (including a timeline and proposed exhibits) on key causes of the civil war, and historical and present-day effects not emphasized in the standard.

- Task: Write a historical letter from a southern plantation owner, freed slave, or northern visitor.

- Task: Write an anniversary newspaper article on visible effects today.

Templates · Stage 1 · Stage 2 · Stage 3 · Peer review · Exercises · Process sheets · Glossary

What Does the Goal Imply for Assessment?

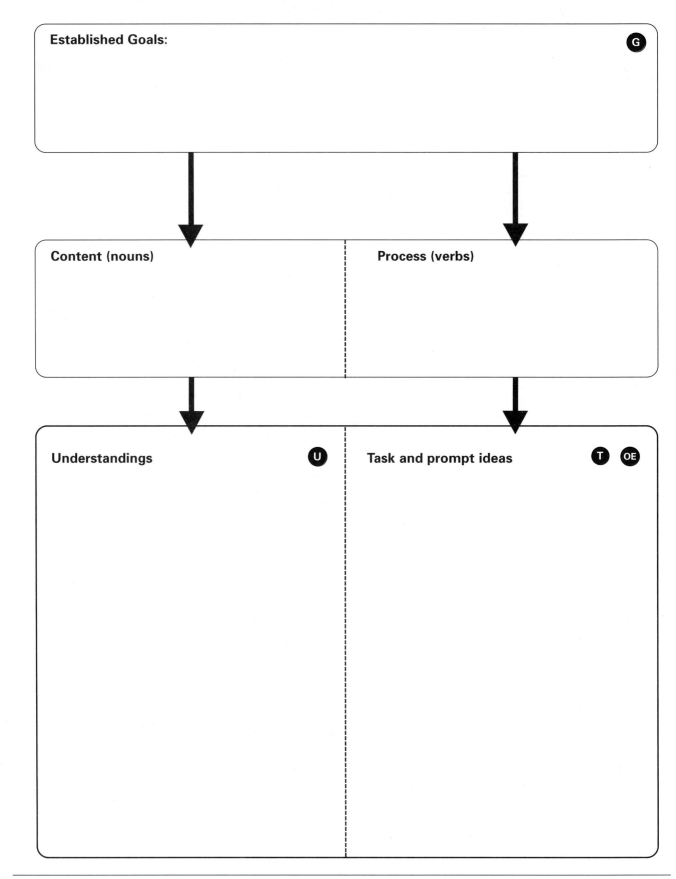

Templates

Stage 1

Stage 2

Stage 3

Peer review

Exercises

Process sheets

Glossary

154

The Six Facets of Understanding

Facet 1—EXPLANATION

Sophisticated and apt explanations and theories that provide knowledgeable and justified accounts of events, actions, and ideas: Why is that so? What explains such events? What accounts for such action? How can we prove it? To what is this connected? How does this work?

Facet 2—INTERPRETATION

Narratives, translations, metaphors, images, and artistry that provide meaning: What does it mean? Why does it matter? What of it? What does it illustrate or illuminate in human experience? How does it relate to me? What makes sense?

Facet 3—APPLICATION

Ability to use knowledge effectively in new situations and diverse contexts: How and where can we use this knowledge, skill, or process? How should my thinking and action be modified to meet the demands of this particular situation?

Facet 4—PERSPECTIVE

Critical and insightful points of view: From whose point of view? From which vantage point? What is assumed or tacit that needs to be made explicit and considered? What is justified or warranted? Is there adequate evidence? Is it reasonable? What are the strengths and weaknesses of the idea? Is it plausible? What are its limits? So what? What is a novel way to look at this?

Facet 5—EMPATHY

The ability to get "inside" another person's feelings and world view: How does it seem to you? What do they see that I don't? What do I need to experience if I am to understand? What was the author, artist, or performer feeling, seeing, and trying to make me feel and see?

Facet 6—SELF-KNOWLEDGE

The wisdom to know one's ignorance and how one's patterns of thought and action inform as well as prejudice understanding: How does who I am shape my views? What are the limits of my understanding? What are my blind spots? What am I prone to misunderstand because of prejudice, habit, or style? How do I learn best? What strategies work for me?

Templates

Stage 1

Stage 2

Stage 3

Peer review

Exercises

Process sheets

Glossary

Questioning for Understanding

Explanation

What is the key idea in _____?
What are examples of_____?
What are the characteristics and parts of_____?
What caused _____? What are the effects of_____?
How might we prove, confirm, justify_____?
How is _____ connected to _____?
What might happen if _____?
What are common misconceptions about _____?
How did this come about? Why is this so?

Interpretation

What is the meaning of _____?
What are the implications of _____?
What does _____ reveal about_____?
How is _____ like_____ (analogy or metaphor)?
How does _____ relate to me or us?
So what? Why does it matter?

Application

How is _____ applied in the larger world?
How might _____ help us to _____?
How could we use _____ to overcome _____?
How and when can we use this (knowledge or process)?

Perspective

What are different points of view about _____?
How might this look from_____'s perspective?
How is _____ similar to or different from _____?
What are other possible reactions to _____?
What are the strengths and weaknesses of _____?
What are the limits of_____?
What is the evidence for _____?
Is the evidence reliable? sufficient?

Empathy

What would it be like to walk in _____'s shoes?
How might _____ feel about _____?
How might we reach an understanding about _____?
What was _____ trying to make us feel and see?

Self-Knowledge

How do I know _____?
What are the limits of my knowledge about _____?
What are my "blind spots" about _____?
How can I best show _____?
How are my views about _____ shaped by _____
(experiences, habits, prejudices, style)?
What are my strengths and weaknesses in _____?

Templates · Stage 1 · Stage 2 · Stage 3 · Peer review · Exercises · Process sheets · Glossary

Performance Task Ideas Based on the Six Facets of Understanding
Samples by Subject

Topic	Explain	Interpret	Apply	Perspective	Empathy	Self-Knowledge
Social Studies: Pioneer Life	Write letters home describing what pioneer life is *really* like vs. what you expected.	Read and interpret real-life journals and stories of pioneers (e.g., *Sarah Plain and Tall*) to infer from vocabulary and images what life was really like.	Create a museum exhibit in which photos and facsimile artifacts tell the story of the hardships of pioneer life.	Stage a debate between settlers and Native Americans on the effects of western settlement.	Write a letter to relatives "back east" describing the death of pioneer neighbors.	"Why Leave Home?" Write on how you have felt or would feel if you had to leave your home.
Friendship	"Who are your true friends? Who are your fair-weather friends?"	Interpret "Spring" in *Frog and Toad are Friends.* What does this episode reveal about friendship?	Place an order for a "true friend" from an imaginary mail-order friendship store.	How do others view me as a friend?	Write an essay or journal entry on why some kids always get picked on and what it feels like to be those kids.	Respond to writing prompts: "Do I know who my true friends are?"
History: U.S. Revolutionary War	Write a newspaper editorial for a 1777 newspaper: Was the break with England inevitable?	"What really happened at Lexington?" Analyze the texts and information available to make sense of the war's opening (facts vs. opinions).		Read Canadian and French accounts of the Revolutionary War era. Defend or oppose their use as teaching resources at a simulated school board meeting.	Write a series of simulated letters back and forth between relatives in United States and England during the pre-Revolutionary War, war, and postwar eras.	Journal writing: "What would I fight for?"
Mathematics: Conic Sections	Explain how slicing a cone produces all conic sections and justifies their algebraic formulae.	Analyze various data sets to determine the "best-fit" conic section curve.	Design a "whisper chamber" for a science museum under various logistical constraints, using your knowledge of conic sections.	Conduct experiments with flashlights, conic section cut-outs, and shadows to explore how conic sections are formed and how their shapes vary.		
Physics: Electricity	Develop a troubleshooting guide for an electric circuit system.	Assume the role of an electrical subcontractor: Interpret and analyze the wiring drawings for building a house.	Build a working set of switches for a model railroad layout.	AC or DC? Argue the merits of each type of current for various users.	Create an imaginary diary entry: "A day in the life of an electron."	
French	Explain the difference between the various forms of past tense and when they should be and should not be used.	Compare French vs. English versions of *Le Petit Prince* to determine if and how language influences the meaning.	Role-play a conversation over the phone (e.g., planning weekend activities for French visitors to your town).		Develop a guide containing lists of colloquialisms and their translations to help French visitors avoid misunderstandings.	Keep a log of your reactions to French customs.

Performance Task Ideas Based on the Six Facets of Understanding (continued)
Samples by Subject

Topic	Explain	Interpret	Apply	Perspective	Empathy	Self-Knowledge
History and Social Studies	Provide conceptual clarification (e.g., freedom compared to license; meaning of the term "third world").	Develop an oral history on the significance of the 1960s using primary sources, and write a historical biography.	Design a museum exhibit on the causes and effects of early 20th century immigration.	Compare your textbook account to British and French textbook accounts of the Revolutionary War.	Role-play a meeting of the minds (e.g., Truman deciding to drop the atomic bomb).	Self-assess your involvement in class discussions and performances, and explain your patterns of participation.
Mathematics	Study a common phenomenon (e.g., weather data). Reveal subtle and easily overlooked patterns in the data.	Do a trend analysis of a finite data set.	Develop a new statistic for evaluating the value of a baseball player in key situations.	Examine the differences when using various measures (e.g., mean, median) for calculating grades.	Read *Flatland* and a set of letters between mathematicians explaining why they fear publishing their findings; write a reflective essay on the difficulty of explaining new ideas, even abstract ones.	Develop a mathematical resume with a brief description of your intellectual strengths and weaknesses.
English and Language Arts	Describe why a particular rhetorical technique is effective in a speech.	"What's wrong with Holden?" Make sense of the main character in *Catcher in the Rye*.	What makes a great book? Make an audiotape review of a favorite book for the school library.	Read and discuss *The Real Story of the Three Little Pigs* by A. Wolf.	Work in a soup kitchen, and write an essay on the experiences of the homeless after reading Charles Dickens.	Attach a self-assessment to each paper you write reflecting on your writing process.
Arts	Explain the role of silence in music.	Represent fear and hope in a visual collage or dance.	Write and perform a one-act play on a school issue.	Critique three different versions of the same Shakespeare play (focus on a key scene).	Imagine you are Juliet from *Romeo and Juliet*, and consider your terrible, final act. What are you thinking and feeling?	Keep a log of the drama class exercises that demand the most from you emotionally.
Science	Link everyday actions and facts to the laws of physics, concentrating on easily misunderstood aspects (e.g., mass compared to weight).	Take readings of pond water to determine whether the algae problem is serious.	Perform a chemical analysis of local stream water to monitor EPA compliance, and present findings.	Conduct thought experiments (e.g., Einstein's—What would the world be like if I were traveling on a beam of light?).	Read and discuss premodern or discredited scientific writings to identify plausible or "logical" theories (given the information available at the time).	Propose solutions to an ineffective cooperative learning activity based on what didn't work in your group.

Transforming Targeted Understandings into Possible Performances
U.S. History

A practical means of generating ideas for performance assessments of understanding involves combining the generalizations to be understood with appropriate verbs. The verbs specify the *kinds* of performances needed to reveal understanding (or its absence) by making the invisible, visible. Performance-oriented verbs are embedded within the six facets of understanding and the higher-order aspects of Bloom's Taxonomy: explain, interpret, apply, show, solve, demonstrate, argue, evaluate, prove, decide, create.

Use the design sheet on the next page to turn a desired understanding into possible performances that may be assessed. (See list of performance verbs based on the six facets of understanding.)

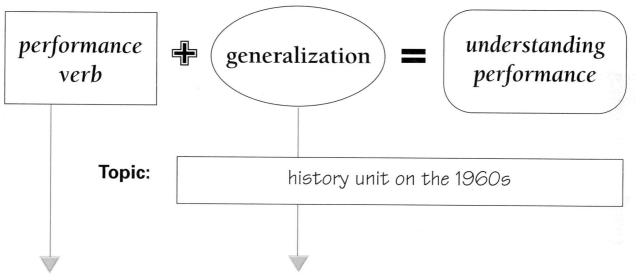

Topic: history unit on the 1960s

Examples of possible performances:

Explain	how U.S. involvement in the Vietnam War caused some people to lose faith in their government.
Argue	for or against the view that the antiwar movement was sparked by the Civil Rights movement.
Apply	your understanding of the era in a role-play recreation of the Kerner Commission report on violence.

Templates | Stage 1 | Stage 2 | Stage 3 | Peer review | Exercises | Process sheets | Glossary

Templates

Stage 1

Stage 2

Stage 3

Peer review

Exercises

Process sheets

Glossary

Transforming Targeted Understandings into Possible Performances

A practical means of generating ideas for performance assessments of understanding involves combining the generalizations to be understood with appropriate verbs. The verbs specify the *kinds* of performances needed to reveal understanding (or its absence) by making the invisible, visible. Performance-oriented verbs are embedded within the six facets of understanding and the higher-order aspects of Bloom's Taxonomy: explain, interpret, apply, show, solve, demonstrate, argue, evaluate, prove, decide, create.

Use the design sheet on the next page to turn a desired understanding into possible performances that may be assessed. (See list of performance verbs based on the six facets of understanding.)

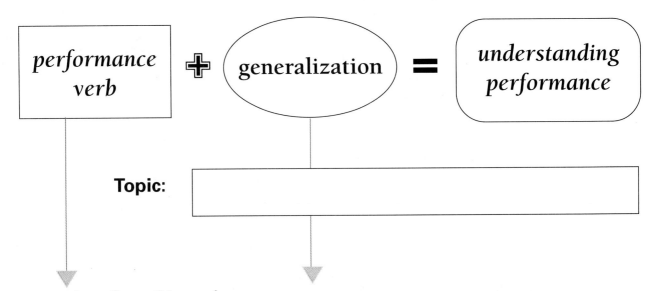

Topic:

Examples of possible performances:

Performance Verbs Based on the Six Facets of Understanding

Consider the following performance verbs when planning possible ways in which students may demonstrate their understanding. (See the design tool on the next page.)

explain
demonstrate
derive
describe
design
exhibit
express
induce
instruct
justify
model
predict
prove
show
synthesize
teach

interpret
analogies (create)
critique
document
evaluate
illustrate
judge
make meaning of
make sense of
metaphors (provide)
read between the lines
represent
tell a story of
translate

apply
adapt
build
create
de-bug
decide
design
exhibit
invent
perform
produce
propose
solve
test
use

perspective
analyze
argue
compare
contrast
criticize
infer

empathy
assume role of
believe
be like
be open to
consider
imagine
relate
role-play

self-knowledge
be aware of
realize
recognize
reflect
self-assess

Templates
Stage 1
Stage 2
Stage 3
Peer review
Exercises
Process sheets
Glossary

Generating Assessment Ideas Using the Six Facets of Understanding
Economics

Stage 1	Stage 2	
If the desired result is for learners to . . .	*Then, you need evidence of the student's ability to . . .*	*So, the assessments need to include some things like . . .*
Understand that: • Price is a function of supply and demand. **And thoughtfully consider the questions . . .** • What determines how much something costs? • What's a "good" price?	• **Explain . . .** why similar items might command very different prices based on supply and demand. • **Interpret . . .** data on prices (e.g., changes in prices for the same item over time). • **Apply by . . .** setting the right prices for items to be sold. • **See from the points of view of . . .** buyers and sellers of the same commodity. • **Empathize with . . .** the inventor of a new product who is trying to set a price. a buyer who has been "taken." • **Overcome the naive or biased idea that . . .** commodities have an inherent value or fixed price. • **Reflect on . . .** the influence of "sale prices" on your buying habits.	• Provide an oral and written explanation of why prices of specific items vary (e.g., Beanie babies, ski lift tickets) as a function of supply and demand. • Develop a PowerPoint presentation to explain fluctuations in prices over time (e.g., for gasoline or housing). • Conduct consumer research to establish prices for a school store or fund raiser. • Role-play a buyer-seller negotiation at a flea market, garage sale, or on e-Bay to illustrate different perspectives on price. • Write a simulated journal entry as a (consumer, inventor, or merchant) to reveal his thoughts and feelings regarding transactions. • Describe a specific case where you (or someone else) came to understand that commodities do not have an inherent value or fixed price.

Generating Assessment Ideas Using the Six Facets of Understanding
Assessment

Stage 1	Stage 2	
If the desired result is for learners to . . .	*Then, you need evidence of the student's ability to . . .*	*So, the assessments need to include some things like . . .*
Understand that: • Valid assessment matches the achievement targets with the evidence. • Effective assessment promotes learning, as well as measures it. • Assessments of understanding require students to apply and explain, not simply recall. • Clear criteria and "anchors" enhance scoring reliability. **And thoughtfully consider the questions . . .** • What is valid assessment? • Are we appropriately assessing everything we value? • What evidence will show that students really understand? • How can we make our judgments more reliable?	**• Explain . . .** any of the desired understandings. **• Interpret . . .** the meaning of results from different assessment measures. **• Apply by . . .** designing a valid assessment for specific achievement targets. **• See from the points of view of . . .** different users of assessment information. **• Empathize with . . .** a student being assessed. **• Overcome the naive or biased idea that . . .** everything that is assessed must be graded. **• Reflect on . . .** your own experiences, attitudes, and biases regarding assessment.	• Plan a presentation for beginning teachers to explain the rationale for using a balance of assessment formats when gathering evidence of learning. • Develop a summary statement to synthesize the results from different assessments. Then, suggest specific improvement actions suggested by the results. • Design an authentic performance assessment task and rubric to judge the degree of understanding of a Big Idea or process. • Express the view of a policy maker (e.g., legislator, board member) regarding the use of standardized tests to evaluate school performance. • Write a simulated journal entry as a student who understands the material but is not a good traditional test taker. • Identify any biases that you have regarding various types of assessment (e.g., multiple-choice, essay, projects, standardized tests), and reflect on if and how these have influenced your work.

Generating Assessment Ideas Using the Facets of Understanding

Stage 1	Stage 2	
If the desired result is for learners to . . .	*Then, you need evidence of the student's ability to . . .*	*So, the assessments need to include some things like . . .*
Understand that: **And thoughtfully consider the questions . . .**	• Explain . . . • Interpret . . . • Apply by . . . • See from the points of view of . . . • Empathize with . . . • Overcome the naive or biased idea that . . . • Reflect on . . .	

Templates · **Stage 1** · **Stage 2** · **Stage 3** · **Peer review** · **Exercises** · **Process sheets** · **Glossary**

Brainstorming Assessment Ideas
Using the Six Facets of Understanding
Electricity

Use the six facets of understanding to generate possible ways in which students might reveal understanding.

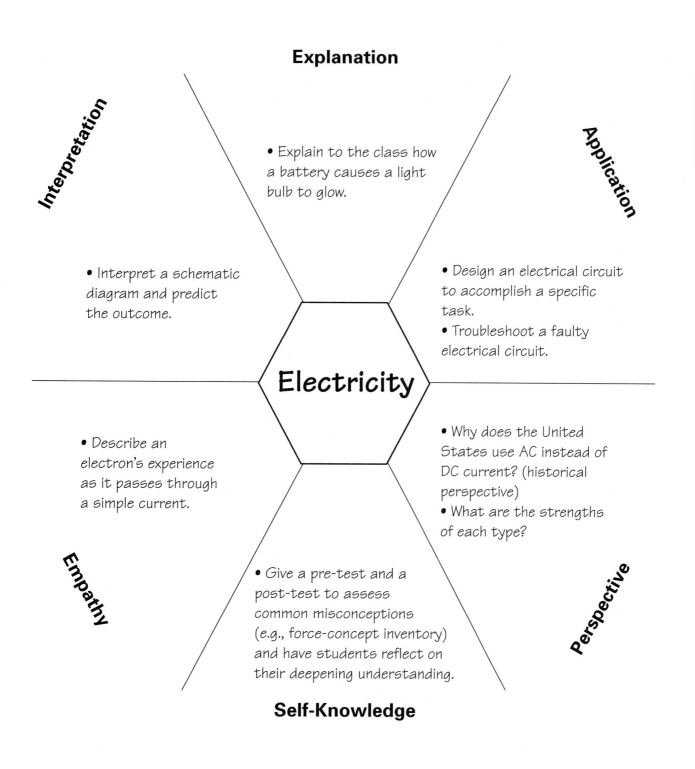

Explanation

• Explain to the class how a battery causes a light bulb to glow.

Interpretation

• Interpret a schematic diagram and predict the outcome.

Application

• Design an electrical circuit to accomplish a specific task.
• Troubleshoot a faulty electrical circuit.

Electricity

Empathy

• Describe an electron's experience as it passes through a simple current.

Perspective

• Why does the United States use AC instead of DC current? (historical perspective)
• What are the strengths of each type?

Self-Knowledge

• Give a pre-test and a post-test to assess common misconceptions (e.g., force-concept inventory) and have students reflect on their deepening understanding.

Templates | Stage 1 | Stage 2 | Stage 3 | Peer review | Exercises | Process sheets | Glossary

Brainstorming Assessment Ideas Using the Six Facets of Understanding

Use the six facets of understanding to generate possible ways in which students might reveal understanding.

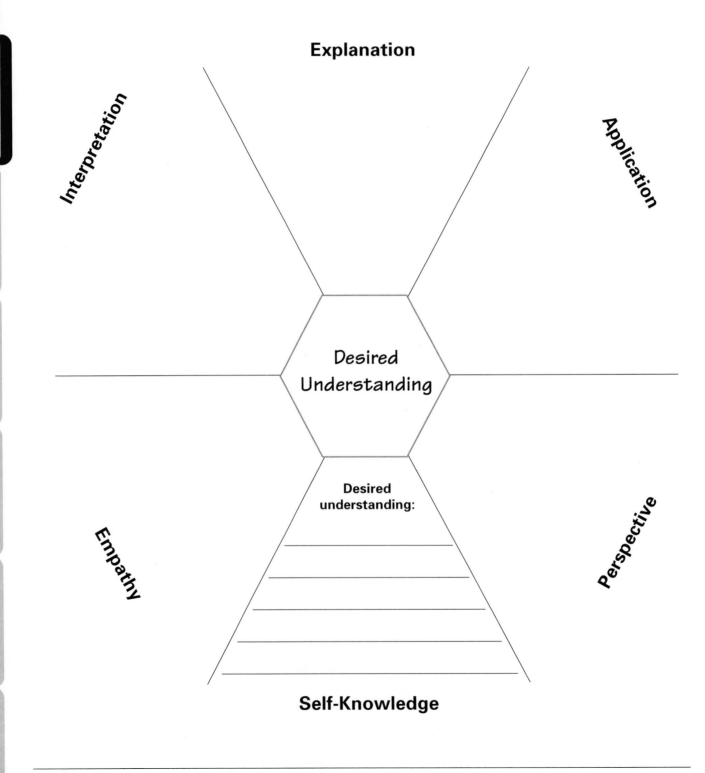

Templates
Stage 1
Stage 2
Stage 3
Peer review
Exercises
Process sheets
Glossary

Characteristics of Performance Tasks

Part 1—Examine the performance task vignettes on the following pages. What distinguishes these tasks from typical test items? What common features or characteristics do these share? List characteristics or features that you observe.

T

Tasks or Vignettes Examined	**Characteristics and Features:**
_____	• _____
	• _____
_____	• _____
	• _____
_____	• _____
	• _____
_____	

Part 2—Share and discuss your observations with members of your group. List the common characteristics or features of the performance tasks you examined.

Characteristics and Features:

- _____
- _____
- _____
- _____
- _____
- _____
- _____

- _____
- _____
- _____
- _____
- _____
- _____
- _____

Templates

Stage 1

Stage 2

Stage 3

Peer review

Exercises

Process sheets

Glossary

Performance Task Samples

Hall of Recognition (Social Studies and Language Arts, grade 4–5)

The state has announced the establishment of a Hall of Recognition to honor the contributions of local citizens to their community, the state, or the nation. Because you are learning about famous individuals from _____, you have been asked to nominate a candidate you believe would be worthy of admission to the Hall.

Your task is to select and research the life of your chosen individual. Submit a nomination letter to the Hall's selection committee explaining the reasons that your candidate should be included in the Hall of Recognition. Be sure to describe your candidate's accomplishments and the contributions your candidate has made.

Chemical Equilibrium (Chemistry, grades 11–12)

You are a researcher hired by a group of expert mountain climbers. Hypoxia is the set of symptoms (headache, fatigue, nausea) that comes from a lack of oxygen in body tissues. It is often felt by mountain climbers as they ascend altitude quickly. Sherpas, longtime residents of high altitudes, seem to feel no hypoxic discomfort. Why might that be? Your group wants to know and to benefit from the knowledge.

Design a series of experiments that would test the difference in hypoxic symptoms between mountain climbers and sherpas. Explain, using chemical equilibrium, why high altitude causes hypoxia in the climbers. How can sherpas avoid these symptoms? How can you test for these possibilities? What would a positive test look like? What inherent errors would you have to be aware of?

Mail-Order Friend (Language Arts, grades K–2)

Imagine that you have an opportunity to "order" a friend by telephone from a mail-order catalog. Think about the qualities that you want in a friend. Before you "order" your friend over the telephone, practice asking for three characteristics that you want in a friend and give an example of each characteristic. Remember to speak clearly and loud enough so that the salesperson will know exactly who to send.

Tour Director (World Languages, Level 1)

You serve on a Welcome Committee to provide tours for new students. Plan a trip to three *places* (e.g., school, town, mall) in the new student's target language. Incorporate the following vocabulary: *directions* (left, right, near, far, next to), *places* (e.g., classrooms, cafeteria, gym, library, labs, churches, police and fire stations, schools, restaurants, stores) and *transportation* (e.g., bus, bike, stairs, escalators, taxi, train, car, elevators).

Remember to include a variety of locations, directions, and forms of *transportation* on your trips. Keep sentences simple, and narrate in the target language.

Mythic Job Search (English, grades 7–10)

Your task is to select an epic hero from the literature we have read and write a letter to the hero in which you apply for a job as a crew member on his expeditions. In the letter, you must be specific about the position for which you are applying, your qualifications for the job, and why you feel you would be an asset to the crew. Be sure to make your letter persuasive by making it clear that you understand the particular struggles and adventures the hero and crew have already undertaken, and how you might be of value to them in handling such situations and difficulties. Write in business-letter form, and include a résumé.

Templates · Stage 1 · Stage 2 · Stage 3 · Peer review · Exercises · Process sheets · Glossary

Performance Task Examples (continued)

We Salute You (*Language Arts, Social Studies, grades 1–3*)

Our room mother, Mrs. _____, has done many things to help us throughout the year. When people do things for you, it is important to show appreciation. We will each be writing a letter to her to thank her and let her know how she has helped our class.

Your letter should include all the parts of a friendly letter. Be sure to tell her at least three ways she has been helpful to our class. Include at least one thing that you especially appreciate about our room mother.

Dry Walling a Home (*Mathematics, grades 7–9*)

When contractors give us an estimate on home repairs, how can we know if the cost is reasonable? A homeowner has asked you to review a dry walling contractor's proposal to determine whether the homeowner is being overcharged. (Students are given room dimensions and cost figures for materials, labor, and a 20 percent profit.)

Examine the proposal and write a letter to the homeowner providing your evaluation of the proposal. Be sure to show your calculations so that the homeowner will understand how you arrived at your conclusion.

From the Mountains to the Seashore (*History, Geography, Math, grades 5–8*)

A group of nine foreign students is visiting your school for one month as part of an international exchange program. (Don't worry, they speak English!) The principal has asked your class to plan and budget a four-day tour of Virginia to help the visitors understand the state's impact on the history and development of our nation. Plan your tour so that the visitors are shown sites that best capture the ways that Virginia has influenced our nation's development.

You should prepare a written tour itinerary, including an explanation of why each site was selected. Include a map tracing the route for the four-day tour and a budget for the trip.

Express Yourself (*Art, grades 4–7*)

You have recently analyzed the narrative work of Faith Ringgold to identify ways she communicated ideas about her world. Think about your own world, your friends, family, daily experiences, and the things that are important to you. Select a drawing or painting medium, or use mixed media to create your own narrative work that communicates personal ideas about your world.

Fitness Consultant (*Physical Education, high school*)

Image that you are a fitness consultant for a local health club. Your task is to design a fitness program for a client. (Students are given client specifications—age, height, weight, fitness goals.) Use our fitness planning format to design a 16-week fitness program for strength, endurance, and flexibility. Explain how your selection of aerobic, anaerobic, and stretching exercises will help your client meet the goal. Be prepared to demonstrate the proper technique for all exercises and stretches that you recommend.

Constructing a Performance Task Scenario Using GRASPS

Mathematics

Goal:

• **The goal (within the scenario) is to** minimize costs for shipping bulk quantities of M&M'S.

Role:

• **You are** an engineer in the packaging department of the M&M'S candy company.

Audience:

• **The target audience** is nonengineer company executives.

Situation:

• **You need to** convince penny-pinching company officers that your container design will provide cost-effective use of the given materials, maximize shipping volume of bulk quantities of M&M'S, and be safe to transport.

Product Performance and Purpose:

• **You need to** design a shipping container from given materials for the safe and cost-effective shipping of the M&M'S. Then you will prepare a written proposal in which you include a diagram and show mathematically how your container design provides effective use of the given materials and maximizes the shipping volume of the M&M'S.

Standards and Criteria for Success:

• **Your** container proposal should . . .
  – Provide cost-effective use of the given materials.
  – Maximize shipping volume of bulk quantities of M&M'S.
  – Be safe to transport.
• **Your** models must make the mathematical case.

Constructing a Performance Task Scenario Using GRASPS

Social Studies

Goal:

• **Your goal is to** help a group of foreign visitors understand the key historic, geographic, and economic features of our region.

Role:

• **You are** an intern at the Regional Office of Tourism.

Audience:

• **The audience** is a group of nine foreign visitors (who speak English).

Situation:

• **You have been asked to** develop a plan, including a budget, for a four-day tour of the region. Plan your tour so that the visitors are shown sites that best illustrate the key historic, geographic, and economic features of our region.

Product Performance and Purpose:

• **You need to** prepare a written tour itinerary and a budget for the trip. You should include an explanation of why each site was selected and how it will help the visitors understand the key historic, geographic, and economic features of our region. Include a map tracing the route for the tour.

Standards and Criteria for Success:

• **Your** proposed tour plan (including itinerary, budget and route map) **needs to include**
  – The key historic, geographic, and economic features of the region.
  – A clear rationale for the selected sites.
  – Accurate and complete budget figures.

Templates

Stage 1

Stage 2

Stage 3

Peer review

Exercises

Process sheets

Glossary

Templates

Stage 1

Stage 2

Stage 3

Peer review

Exercises

Process sheets

Glossary

Constructing a Performance Task Scenario Using GRASPS

Consider the following set of stem statements as you construct a scenario for a performance task. Refer to the previous idea sheets to help you brainstorm possible scenarios. (Note: These are idea starters. Resist the urge to fill in all of the blanks.)

Goal:

- Your task is_____

- The goal is to _____

- The problem or challenge is _____

- The obstacles to overcome are _____

Role:

- You are _____

- You have been asked to _____

- Your job is _____

Audience:

- Your clients are _____

- The target audience is _____

- You need to convince _____

Situation:

- The context you find yourself in is _____

- The challenge involves dealing with _____

Product, Performance, and Purpose:

- You will create a _____

  in order to _____

- You need to develop _____

  so that _____

Standards and Criteria for Success:

- Your performance needs to _____

- Your work will be judged by _____

- Your product must meet the following standards: _____

- A successful result will _____

Possible Student Roles and Audiences

KEY: ○ = ROLES and ❑ = AUDIENCES

○ ❑ actor
○ ❑ advertiser
○ ❑ artist/illustrator
○ ❑ author
○ ❑ biographer
○ ❑ board member
○ ❑ boss
○ ❑ Boy/Girl Scout
○ ❑ businessperson
○ ❑ candidate
○ ❑ carpenter
○ ❑ cartoon character
○ ❑ cartoonist
○ ❑ caterer
○ ❑ celebrity
○ ❑ CEO
○ ❑ chairperson
○ ❑ chef
○ ❑ choreographer
○ ❑ coach
○ ❑ community member
○ ❑ composer
○ ❑ client/customer
○ ❑ construction worker
○ ❑ dancer
○ ❑ designer
○ ❑ detective
○ ❑ editor
○ ❑ elected official
○ ❑ embassy staff
○ ❑ engineer
○ ❑ expert (in _____)
○ ❑ eyewitness

○ ❑ family member
○ ❑ farmer
○ ❑ filmmaker
○ ❑ firefighter
○ ❑ forest ranger
○ ❑ friend
○ ❑ geologist
○ ❑ government official
○ ❑ historian
○ ❑ historical figure
○ ❑ illustrator
○ ❑ intern
○ ❑ interviewer
○ ❑ inventor
○ ❑ judge
○ ❑ jury
○ ❑ lawyer
○ ❑ library patron
○ ❑ literary critic
○ ❑ lobbyist
○ ❑ meteorologist
○ ❑ museum director/
        curator
○ ❑ museum goer
○ ❑ neighbor
○ ❑ newscaster
○ ❑ novelist
○ ❑ nutritionist
○ ❑ observer
○ ❑ panelist
○ ❑ parent
○ ❑ park ranger
○ ❑ pen pal

○ ❑ photographer
○ ❑ pilot
○ ❑ playwright
○ ❑ poet
○ ❑ police officer
○ ❑ pollster
○ ❑ radio listener
○ ❑ reader
○ ❑ reporter
○ ❑ researcher
○ ❑ reviewer
○ ❑ sailor
○ ❑ school official
○ ❑ scientist
○ ❑ ship's captain
○ ❑ social scientist
○ ❑ social worker
○ ❑ statistician
○ ❑ storyteller
○ ❑ student
○ ❑ taxi driver
○ ❑ teacher
○ ❑ tour guide
○ ❑ trainer
○ ❑ travel agent
○ ❑ traveler
○ ❑ tutor
○ ❑ t.v. viewer
○ ❑ t.v. or movie
        character
○ ❑ visitor
○ ❑ Web site designer
○ ❑ zookeeper

173

Templates

Stage 1

Stage 2

Stage 3

Peer review

Exercises

Process sheets

Glossary

Possible Products and Performances

What student products and performances will provide appropriate evidence of understanding and proficiency? The following lists offer possibilities. (Remember that student products and performances should be framed by an explicit purpose or goal and an identified audience.)

Templates

Stage 1

Stage 2

Stage 3

Peer review

Exercises

Process sheets

Glossary

Written	Oral	Visual
◯ advertisement	◯ audiotape	◯ advertisement
◯ biography	◯ conversation	◯ banner
◯ book report or review	◯ debate	◯ cartoon
◯ brochure	◯ discussion	◯ collage
◯ collection	◯ dramatic reading	◯ computer graphic
◯ crossword puzzle	◯ dramatization	◯ data display
◯ editorial	◯ interview	◯ design
◯ essay	◯ oral presentation	◯ diagram
◯ experiment record	◯ oral report	◯ diorama
◯ historical fiction	◯ poetry reading	◯ display
◯ journal	◯ puppet show	◯ drawing
◯ lab report	◯ radio script	◯ filmstrip
◯ letter	◯ rap	◯ flyer
◯ log	◯ skit	◯ game
◯ magazine article	◯ song	◯ graph
◯ memo	◯ speech	◯ map
◯ newscast	◯ teach a lesson	◯ model
◯ newspaper article		◯ painting
◯ play		◯ photograph
◯ poem		◯ poster
◯ position paper		◯ PowerPoint show
◯ proposal		◯ questionnaire
◯ research report		◯ scrapbook
◯ script		◯ sculpture
◯ story	Other:	◯ slide show
◯ test		◯ storyboard
◯ Web site	◯ _____	◯ videotape
	◯ _____	◯ Web site

Assessment Task Blueprint
Nutrition

What understandings or goals will be assessed through this task? (G)

> Students will plan appropriate diets for themselves and others.

What criteria are implied in the standards and understandings regardless of the task specifics? What qualities must student work demonstrate to signify that standards were met?

> - Nutritionally sound
> - Comparison of taste vs. nutrition
> - Feasible

Through what authentic performance task will students demonstrate understanding?

> **Task Overview:** (T)
>
> Since we have been learning about nutrition, the camp director at the Outdoor Ed Center has asked us to propose a nutritionally balanced menu for our three-day trip to the center later this year. Using the USDA Food Pyramid guidelines and the nutrition facts on food labels, design a plan for three days, including the three main meals and three snacks (a.m., p.m., and campfire). Your goal is a tasty and nutritionally balanced menu. In addition to your menu, prepare a letter to the camp director explaining how your menu meets the USDA nutritional guidelines. Include a chart showing a breakdown of the fat, protein, carbohydrates, vitamins, minerals, and calories.

What student products and performances will provide evidence of desired understandings?

> Menu with chart of nutritional values

> Letter to camp director

By what criteria will student products and performances be evaluated?

> - Menu meets USDA guidelines
> - Nutritional values chart is accurate and complete
> - Menu addresses the audience and the situation

> - Effective explanation of nutritional value and taste appeal of proposed menu
> - Proper letter form
> - Correct spelling and conventions

175

Templates · Stage 1 · Stage 2 · Stage 3 · Peer review · Exercises · Process sheets · Glossary

Assessment Task Blueprint

What understandings or goals will be assessed through this task? **G**

What criteria are implied in the standards and understandings *regardless* of the task specifics? What qualities must student work demonstrate to signify that standards were met?

Through what authentic performance task will students demonstrate understanding?

Task Overview: **T**

What student products and performances will provide evidence of desired understandings?

By what criteria will student products and performances be evaluated?

Templates

Stage 1

Stage 2

Stage 3

Peer review

Exercises

Process sheets

Glossary

Checking for Validity
Virginia History
(Note: This is a flawed example.)

G **U**

What understandings or goals will be assessed through this task?

Virginia History Standard 5.7: The student will understand the causes and effects of the Civil War with emphasis on slavery, states' rights, leadership, settlement of the West. . . secession, military events.

Students will demonstrate knowledge of and skill in using topographical maps.

What criteria are implied in the standards and understandings *regardless* of the task specifics? What qualities must student work demonstrate to signify that standards were met?

- Thorough analysis of cause and effect
- Historically accurate

- Accurate map
- Drawn to scale

Through what authentic performance task will students demonstrate understanding?

T

Task Overview:

You are opening a new museum on the Civil War designed to inform and engage young people. Your task is to select a decisive Civil War battle, research the battle, and construct a diorama of the battle. Attach an index card to your diorama containing the date of the battle, the names of the opposing generals, the number of casualties on each side and the victor. Finally, create a topographical map to show an aerial view of the battlefields.

Remember: Your map must be drawn to scale. Neatness and spelling count!

What student products and performances will provide evidence of desired understandings?

Diorama of Civil War battle

Topographical map of battlefield

By what criteria or indicators will task-derived student products and performances be evaluated? (Consider criteria that refer to desired task content, process, and results.)

- Actual Civil War battle depicted
- Accurate information on index card
- Neat and colorful
- Correct spelling

- Accurate topography
- Drawn to scale
- Includes compass rose
- Correct placement of armies
- Neat and colorful

Validity requires that all these elements must align

177

Side tab labels: Templates / Stage 1 / Stage 2 / Stage 3 / Peer review / Exercises / Process sheets / Glossary

Checking for Validity—Analysis

Check for alignment: Does the task enable inference about the goals?

Civil War Museum Exhibit

Established Goals: **G**

Virginia SOL History Standard 5.7:
The student will understand the causes and effects of the Civil War with emphasis on slavery, states' rights, leadership, settlement of the West, secession, military events.

Understandings: **U**

Students will understand the causes and effects of the Civil War.
Students will demonstrate knowledge of topographical maps.

Performance Task: **T**

You are opening a new museum on the Civil War designed to inform and engage young people. Your task is to select a decisive Civil War battle, research the battle, and construct a diorama of the battle. Attach an index card to your diorama containing the date of the battle, the names of the opposing generals, the number of casualties on each side, and the victor. Finally, create a topographical map to show an aerial view of the battlefield.

Student Products and Performances:

| Diorama of Civil War battle | Topographical map of battlefield |

Criteria:

- Key Civil War battle depicted
- Accurate information on index card
- Neat and colorful
- Correct spelling

- Accurate topography
- Drawn to scale
- Includes compass rose
- Correct placement of armies
- Neat and colorful

Could the task be performed well without understanding? ❑ *yes* ❑ *no*

Could the task be performed poorly in spite of understanding? ❑ *yes* ❑ *no*

COMMENTS

The standard requires evidence that shows analysis of and justification for a number of key events and how those events are connected causally.

While engaging and related to the topic, the task does not allow valid inferences to be made about the standard; for example, the student could do well on the diorama without demonstrating an understanding of cause-and-effect. Furthermore, with a focus on a single battle, it is unlikely that even the best diorama would yield insight into the war's cause and effect. Finally, the focus on a single task involving small-motor and aesthetic skills is problematic: students may do poorly or well at the task (i.e., constructing the diorama) for reasons having little to do with their content understanding or lack of it.

Even if the task were adequate for making inferences about the standard, the criteria used to judge the diorama product are somewhat inappropriate. The emphasis here is on accuracy and neatness, with no explicit link in the scoring back to the desired understanding (cause-and-effect reasoning). A more appropriate criterion might involve "sophistication of analysis of battle and its impact" tied to a task about the battle's importance (e.g., having the student write and produce the audiotape for patrons as they walk in a museum about the war).

Checking for Validity—Revision

What understandings or goals will be assessed through this task?

> Virginia Standards of Learning History
> Standard 5.7: The student will understand the causes and effects of the Civil War with emphasis on slavery, states' rights, leadership, settlement of the West, secession, military events.

> Students will understand that there were complex social, economic, and political causes of the Civil War and that some effects are still with us.

What criteria are implied in the standards and understandings *regardless* of the task specifics? What qualities must student work demonstrate to signify that standards were met?

> • Thorough analysis of cause and effect
> • Historically accurate

Through what authentic performance task will students demonstrate understanding?

> **Task Overview:**   T
>
> You are part of a team opening a new museum on the Civil War designed to inform and engage young people. Your task is to select three to four decisive trends and events that caused the war and three to four effects of the war that have lasted until today. Provide a sketch of each exhibit and a visual flowchart or timeline of cause-and-effect, and develop a virtual or real model of one of the exhibits. (An individual exhibit might be devoted to more than one cause, effect, or combination.) Make your pitch to the museum directors for your choices and designs, using whatever media will best make your case.

What student products and performances will provide evidence of desired understandings?

> Exhibit proposal

> Exhibit model

By what criteria or indicators will task-derived student products and performances be evaluated? (Consider criteria that refer to desired task content, process, and results.)

> • Sophisticated analysis of cause-and-effect
> • Historically accurate
> • Justified choices

> • Polish of presentation
> • Craftsmanship of sketches
> • Craftsmanship of exhibit

Templates · Stage 1 · Stage 2 · Stage 3 · Peer review · Exercises · Process sheets · Glossary

Templates

Stage 1

Stage 2

Stage 3

Peer review

Exercises

Process sheets

Glossary

Self-Test Assessment Ideas

Stage 1

Desired Results:

Stage 2

Proposed Assessment:

	very likely	somewhat likely	very unlikely
How likely is it that a student could do well *on the assessment by*			
1. Making clever guesses based on limited understanding?	❑	❑	❑
2. Parroting back or plugging in what was learned, with accurate recall but limited or no understanding?	❑	❑	❑
3. Making a good-faith effort, with lots of hard work and enthusiasm, but with limited understanding?	❑	❑	❑
4. Producing lovely products and performances, but with limited understanding?	❑	❑	❑
5. Applying natural ability to be articulate and intelligent, with limited understanding of the content in question?	❑	❑	❑
How likely is it that a student could do poorly *on the assessment by*			
6. Failing to meet the performance goals despite having a deep understanding of the big ideas? (i.e., the task is not relevant to the goals)	❑	❑	❑
7. Failing to meet the scoring and grading criteria used, despite having a deep understanding of the Big Ideas? (i.e., some of the criteria are arbitrary, placing undue or inappropriate emphasis on things that have little to do with the desired results or true excellence at such a task)	❑	❑	❑

Goal: Make all your answers "very unlikely"

Criterion-Based Performance List

Performance lists offer a practical means of judging student performance based upon identified criteria. A performance list consists of criteria, elements, or traits, and a rating scale. The rating scale is quite flexible, ranging from three to 100 points.

Teachers can assign points to the various elements, in order to "weight" certain elements over others (e.g., accuracy counts more than neatness) based on the relative importance given the achievement target. The lists may be configured to easily convert to conventional grades. For example, a teacher could assign point values and weights that add up to 25, 50, or 100 points, enabling a straightforward conversion to a district or school grading scale (e.g., 90–100 = A, 80–89 = B and so on). When the lists are shared with students in advance, they provide a clear performance target, signaling to students what elements should be present in their work.

Despite these benefits, performance lists do not provide detailed descriptions of *performance levels*. Thus, despite identified criteria, different teachers using the same performance list may rate the same student's work quite differently.

Performance List for Graphic Display of Data

	Yes	No	Points:
1. The graph contains a title that tells what the data show.	☐	☐	☐
2. All parts of the graph (i.e., units of measurement, rows) are correctly labeled.	☐	☐	☐
3. All data are accurately represented on the graph.	☐	☐	☐
4. The graph is neat and easy to read.	☐	☐	+ ☐
		Total	☐

Holistic Rubric

A holistic rubric provides an overall impression of a student's work. Holistic rubrics yield a *single* score or rating for a product or performance. Holistic rubrics are well suited to judging simple products or performances, such as a student's response to an open-ended test prompt. They provide a quick snapshot of overall quality or achievement, and are thus often used in large-scale assessment contexts (national, state, or district levels) to evaluate a large number of student responses. Holistic rubrics are also effective for judging the effect of a product or performance (e.g., To what extent was the essay persuasive? Did the play entertain?).

Despite these advantages, holistic rubrics have limitations. They do not provide a detailed analysis of the strengths and weaknesses of a product or performance. Because a single score is generally inadequate for conveying to students what they have done well and what they need to work on to improve, scores are less effective at providing specific feedback to students.

Holistic Rubric for Graphic Display of Data

3	All data are accurately represented on the graph. All parts of the graph (units of measurement, rows) are correctly labeled. The graph contains a title that clearly tells what the data show. The graph is very neat and easy to read.
2	Data are accurately represented on the graph *or* the graph contains minor errors. All parts of the graph are correctly labeled *or* the graph contains minor inaccuracies. The graph contains a title that generally tells what the data show. The graph is generally neat and readable.
1	The data are inaccurately represented, contain major errors or are missing. Only some parts of the graph are correctly labeled, or labels are missing. The title does not reflect what the data show, or the title is missing. The graph is sloppy and difficult to read.

Analytic-Trait Rubric

An analytic-trait rubric divides a product or performance into distinct traits or dimensions and judges each separately. Because an analytic rubric rates each of the identified traits independently, a separate score is provided for each (even if a single total score is also calculated).

Analytic rubrics are better suited to judging complex performances (e.g., research) involving several significant dimensions. As evaluation tools, they provide more specific information or feedback to students, parents, and teachers about the strengths and weaknesses of a performance. Teachers can use the information provided by analytic evaluation to target instruction to particular areas of need. From an instructional perspective, analytic rubrics help students come to better understand the nature of quality work because they identify the important dimensions of a product or performance.

However, analytic rubrics are typically more time-consuming to learn and apply. Because several traits are to be considered, analytic scoring may yield lower inter-rater reliability (degree of agreement among different judges) than holistic scoring. Thus, analytic scoring may be less desirable for use in large-scale assessment contexts, where speed and reliability are necessary.

Format Note: Don't confuse the concept of analytic-trait scoring with the format of the rubrics. Analytic-trait scoring of multiple traits can be done on a single page *if* the separate traits can be identified within the overall paragraph for that score point, and are meant to be scored separately. Similarly, we may choose to assess only *one* criterion on a particular assignment, but the single rubric focuses on one analytic trait, rather than a holistic view of the entire performance.

Analytic-Trait Rubric for Graphic Display of Data

	title	labels	accuracy	neatness
weight:	*10%*	*20%*	*50%*	*20%*
3	The graph contains a title that clearly tells what the data show.	All parts of the graph (units of measurement, rows) are correctly labeled.	All data are accurately represented on the graph.	The graph is very neat and easy to read.
2	The graph contains a title that generally tells what the data show.	Some parts of the graph are inaccurately labeled.	Data representation contains minor errors.	The graph is generally neat and readable.
1	The title does not reflect what the data show *or* the title is missing.	Only some parts of the graph are correctly labeled *or* labels are missing.	The data are inaccurately represented, contain major errors *or* are missing.	The graph is sloppy and difficult to read.

Templates · Stage 1 · Stage 2 · Stage 3 · Peer review · Exercises · Process sheets · Glossary

Templates

Stage 1

Stage 2

Stage 3

Peer review

Exercises

Process sheets

Glossary

Identifying Important Performance Qualities

Part 1—Individually, list the important qualities or traits for _____.

❑ _____

❑ _____

❑ _____

❑ _____

❑ _____

❑ _____

❑ _____

❑ _____

- -

Part 2—With your group, agree to four to six of the most important traits. List them below.

1. _____

2. _____

3. _____

4. _____

5. _____

6. _____

Naive vs. Sophisticated Understanding
Civil War

Use the following worksheet to develop a simple rubric to assess understanding of a targeted Big Idea or complex process. Begin by identifying the indicators of a sophisticated, expert understanding. Then list the indicators of the understandings (and probable misunderstandings) of a novice. These lists provide descriptors for the top and bottom levels of a rubric scale.

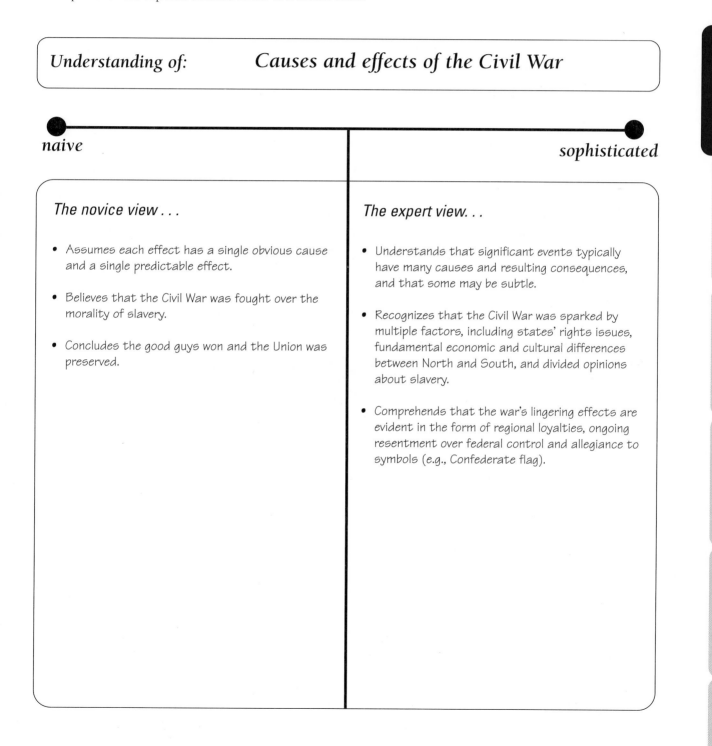

Understanding of: *Causes and effects of the Civil War*

naive   **sophisticated**

The novice view . . .

- Assumes each effect has a single obvious cause and a single predictable effect.

- Believes that the Civil War was fought over the morality of slavery.

- Concludes the good guys won and the Union was preserved.

The expert view. . .

- Understands that significant events typically have many causes and resulting consequences, and that some may be subtle.

- Recognizes that the Civil War was sparked by multiple factors, including states' rights issues, fundamental economic and cultural differences between North and South, and divided opinions about slavery.

- Comprehends that the war's lingering effects are evident in the form of regional loyalties, ongoing resentment over federal control and allegiance to symbols (e.g., Confederate flag).

Templates

Stage 1

Stage 2

Stage 3

Peer review

Exercises

Process sheets

Glossary

Naive vs. Sophisticated Understanding
Persuasion

Use the following worksheet to develop a simple rubric to assess understanding of a targeted Big Idea or complex process. Begin by identifying the indicators of a sophisticated, expert understanding. Then list the indicators of the understandings (and probable misunderstandings) of a novice. These lists provide descriptors for the top and bottom levels of a rubric scale.

Understanding of: *Persuasion*

naive ●————————————————————● **sophisticated**

The novice view...	*The expert...*
• Assumes that making a logical argument is sufficient to persuade	• Understands that persuasion often works at the subliminal levels, based on an insight into the audience's emotions
•	•
•	•
•	•
•	•
•	•
•	•
•	•
•	•
•	•
•	•

Naive vs. Sophisticated Understanding

Use the following worksheet to develop a simple rubric to assess understanding of a targeted Big Idea or complex process. Begin by identifying the indicators of a sophisticated, expert understanding. Then list the indicators of the understandings (and probable misunderstandings) of a novice. These lists provide descriptors for the top and bottom levels of a rubric scale.

Understanding of:

naive   *sophisticated*

The novice view . . .

- _____
  _____
- _____
  _____
- _____
  _____
- _____
  _____
- _____
  _____
- _____
  _____

The expert view. . .

- _____
  _____
- _____
  _____
- _____
  _____
- _____
  _____
- _____
  _____
- _____
  _____

Templates

Stage 1

Stage 2

Stage 3

Peer review

Exercises

Process sheets

Glossary

An Analytic Scoring Rubric with Two Basic Traits

Use the frame to evaluate the (1) degree of student understanding and (2) effectiveness of performance or product.

Traits	Understanding	Performance or performance quality
Scale	*Weights* → **65 percent**	**35 percent**
4	Shows a sophisticated understanding of the relevant ideas or processes. The concepts, evidence, arguments, qualifications made, questions posed and methods used are advanced, going well beyond the grasp of the subject typically found at this age level.	The performance or product is highly effective. The ideas are presented in an engaging, polished, clear, and thorough manner, mindful of the audience, context, and purpose. There is unusual craftsmanship in the final product or performance.
3	Shows a solid understanding of the relevant ideas or processes. The concepts, evidence, arguments, and methods used are appropriate for addressing the issues and problems. There are no misunderstandings of key ideas or overly simplistic approaches.	The performance or product is effective. The ideas are presented in a clear and thorough manner, showing awareness of the audience, context, and purpose.
2	Shows a somewhat naive or limited understanding of the relevant ideas or processes. The concepts, evidence, arguments, and methods used are somewhat simple, crude, or inadequate for addressing the issues or problems. Response may reveal some misunderstanding of key ideas or methods.	The performance or product is somewhat effective. There are some problems with clarity, thoroughness, delivery, and polish. It is unclear whether audience, context, and purpose have been considered.
1	Shows little apparent understanding of the relevant ideas and issues. The concepts, evidence, arguments, and methods used are inadequate for addressing the issues and problems. Response reveals major misunderstandings of key ideas or methods.	The performance or product is ineffective. The performance is unpolished, providing little evidence of prior planning, practice, and consideration of purpose and audience, *or* the presentation is so unclear and confusing as to make it difficult to determine the key points.

Templates   Stage 1   Stage 2   Stage 3   Peer review   Exercises   Process sheets   Glossary

Criteria and Rubric Ideas

By what criteria should understanding performances be assessed? The challenge in answering is to ensure that we assess what is *central* to the understanding, not just what is easy to score. In addition, we need to make sure that we identify the *separate* traits of performance (e.g., a paper can be well-organized but not informative, and vice versa) to ensure that the student gets specific and valid feedback. Finally, we need to make sure that we consider the different *types* of criteria (e.g., the quality of the *understanding* vs. the quality of the *performance* in which it is revealed). Ideas for criteria and rubrics are provided on the next three pages; sample rubrics follow.

Four Types of Performance Criteria with Sample Indicators

Content	Process	Quality	Result
Describes the degree of knowledge of factual information or understanding of concepts, principles, and processes.	Describes the degree of skill or proficiency. Also refers to the effectiveness of the process or method used.	Describes the degree of quality evident in products and performances.	Describes the overall impact and the extent to which goals, purposes, or results are achieved.
accurate	careful	attractive	beneficial
appropriate	clever	competent	conclusive
authentic	coherent	creative	convincing
complete	collaborative	detailed	decisive
correct	concise	extensive	effective
credible	coordinated	focused	engaging
explained	effective	graceful	entertaining
justified	efficient	masterful	informative
important	flawless	neat	inspiring
in-depth	followed process	novel	meets standards
insightful	logical or reasoned	organized	memorable
logical	mechanically correct	polished	moving
makes connections	methodical	precise	persuasive
precise	meticulous	proficient	proven
relevant	organized	rigorous	responsive
sophisticated	planned	skilled	satisfactory
supported	purposeful	stylish	satisfying
thorough	rehearsed	smooth	significant
valid	sequential	unique	understood
	skilled	well-crafted	useful

Templates

Stage 1

Stage 2

Stage 3

Peer review

Exercises

Process sheets

Glossary

Criteria and Rubric Ideas (continued)

Quality of the understanding	Quality of the performance
accurate	comprehensive
credible	effective
critical	efficient
illuminating	elegant
illustrative	engaging
insightful	fluent
grounded	graceful
justified	mechanically sound
meaningful	persuasive
perceptive	poised
plausible	polished
revealing	practical
sensitive	precise
significant	skilled
sophisticated	solved
unusual	thorough

Criteria Related to the Six Facets of Understanding					
Facet 1	Facet 2	Facet 3	Facet 4	Facet 5	Facet 6
Explanation	**Interpretation**	**Application**	**Perspective**	**Empathy**	**Self-knowledge**
accurate	illuminating	appropriate	credible	open	insightful
coherent	illustrative	effective	critical	perceptive	metacognitive
elegant	important	efficient	insightful	receptive	reflective
justified	meaningful	fluent	plausible	responsive	self-adjusting
predictive	revealing	graceful	revealing	sensitive	self-aware
thorough	significant	practical	unusual	tactful	wise

Templates · Stage 1 · Stage 2 · Stage 3 · Peer review · Exercises · Process sheets · Glossary

An Analytic Rubric Frame

Understanding: _____

Specific Product or Performance: _____

traits / scale				
weights →				
4				
3				
2				
1				

Templates · Stage 1 · Stage 2 · Stage 3 · Peer review · Exercises · Process sheets · Glossary

Templates

Stage 1

Stage 2

Stage 3

Peer review

Exercises

Process sheets

Glossary

Descriptive Terms for Differences in Degree

Use the following general terms to describe differences in degree when constructing a "first-time" scoring rubric with a four-point scale. Once the rubric is applied, an analysis of student work will yield more precise descriptive language and a rubric with more gradations.

Degrees of Understanding

- Thorough and complete
- Substantial
- Partial or incomplete
- Misunderstanding or serious misconceptions

Degrees of Frequency

- Always or consistently
- Frequently or generally
- Sometimes or occasionally
- Rarely or never

Degrees of Effectiveness

- Highly effective
- Generally effective
- Somewhat effective
- Ineffective

Degrees of Independence

Student successfully completes the task

- Independently
- With minimal assistance required
- With moderate assistance required
- With considerable assistance required

Degrees of Accuracy

- Completely accurate; all (facts, concepts, mechanics, computations) correct
- Generally accurate; minor inaccuracies do not affect overall result
- Inaccurate; numerous errors detract from result
- Major inaccuracies; significant errors throughout

Degrees of Clarity

- Exceptionally clear; easy to follow
- Generally clear; able to follow
- Lacks clarity; difficult to follow
- Unclear; impossible to follow

Generic Rubric for Understanding

SOPHISTICATED

5: Student work shows a sophisticated understanding of the subject matter involved. The concepts, evidence, arguments, qualifications made, questions posed, and methods used are expertly insightful, going well beyond the grasp of the subject typically found at this level of experience. Student grasps the essence of the idea or problem and applies the most powerful tools for solving it. The work shows that the student is able to make subtle distinctions, and to relate the particular challenge to more significant, complex, and comprehensive principles.

4: Student work shows a good understanding of the subject matter involved. The concepts, evidence, arguments, and methods used involve an advanced degree of difficulty and power. Frames the matter appropriately for someone at this level of experience. There may be limits to the understanding or some naivete or glibness in the response, but no misunderstandings or overly simplistic aspects appear in the work.

3: Student work shows an adequate understanding of the issues involved. Work reveals control of knowledge, concepts, and methods that enable the problems to be solved at the intended level of difficulty. There is less subtlety, discrimination, or nuance than found in the more sophisticated work, and there may be evidence of some misunderstanding of key ideas. The work may yield correct answers, but the approach, concepts, or methods used are more simplistic than expected at this level of experience.

2: Student work shows a naive or limited understanding of the ideas and issues involved. Simple rules, formulae, approaches, and concepts are used where more sophisticated ones are called for and available from previous learning. Important ideas may be misunderstood or misapplied. The student's work may be adequate to address all or most aspects of the problem, but the concepts and methods used are simplistic.

1: Student work shows no apparent understanding of the underlying ideas and issues involved in the problem. Brings to bear inappropriate and inadequate knowledge to the problem.

0: Insufficient evidence in the response to judge the student's knowledge of subject matter involved in this problem (typically due to a failure to complete the work).

Source: The *Assessment Wizard*, a joint venture of *Relearning by Design* and the *Educational Testing Service*, contains more than 40 rubrics and 150 assessments, and enables the design and sharing of preexisting and teacher-designed assessments.

Templates

Stage 1

Stage 2

Stage 3

Peer review

Exercises

Process sheets

Glossary

Templates

Stage 1

Stage 2

Stage 3

Peer review

Exercises

Process sheets

Glossary

Adding Specific Indicators to Generic Trait Rubrics
Persuasive Writing

An effective and efficient approach involves identifying sets of district-level rubrics of a fairly general kind. These generic rubrics can then be customized for specific grade or benchmark levels. In addition, teachers can make them more precise by adding specific indicators to suit each individual assessment task.

Persuasive Essay (with teacher-added bulleted indicators shown)

1. The performance is unusually persuasive. The ideas and arguments are exceptionally strong, and they are presented in a highly effective and clear manner. The performance is a sensitive one, clearly mindful of purpose, audience, and situation. This is sophisticated work.

- The essay makes excellent use of sophisticated rhetorical and syntactical elements.
- There is a thorough bibliography and a rich array of footnotes.
- Key counterarguments have been considered and rebutted in the essay.
- Sentence structure is varied and complex.
- Minor errors in mechanics and spelling, if they occur, do not interfere with the fluency of the paper.

4. The performance is unpersuasive. The ideas and arguments have significant weaknesses or gaps as presented. There are numerous content and rhetorical errors in the work, or the supporting evidence and resources used are inadequate or inappropriate.

- The techniques used to persuade are minimal or naive (e.g., stating a strong belief, attacking critics of other views, appealing to one authority).
- The weaknesses in the essay suggest a lack of adequate planning and revision or a misunderstanding of the purpose, audience, and situation of the writing assignment, and an inadequate understanding of the techniques of persuasive writing.
- Major errors in sentence structure, usage, mechanics, or spelling interfere with the readability of the paper.
- Many places in the essay contain logic that is hard to follow.
- Language may be too imprecise, inappropriate, or immature to convey the intended message.

Tips for Designing Effective Scoring Tools

1. Make sure that the scoring tool (rubric or checklist) includes the most important traits, given the **purpose** of the assessment and the **qualities of excellent performance.** Consider
   - Are you scoring what is easy to score rather than what is most important?
   - Could a student meet all the scoring criteria and get high scores *without* really demonstrating the desired understandings or producing excellent work?
   - Are any of the criteria or reasons for the score arbitrary? In other words, are you giving or taking away points based on characteristics that have little to do with excellence at this particular task?

2. Beware of the following common problems with scoring tools:
   - Scoring the length of the paper instead of its quality
   - Focusing on mechanics, organization, and presentation rather than content, substance, and effect (e.g., a science project display could be attractive but superficial)
   - Looking for quantity rather than results (e.g., the number of information sources used in research instead of the appropriateness and thoroughness of those sources; number of reasons in a persuasive essay instead of the logic of the reasoning)
   - Demanding that the performance follow an arbitrary format (e.g., five-paragraph essay), although successful expert performance may take a different form or use an unorthodox approach

3. Check for consistency of the descriptive terms throughout the scoring scale. For example, if the top score point includes the descriptors, *consistently* and *thorough*, expect to see parallel descriptors in the lower score points—*sometimes* and *incomplete*.

4. Use the following prompts to help avoid these problems:
   - *Because the aim of [the performance] is to provide evidence of* _____, *we need to assess whether the performance has been* _____. (List appropriate traits, given the purpose of the task and the evidence it demands.)

   - *The best pieces of work are those that are always* _____ (insert trait[s] from your list) _____. Does the sentence make sense or not? If yes, the trait is appropriate; if not, it is probably arbitrary.

Templates

Stage 1

Stage 2

Stage 3

Peer review

Exercises

Process sheets

Glossary

Check for Understanding

Review this flawed rubric. What problems do you notice? How could this rubric be improved?

Rubric for a Civil War Reenactor
(flawed)

4 The reenactor always wears wool from head-to-toe while on the battlefield or in camp. He eliminates all 20th-century terms from vocabulary while in role. Subsists entirely on hardtack and coffee. Contracts lice and annoying intestinal ailments during extended reenactments.

3 The reenactor dresses in wool from head-to-toe in July. She usually follows drill orders to march and fire rifle. Carries hardtack and coffee in haversack. Can correctly identify Union and Confederate troops while in the field.

2 The reenactor wears a blue uniform made of synthetic materials. He executes most orders, but three to five seconds after the rest of the company. Hides a Snickers bar in his haversack and carries beer in canteen. Sometimes cannot remember which side wears blue and which wears gray.

1 The reenactor wears an Orioles cap, Hard Rock Cafe t-shirt and Reeboks with uniform. She cannot tell Union from Confederate troops. Has been heard asking, "Are you a Union or Confederate soldier?" Fires upon her fellow soldiers and frequently wounds self or fellow soldiers. Litters the 19th-century campground with Twinkie and Big Mac wrappers.

—Adapted from a humorous rubric created by Dr. Tim Dangel, Anne Arundel Schools (MD)

Steps in Designing a Draft Performance Task

A variety of worksheets have been provided to assist in the design of performance assessment tasks to provide evidence of student understanding. The following process illustrates a sequence for using the various UbD worksheets to develop a draft task.

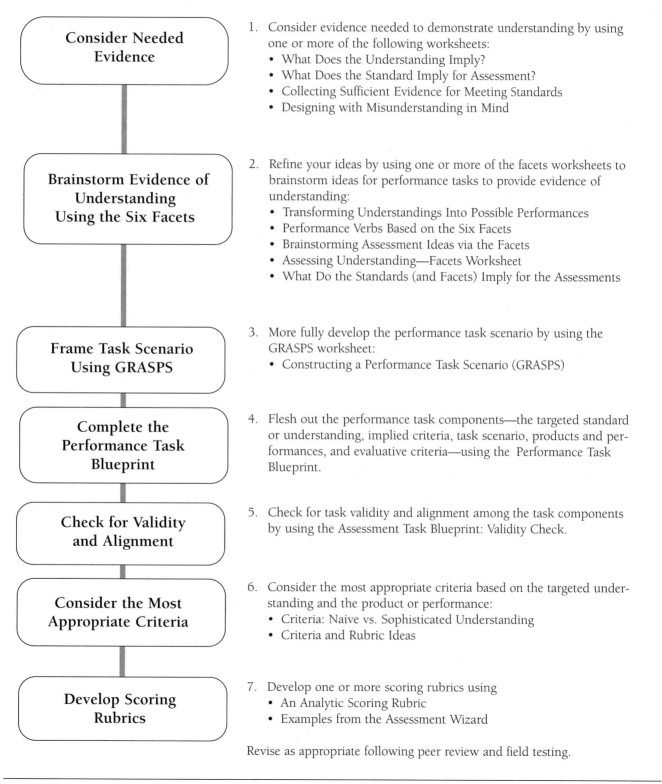

Consider Needed Evidence

1. Consider evidence needed to demonstrate understanding by using one or more of the following worksheets:
   • What Does the Understanding Imply?
   • What Does the Standard Imply for Assessment?
   • Collecting Sufficient Evidence for Meeting Standards
   • Designing with Misunderstanding in Mind

Brainstorm Evidence of Understanding Using the Six Facets

2. Refine your ideas by using one or more of the facets worksheets to brainstorm ideas for performance tasks to provide evidence of understanding:
   • Transforming Understandings Into Possible Performances
   • Performance Verbs Based on the Six Facets
   • Brainstorming Assessment Ideas via the Facets
   • Assessing Understanding—Facets Worksheet
   • What Do the Standards (and Facets) Imply for the Assessments

Frame Task Scenario Using GRASPS

3. More fully develop the performance task scenario by using the GRASPS worksheet:
   • Constructing a Performance Task Scenario (GRASPS)

Complete the Performance Task Blueprint

4. Flesh out the performance task components—the targeted standard or understanding, implied criteria, task scenario, products and performances, and evaluative criteria—using the Performance Task Blueprint.

Check for Validity and Alignment

5. Check for task validity and alignment among the task components by using the Assessment Task Blueprint: Validity Check.

Consider the Most Appropriate Criteria

6. Consider the most appropriate criteria based on the targeted understanding and the product or performance:
   • Criteria: Naive vs. Sophisticated Understanding
   • Criteria and Rubric Ideas

Develop Scoring Rubrics

7. Develop one or more scoring rubrics using
   • An Analytic Scoring Rubric
   • Examples from the Assessment Wizard

Revise as appropriate following peer review and field testing.

Templates · Stage 1 · Stage 2 · Stage 3 · Peer review · Exercises · Process sheets · Glossary

Generating Ideas for Performance Tasks, Part 1
Pioneer Life

T

Students show they understand that	The life of pioneers on the prairie was filled with hardships and dangers.

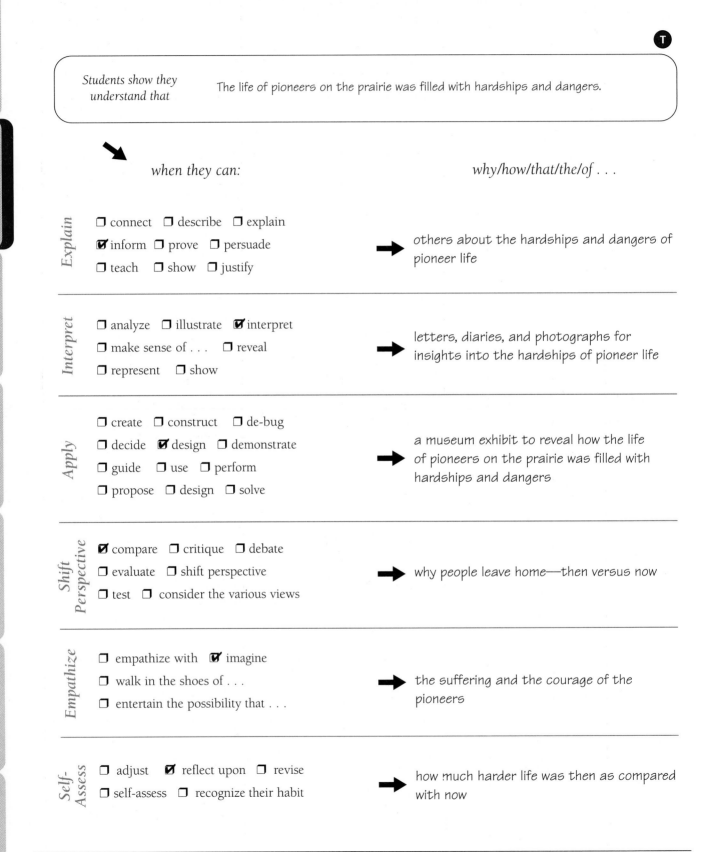

when they can: *why/how/that/the/of . . .*

Explain
- ❏ connect ❏ describe ❏ explain
- ☑ inform ❏ prove ❏ persuade
- ❏ teach ❏ show ❏ justify

→ others about the hardships and dangers of pioneer life

Interpret
- ❏ analyze ❏ illustrate ☑ interpret
- ❏ make sense of . . . ❏ reveal
- ❏ represent ❏ show

→ letters, diaries, and photographs for insights into the hardships of pioneer life

Apply
- ❏ create ❏ construct ❏ de-bug
- ❏ decide ☑ design ❏ demonstrate
- ❏ guide ❏ use ❏ perform
- ❏ propose ❏ design ❏ solve

→ a museum exhibit to reveal how the life of pioneers on the prairie was filled with hardships and dangers

Shift Perspective
- ☑ compare ❏ critique ❏ debate
- ❏ evaluate ❏ shift perspective
- ❏ test ❏ consider the various views

→ why people leave home—then versus now

Empathize
- ❏ empathize with ☑ imagine
- ❏ walk in the shoes of . . .
- ❏ entertain the possibility that . . .

→ the suffering and the courage of the pioneers

Self-Assess
- ❏ adjust ☑ reflect upon ❏ revise
- ❏ self-assess ❏ recognize their habit

→ how much harder life was then as compared with now

Generating Ideas for Performance Tasks, Part 2
Pioneer Life

Key: ○ Roles
Δ Audiences

○Δ actor
○Δ advertiser
○Δ artist or illustrator
○Δ author
○Δ biographer
○Δ board members
○Δ boss
○Δ Boy or Girl Scout
○Δ businessperson
○Δ candidate
○Δ cartoon character
○Δ cartoonist
○Δ caterer
○Δ celebrities
○Δ chair
○Δ CEO
○Δ chef
○Δ coach
○Δ community members
○Δ composer
○Δ clients or customers
○Δ construction worker
○Δ detective
○Δ editor
○Δ elected official
○Δ engineer
○Δ expert (in _____)
○Δ eyewitness

○Δ family members
○Δ filmmaker
○Δ firefighter
○Δ foreign embassy staff
○Δ friends
○Δ government officials
○Δ historian
○Δ historical figures
○Δ intern
○Δ interviewer
○Δ inventor
○Δ judge
○Δ jury
○Δ lawyer
○Δ literary critic
○Δ lobbyist
☑Δ museum director or curator
○Δ museum goer
○Δ neighbor
○Δ newscaster
○Δ novelist
○Δ nutritionist
○Δ panelist
○Δ park ranger
○Δ pen pals
○Δ photographer
○Δ pilot
○Δ playwright

○Δ poet
○Δ police officer
○Δ product designer
○Δ radio listeners
○Δ reader
○Δ reporter
○Δ researcher
○Δ reviewer
○Δ school official
○Δ scientist
○Δ ship's captain
○Δ social scientist
○Δ student
○Δ taxi driver
○Δ teacher
○Δ television viewers
○Δ tour guide
○Δ travel agent
○Δ traveler
○Δ television or movie
   character
○Δ tutor
○Δ viewers
○☑ visitors
○Δ Web page designer
○Δ zookeeper
○Δ other: _____

PRODUCTS and PERFORMANCES

❏ advertisement ❏ article ❏ audiotape ❏ book report ❏ brochure ❏ cartoon ❏ collage ❏ construction

❏ data display ❏ demonstration ❏ design ❏ diagram ☑ diary ❏ diorama ❏ directions ❏ display

❏ dramatization ☑ drawing ❏ editorial ❏ e-mail message ❏ essay ☑ exhibit ❏ experiment ❏ game

❏ graph ❏ graphic ❏ interview ❏ investigation ❏ journal ❏ lesson ☑ letter ❏ log ❏ map ❏ memo

❏ model ❏ museum exhibit ❏ newscast ❏ painting ❏ photograph ❏ plan ❏ play ❏ poem

❏ position paper ❏ poster ❏ PowerPoint presentation ❏ proposal ❏ rap song ❏ report ❏ review

❏ script ❏ skit ❏ slide show ❏ song ❏ speech ❏ story ❏ test or exam ❏ videotape ❏ Web site

Generating Ideas for Performance Tasks, Part 3
Pioneer Life

Performance Task Ideas

> You are a curator in a U.S. History museum.
> Design a museum exhibit on pioneer life containing drawings, simulated diary entries, and letters back home. The goal of your exhibit is to inform visitors about the challenges faced by the pioneers.
>   Your exhibit should . . .

meet the following criteria

☑ accurate   ○ appropriate   ○ apt   ○ clear   ○ convincing   ○ correct   ○ creative

○ defensible   ○ effective   ○ efficient   ○ elegant   ○ empathetic   ○ entertaining

☑ informative   ○ insightful   ○ justified   ○ novel   ○ organized   ○ perceptive

○ persuasive   ○ polished   ○ precise   ○ proficient   ○ reflective   ○ responsive

○ revealing   ☑ sensitive   ○ skilled   ○ sophisticated   ○ supported   ○ thorough

○ understandable   ○ unique   ○ valid   ○ verified   ☑ well-crafted

○ other: _____

so that

the museum visitors better understand the dangers and hardships of pioneer life on the prairie

Generating Ideas for Performance Tasks, Part 1
Scientific Method

T

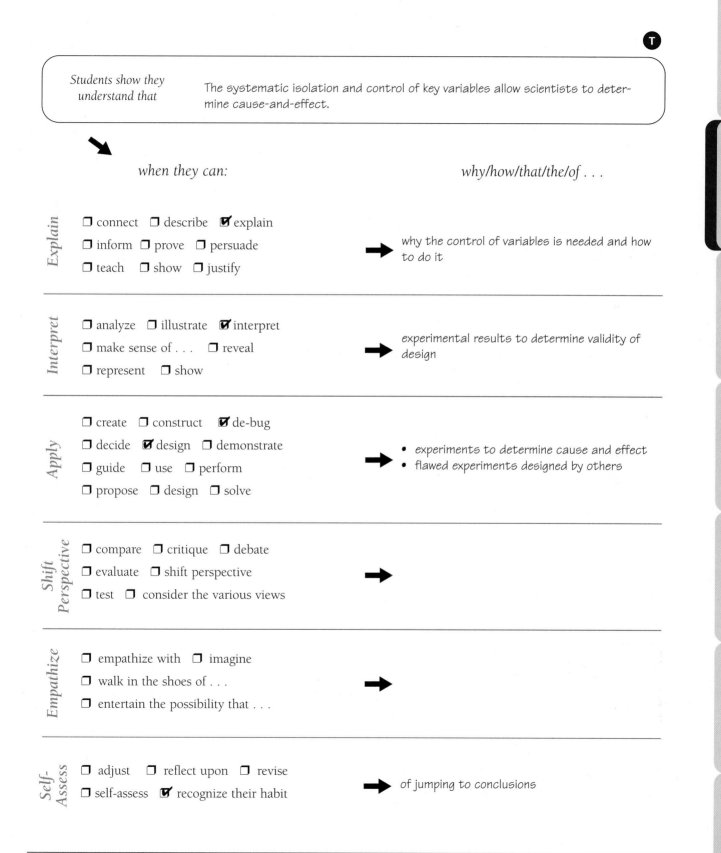

Students show they understand that | The systematic isolation and control of key variables allow scientists to determine cause-and-effect.

when they can: *why/how/that/the/of . . .*

Explain
☐ connect ☐ describe ☑ explain
☐ inform ☐ prove ☐ persuade
☐ teach ☐ show ☐ justify

→ why the control of variables is needed and how to do it

Interpret
☐ analyze ☐ illustrate ☑ interpret
☐ make sense of . . . ☐ reveal
☐ represent ☐ show

→ experimental results to determine validity of design

Apply
☐ create ☐ construct ☑ de-bug
☐ decide ☑ design ☐ demonstrate
☐ guide ☐ use ☐ perform
☐ propose ☐ design ☐ solve

→ • experiments to determine cause and effect
• flawed experiments designed by others

Shift Perspective
☐ compare ☐ critique ☐ debate
☐ evaluate ☐ shift perspective
☐ test ☐ consider the various views

→

Empathize
☐ empathize with ☐ imagine
☐ walk in the shoes of . . .
☐ entertain the possibility that . . .

→

Self-Assess
☐ adjust ☐ reflect upon ☐ revise
☐ self-assess ☑ recognize their habit

→ of jumping to conclusions

Generating Ideas for Performance Tasks, Part 2
Scientific Method

Key: ○ Roles
△ Audiences

T

○△ actor
○△ advertiser
○△ artist or illustrator
○△ author
○△ biographer
○△ board members
○△ boss
○△ Boy or Girl Scout
○△ businessperson
○△ candidate
○△ cartoon character
○△ cartoonist
○△ caterer
○△ celebrities
○△ chair
○△ CEO
○△ chef
○△ coach
○△ community members
○△ composer
○△ clients or customers
○△ construction worker
○△ detective
○△ editor
○△ elected official
○△ engineer
○△ expert (in _____)
○△ eyewitness

○△ family members
○△ filmmaker
○△ firefighter
○△ foreign embassy staff
○△ friends
○△ government officials
○△ historian
○△ historical figures
○△ intern
○△ interviewer
○△ inventor
○△ judge
○△ jury
○△ lawyer
○△ literary critic
○△ lobbyist
○△ museum director or curator
○△ museum goer
○△ neighbor
○△ newscaster
○△ novelist
○△ nutritionist
○△ panelist
○△ park ranger
○△ pen pals
○△ photographer
○△ pilot
○△ playwright

○△ poet
○△ police officer
○△ product designer
○△ radio listeners
○△ reader
○△ reporter
○△ researcher
○△ reviewer
○△ school official
☑△ scientist
○△ ship's captain
○△ social scientist
○☑ student
○△ taxi driver
○△ teacher
○△ television viewers
○△ tour guide
○△ travel agent
○△ traveler
○△ television or movie
   character
○△ tutor
○△ viewers
○△ visitors
○△ Web page designer
○△ zookeeper
○△ other: _____

PRODUCTS and PERFORMANCES

❑ advertisement ❑ article ❑ audiotape ❑ book report ❑ brochure ❑ cartoon ❑ collage ❑ construction

❑ data display ❑ demonstration ☑ design ❑ diagram ❑ diary ❑ diorama ☑ directions ☑ display

❑ dramatization ☑ drawing ❑ editorial ❑ e-mail message ❑ essay ❑ exhibit ❑ experiment ❑ game

❑ graph ❑ graphic ❑ interview ❑ investigation ❑ journal ❑ lesson ❑ letter ❑ log ❑ map ❑ memo

❑ model ❑ museum exhibit ❑ newscast ❑ painting ❑ photograph ❑ plan ❑ play ❑ poem

❑ position paper ❑ poster ❑ PowerPoint presentation ❑ proposal ❑ rap song ❑ report ❑ review

❑ script ❑ skit ❑ slide show ❑ song ❑ speech ❑ story ❑ test or exam ❑ videotape ❑ Web site

Generating Ideas for Performance Tasks, Part 3
Scientific Method

Performance Task Ideas　　　　　　　　　　　　　　**T**

Design an experiment to determine which of four brands of detergent will most effectively remove three different types of stains on cotton fabric. Provide written directions and a graphic display to guide an absent classmate through your procedure.

　　　Your experimental procedure should . . .

| *meet the following criteria* |

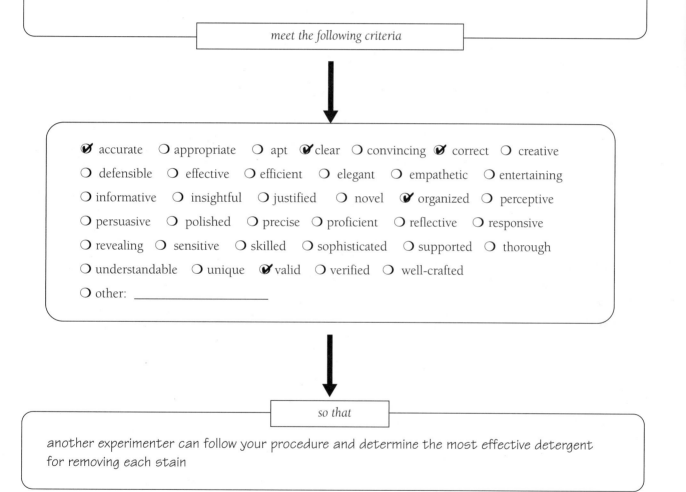

☑ accurate　○ appropriate　○ apt　☑ clear　○ convincing　☑ correct　○ creative

○ defensible　○ effective　○ efficient　○ elegant　○ empathetic　○ entertaining

○ informative　○ insightful　○ justified　○ novel　☑ organized　○ perceptive

○ persuasive　○ polished　○ precise　○ proficient　○ reflective　○ responsive

○ revealing　○ sensitive　○ skilled　○ sophisticated　○ supported　○ thorough

○ understandable　○ unique　☑ valid　○ verified　○ well-crafted

○ other: _____

| *so that* |

another experimenter can follow your procedure and determine the most effective detergent for removing each stain

203

Templates　Stage 1　Stage 2　Stage 3　Peer review　Exercises　Process sheets　Glossary

Generating Ideas for Performance Tasks, Part 1

Templates

Stage 1

Stage 2

Stage 3

Peer review

Exercises

Process sheets

Glossary

T

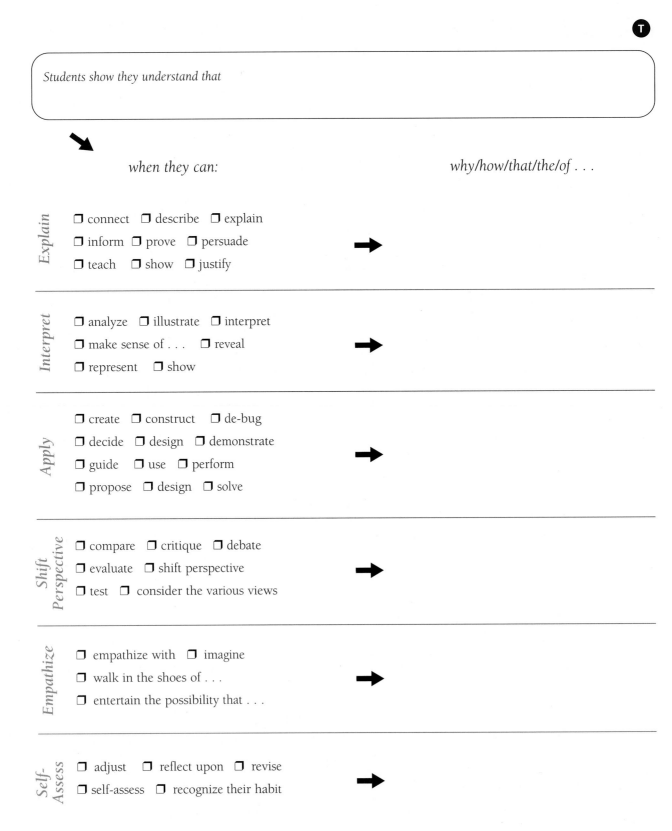

Students show they understand that

when they can: *why/how/that/the/of . . .*

Explain
❏ connect   ❏ describe   ❏ explain
❏ inform   ❏ prove   ❏ persuade
❏ teach   ❏ show   ❏ justify

➤

Interpret
❏ analyze   ❏ illustrate   ❏ interpret
❏ make sense of . . .   ❏ reveal
❏ represent   ❏ show

➤

Apply
❏ create   ❏ construct   ❏ de-bug
❏ decide   ❏ design   ❏ demonstrate
❏ guide   ❏ use   ❏ perform
❏ propose   ❏ design   ❏ solve

➤

Shift Perspective
❏ compare   ❏ critique   ❏ debate
❏ evaluate   ❏ shift perspective
❏ test   ❏ consider the various views

➤

Empathize
❏ empathize with   ❏ imagine
❏ walk in the shoes of . . .
❏ entertain the possibility that . . .

➤

Self-Assess
❏ adjust   ❏ reflect upon   ❏ revise
❏ self-assess   ❏ recognize their habit

➤

Generating Ideas for Performance Tasks, Part 2

Key: ○ Roles
 △ Audiences

T

○△ actor
○△ advertiser
○△ artist or illustrator
○△ author
○△ biographer
○△ board members
○△ boss
○△ Boy or Girl Scout
○△ businessperson
○△ candidate
○△ cartoon character
○△ cartoonist
○△ caterer
○△ celebrities
○△ chair
○△ CEO
○△ chef
○△ coach
○△ community members
○△ composer
○△ clients or customers
○△ construction worker
○△ detective
○△ editor
○△ elected official
○△ engineer
○△ expert (in _____)
○△ eyewitness

○△ family members
○△ filmmaker
○△ firefighter
○△ foreign embassy staff
○△ friends
○△ government officials
○△ historian
○△ historical figures
○△ intern
○△ interviewer
○△ inventor
○△ judge
○△ jury
○△ lawyer
○△ literary critic
○△ lobbyist
○△ museum director or curator
○△ museum goer
○△ neighbor
○△ newscaster
○△ novelist
○△ nutritionist
○△ panelist
○△ park ranger
○△ pen pals
○△ photographer
○△ pilot
○△ playwright

○△ poet
○△ police officer
○△ product designer
○△ radio listeners
○△ reader
○△ reporter
○△ researcher
○△ reviewer
○△ school official
○△ scientist
○△ ship's captain
○△ social scientist
○△ student
○△ taxi driver
○△ teacher
○△ television viewers
○△ tour guide
○△ travel agent
○△ traveler
○△ television or movie
     character
○△ tutor
○△ viewers
○△ visitors
○△ Web page designer
○△ zookeeper
○△ other: _____

PRODUCTS and PERFORMANCES

❏ advertisement ❏ article ❏ audiotape ❏ book report ❏ brochure ❏ cartoon ❏ collage ❏ construction

❏ data display ❏ demonstration ❏ design ❏ diagram ❏ diary ❏ diorama ❏ directions ❏ display

❏ dramatization ❏ drawing ❏ editorial ❏ e-mail message ❏ essay ❏ exhibit ❏ experiment ❏ game

❏ graph ❏ graphic ❏ interview ❏ investigation ❏ journal ❏ lesson ❏ letter ❏ log ❏ map ❏ memo

❏ model ❏ museum exhibit ❏ newscast ❏ painting ❏ photograph ❏ plan ❏ play ❏ poem

❏ position paper ❏ poster ❏ PowerPoint presentation ❏ proposal ❏ rap song ❏ report ❏ review

❏ script ❏ skit ❏ slide show ❏ song ❏ speech ❏ story ❏ test or exam ❏ videotape ❏ Web site

Templates · Stage 1 · Stage 2 · Stage 3 · Peer review · Exercises · Process sheets · Glossary

Generating Ideas for Performance Tasks, Part 3

Performance Task Ideas

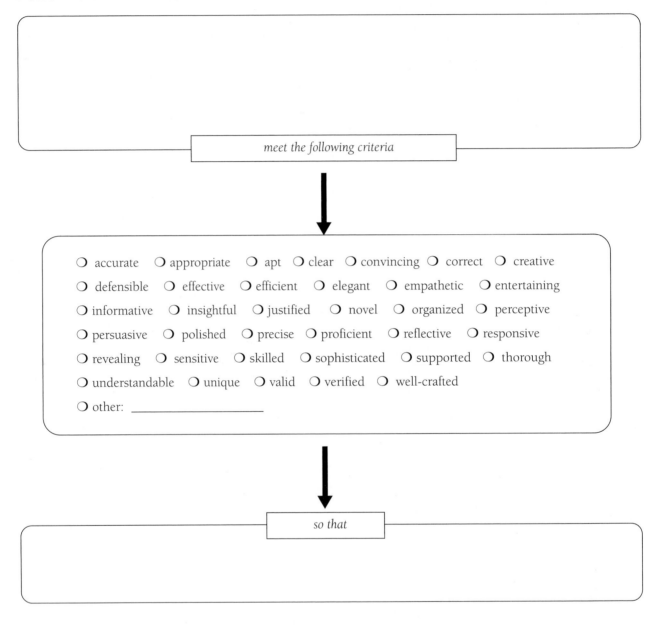

meet the following criteria

- ⭘ accurate   ⭘ appropriate   ⭘ apt   ⭘ clear   ⭘ convincing   ⭘ correct   ⭘ creative
- ⭘ defensible   ⭘ effective   ⭘ efficient   ⭘ elegant   ⭘ empathetic   ⭘ entertaining
- ⭘ informative   ⭘ insightful   ⭘ justified   ⭘ novel   ⭘ organized   ⭘ perceptive
- ⭘ persuasive   ⭘ polished   ⭘ precise   ⭘ proficient   ⭘ reflective   ⭘ responsive
- ⭘ revealing   ⭘ sensitive   ⭘ skilled   ⭘ sophisticated   ⭘ supported   ⭘ thorough
- ⭘ understandable   ⭘ unique   ⭘ valid   ⭘ verified   ⭘ well-crafted
- ⭘ other: _____

so that

Templates | Stage 1 | Stage 2 | Stage 3 | Peer review | Exercises | Process sheets | Glossary

Design Checklist—Stage 2

Performance Tasks · **T**

1. _____ The performance tasks in **T** are aligned with one or more desired results in Stage 1. The tasks will yield appropriate evidence of the identified understandings.

2. _____ The tasks involve a complex, real-world (authentic) application of the identified knowledge, skill, and understandings.

3. _____ The tasks are written in the GRASPS form.

4. _____ The tasks allow students to demonstrate understanding with some choice, options, or variety in the performances and products.

5. _____ The tasks are *not likely to be performed well* without a clear grasp of the understandings the task is meant to assess.

6. _____ The tasks require one or more of the six facets of understanding.

7. _____ The scoring rubric includes distinct traits of understanding *and* successful performance.

8. _____ The scoring rubric highlights what is appropriate, given the evidence needs suggested by the Desired Results of Stage 1.

Other Evidence · **OE**

9. _____ Other appropriate evidence has been identified in summary form (e.g., key quizzes, exams, student self-assessments) to supplement the evidence provided by the performance tasks.

10. _____ Students are given the opportunity to self-assess and reflect upon their learning and performance.

Notes

_____

_____

_____

_____

_____

_____

_____

_____

Templates

Stage 1

Stage 2

Stage 3

Peer review

Exercises

Process sheets

Glossary

Frequently Asked Questions About Stage 2

1. What is relationship between the six Facets of Understanding and Blooms' Taxonomy?

Although both function as frameworks for assessment, one key difference is that Bloom's Taxonomy presents a hierarchy of cognitive complexity. Bloom's Taxonomy was initially developed for analyzing assessments given at the university level, with the six categories used to determine the intellectual level of test items.

The facets of understanding were conceived as six equal indicators of understanding, and thus are used to develop or select assessment tasks and prompts. They were never intended to be a hierarchy. Rather, one selects the appropriate facet or facets depending on the nature of the content and the desired understandings about it.

"Application" means the same in both frameworks, but "analysis," "synthesis," and "evaluation" tend to be called for simultaneously in many assessment tasks (e.g., as in products and performances requiring an "explanation" or "perspective").

2. Why do we need to construct assessment tasks using GRASPS?

A basic contention in Understanding by Design (UbD) is that understanding is best revealed through contextualized performance; that is, applying what is known in novel situations. Simply giving back information as it was learned or selecting the "correct" answer from a set of alternatives does not ensure that true understanding exists.

A second consideration regarding the design of assessments in UbD is to make them as meaningful, authentic, and engaging as possible so that students will put forth their best efforts. One means of addressing these two intentions is through contexualized performance tasks whereby students may display their understanding. GRASPS is simply a design tool to assist in the construction of such tasks.

We are not suggesting that every assessment task must be developed using GRASPS. We propose, however, that at least *one* core performance task for a UbD unit be framed in such an authentic manner. Of course, the GRASPS performance task should be supplemented by other assessment evidence as needed, including traditional tests and quizzes.

3. How can we translate rubric scores into letter grades?

Since most grading and reporting systems rely on letter grades, teachers who use rubrics confront the task of translating the scores to grades. Before we respond directly, consider these questions: What does a letter grade, such as a *B* represent? How about a numerical score of *3*? In both cases, these are symbols reflecting an evaluation of performance based on some performance standard. For instance, a grade of *B* on a multiple-choice test represents the score for a student who answered 83 percent of the items correctly. In this case, the performance standard for *B* is from 80 to 89 percent. A *3* on a 4-point rubric for persuasive writing could describe a solid, but not exemplary, essay. The two symbol systems are compatible, but not identical.

It seems natural to derive a letter grade from a rubric by simply determining the total number of points earned divided by the number of points possible on the rubric. In the previous example, a holistic rubric score of 3 on a 4-point scale would translate to a 75 percent or a *C* in most school districts. Similarly, on a four-trait writing rubric (e.g., organization, language choices, ideas and persuasiveness, and mechanics) with a 4-point scale, a student who was rated 11 (out of 16 possible points) would get 68.75 percent, a *D* by most grading standards. In both cases, however, the resulting letter grade seems lower than what the actual performance deserved. So, we need to reflect on what we want the score or grade to communicate before we unthinkingly make scores equivalent to grades.

Another way to make the conversion is to weight the traits in an analytic rubric, based on their relative importance. For example, using a common rubric, all of the teachers in the mathematics department evaluate student problem solving according to the following traits: computational accuracy, reasoning and strategic thinking, representation, communication, and connections. The department could decide that the first two criteria are worth 30 percent and the remaining criteria each worth 20 percent (or whatever percentages seem most appropriate to a particular problem). Then the final weighted rubric score can be converted into a grade. This way the feedback is more precise and useful to the student, while allowing for a single-letter grade in systems that require it.

A related approach involves deciding on the letter grade equivalents in advance based on the rubric descriptions. For example, the foreign language department in Fairfax County (Va.) Public Schools has developed grading conversion charts for rubrics based on performance expectations and rubric descriptions. For instance, on a 4-point holistic rubric, they use these conversions:

Rubric Score 4: Exceeds Expectations = from 93.5 to 100 percent
Rubric Score 3: Meets Expectations = from 84 to 93 percent
Rubric Score 2: Almost Meets Expectations = from 74 to 83 percent
Rubric Score 1: Does Not Meet Expectations = from 54 to 73 percent

Every foreign language teacher in this large district uses the same rubrics and grade conversion system. This systemic approach results in greater evaluative consistency across classrooms and schools, leading to more effective communication to students and parents.

Templates · Stage 1 · Stage 2 · Stage 3 · Peer review · Exercises · Process sheets · Glossary

Templates

Stage 1

Stage 2

Stage 3

Peer review

Exercises

Process sheets

Glossary

Regardless of the particular conversion method, it is important not to lose sight of the overall goal of grading—to provide a clear, consistent, and fair representation of student performance based on established performance standards. A well-developed rubric, with clear descriptions of the key traits and performance levels, renders any grading system more reliable and defensible.

*To view additional examples and information about Fairfax County Publics Schools and their grading conversion system, visit http://www.fcps.edu/DIS/OHSICS/forlang/PALS/rubrics/index.htm.

Stage 3— Learning Plan

Design Tools and Samples

Backward Design: Stage 3

Stage 3—Learning Plan

Teaching and Learning Activities: **L**

In Stage 3 we consider the instructional strategies and learning experiences needed to achieve the desired results (Stage 1) as reflected in the assessment evidence to be gathered (Stage 2). The activities **L** are planned to develop the targeted understandings and the knowledge and skills identified in Stage 1 *and* to equip students for the performances of learning specified in Stage 2. The acronym WHERETO summarizes key elements to consider when designing an effective and engaging learning plan.

Design Standards for Stage 3

To what extent is the learning plan effective and engaging? Consider:
  Will the students . . .
W ○ Know *where* they're going (the learning goals), *why* (reason for learning the content), and *what* is required of them (unit goal, performance requirements, and evaluative criteria)?
H ○ Be *hooked*—engaged in digging into the Big Ideas (e.g., through inquiry, research, problem-solving, experimentation)?
E ○ Have adequate opportunities to *explore* and *experience* Big Ideas and receive instruction to *equip* them for the required performances?
R ○ Have sufficient opportunities to *rethink*, *rehearse*, *revise* and *refine* their work based upon timely feedback?
E ○ Have an opportunity to *evaluate* their work and set future goals?

  Consider the extent to which the learning plan is
T ○ *Tailored* and flexible to address the interests and learning styles of all students.
O ○ *Organized* and sequenced to maximize engagement and effectiveness.

Templates
Stage 1
Stage 2
Stage 3
Peer review
Exercises
Process sheets
Glossary

Stage 3: Key Design Elements

Consider the following as you develop the learning plan, mindful of the desired results identified in Stage 1 and the needed evidence in Stage 2. There are a variety of ways to "teach for understanding," and UbD is compatible with many instructional frameworks. Regardless of the instructional approach and specific teaching techniques, designers are encouraged to consider the WHERETO elements as they plan.

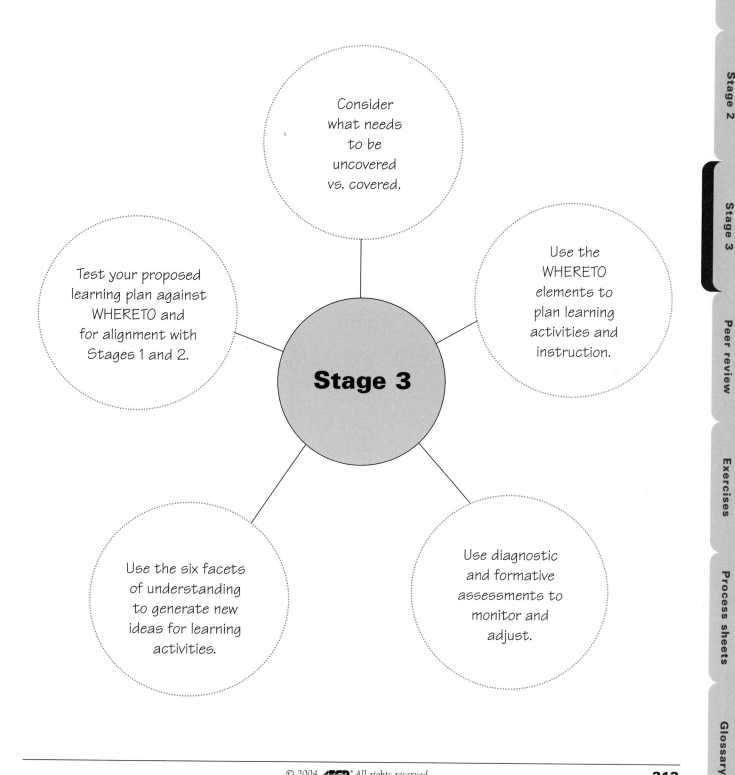

Consider what needs to be uncovered vs. covered.

Use the WHERETO elements to plan learning activities and instruction.

Use diagnostic and formative assessments to monitor and adjust.

Stage 3

Use the six facets of understanding to generate new ideas for learning activities.

Test your proposed learning plan against WHERETO and for alignment with Stages 1 and 2.

Templates · Stage 1 · Stage 2 · Stage 3 · Peer review · Exercises · Process sheets · Glossary

WHERETO
Considerations for the Learning Plan

The acronym WHERETO summarizes the key elements that should be found in your learning plan, given the desired results and assessments drafted in Stages 1 and 2. Note that the elements need not appear in the same order as the letters of the acronym. Think of WHERETO as a checklist for building and evaluating the final learning plan, not a suggested sequence. For example, the learning might start with a Hook (H), followed by instruction on the final performance requirements (W), then perhaps some rethinking of earlier work (R).

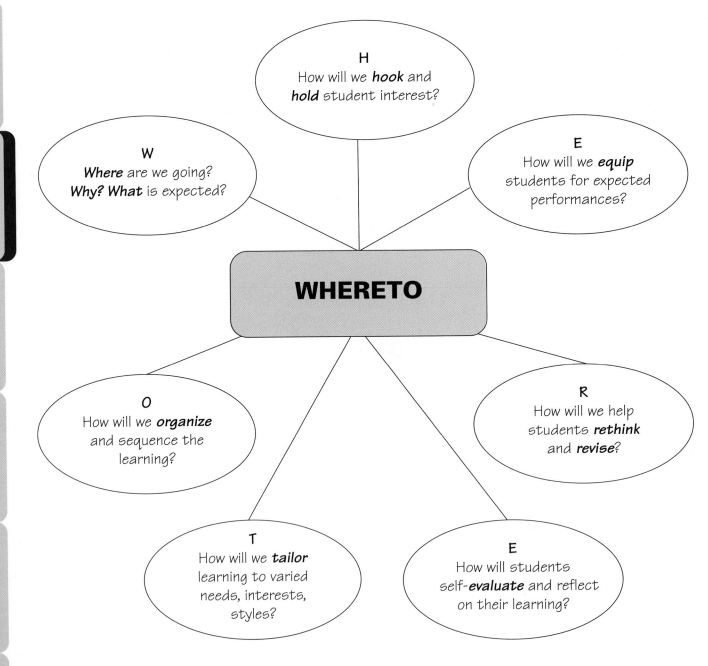

H
How will we *hook* and *hold* student interest?

W
Where are we going? *Why? What* is expected?

E
How will we *equip* students for expected performances?

WHERETO

O
How will we *organize* and sequence the learning?

R
How will we help students *rethink* and *revise*?

T
How will we *tailor* learning to varied needs, interests, styles?

E
How will students self-*evaluate* and reflect on their learning?

Templates

Stage 1

Stage 2

Stage 3

Peer review

Exercises

Process sheets

Glossary

WHERETO
Questions to Consider for *W*

The *W* in WHERETO should be considered from the students' perspective. By working through backward design, designers should be clear about their goals and the evidence needed to show the extent that students have achieved them. Now, we seek to help the students become clear about the goals and expectations and the purpose and benefits of achieving them. Research and experience show that students are more likely to focus and put forth effort when they have clarity on the goals and expectations and see a purpose and value for the intended learning.

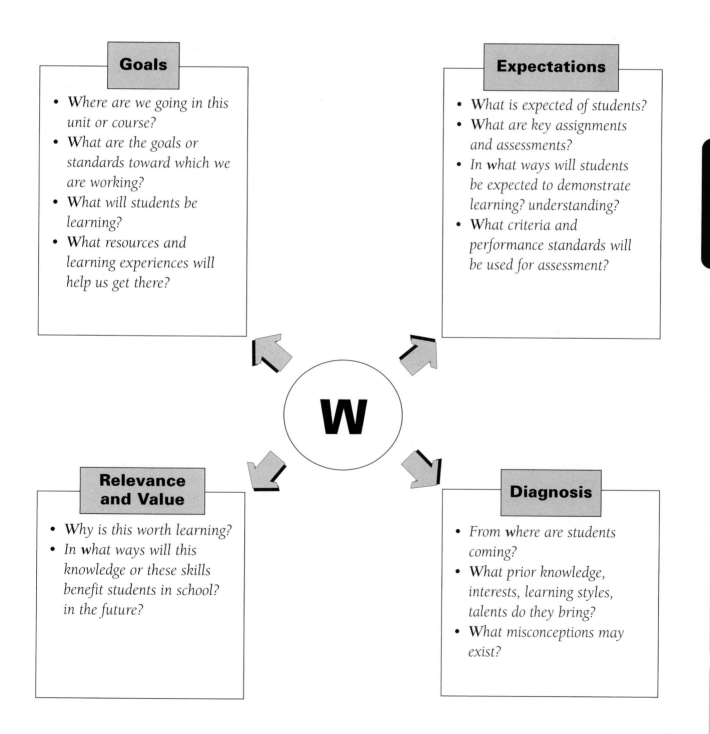

Goals

- *Where are we going in this unit or course?*
- *What are the goals or standards toward which we are working?*
- *What will students be learning?*
- *What resources and learning experiences will help us get there?*

Expectations

- *What is expected of students?*
- *What are key assignments and assessments?*
- *In* **what** *ways will students be expected to demonstrate learning? understanding?*
- *What criteria and performance standards will be used for assessment?*

W

Relevance and Value

- *Why is this worth learning?*
- *In* **what** *ways will this knowledge or these skills benefit students in school? in the future?*

Diagnosis

- *From* **where** *are students coming?*
- *What prior knowledge, interests, learning styles, talents do they bring?*
- *What misconceptions may exist?*

215

WHERETO
Examples for *W*

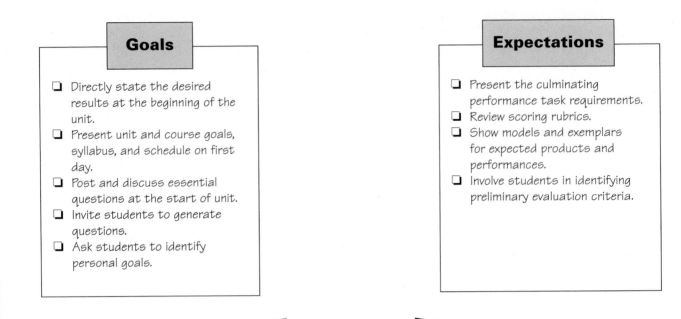

Goals

- Directly state the desired results at the beginning of the unit.
- Present unit and course goals, syllabus, and schedule on first day.
- Post and discuss essential questions at the start of unit.
- Invite students to generate questions.
- Ask students to identify personal goals.

Expectations

- Present the culminating performance task requirements.
- Review scoring rubrics.
- Show models and exemplars for expected products and performances.
- Involve students in identifying preliminary evaluation criteria.

Relevance and Value

- Present the rationale for the unit and course goals.
- Discuss the benefits to students.
- Identify people and places beyond the classroom where this knowledge and these skills are applied.
- Use K-W-L to have students identify things they want to learn.

Diagnosis

- Give a pretest on content knowledge.
- Give a diagnostic skills test.
- Use K-W-L to see what students already know (or think they know).
- Have students create a visual organizer to reveal their initial knowledge and understandings.
- Check for possible and probable misconceptions.

Side tabs: Templates · Stage 1 · Stage 2 · Stage 3 · Peer review · Exercises · Process sheets · Glossary

wHERETO
Hooking and Holding Students

Effective teachers recognize the importance of *hooking* students at the beginning of a new learning experience and *holding* their interest throughout. The *H* in WHERETO directs designers to consider ways of engaging students in the topic and pointing toward Big Ideas, Essential Questions, and performance tasks—by design. Use the list below to brainstorm possible hooks for your unit design.

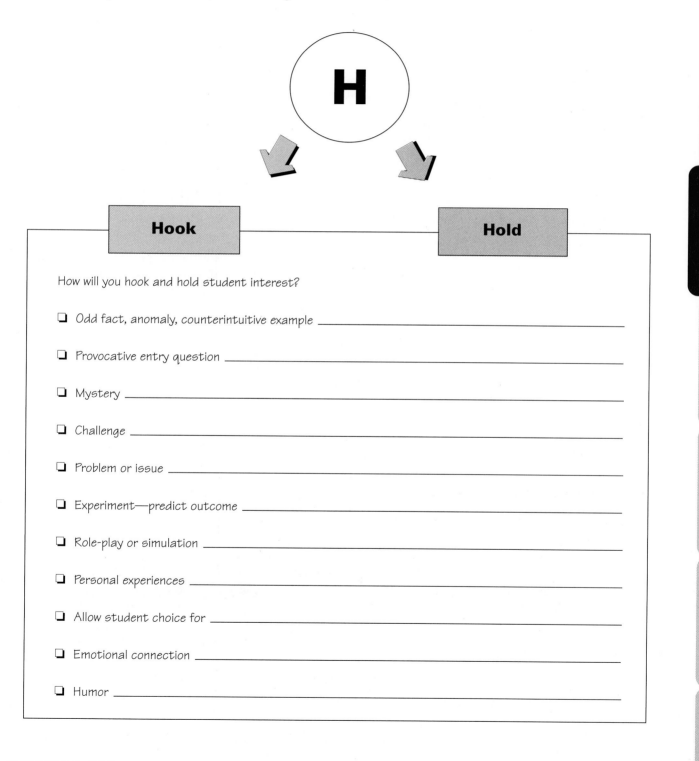

Hook   **Hold**

How will you hook and hold student interest?

❑ Odd fact, anomaly, counterintuitive example _____

❑ Provocative entry question _____

❑ Mystery _____

❑ Challenge _____

❑ Problem or issue _____

❑ Experiment—predict outcome _____

❑ Role-play or simulation _____

❑ Personal experiences _____

❑ Allow student choice for _____

❑ Emotional connection _____

❑ Humor _____

Templates

Stage 1

Stage 2

Stage 3

Peer review

Exercises

Process sheets

Glossary

Templates

Stage 1

Stage 2

Stage 3

Peer review

Exercises

Process sheets

Glossary

WHERETO, Page 1
Equipping Students

The first *E* in WHERETO prompts designers to think about (1) ways they will help students to *explore* the Big Ideas and Essential Questions, and (2) how they will *equip* students for their final performances. In order for students to come to an understanding of important ideas, they must engage in some inductive learning experiences that facilitate the "construction of meaning." In addition, direct instruction and out-of-class activities can play a role in equipping students with the knowledge and skills needed to perform. Consider using the six facets of understanding to generate effective and engaging learning activities.

Experiential and Inductive Learning

- What **experiential** or inductive learning will help students to **explore** the big ideas and questions
  —to achieve desired understandings (Stage 1)?
  —for their expected performances (Stage 2)?

Direct Instruction

- What information or skills need to be taught explicitly to **equip** students
  —to achieve the desired results (Stage 1)?
  —for their expected performances (Stage 2)?

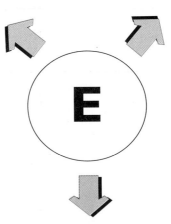

Homework and Other Out-of-Class Experiences

- What homework and other out-of-class **experiences** are needed to **equip** students
  —to achieve the desired results (Stage 1)?
  —for their expected performances (Stage 2)?

WH**E**RETO, Page 2
Equipping Students

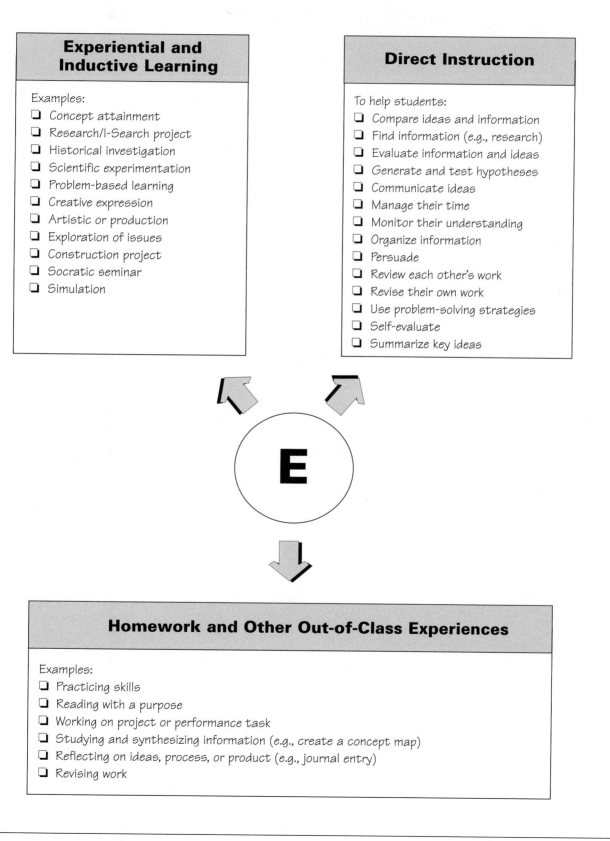

Experiential and Inductive Learning

Examples:
- ❑ Concept attainment
- ❑ Research/I-Search project
- ❑ Historical investigation
- ❑ Scientific experimentation
- ❑ Problem-based learning
- ❑ Creative expression
- ❑ Artistic or production
- ❑ Exploration of issues
- ❑ Construction project
- ❑ Socratic seminar
- ❑ Simulation

Direct Instruction

To help students:
- ❑ Compare ideas and information
- ❑ Find information (e.g., research)
- ❑ Evaluate information and ideas
- ❑ Generate and test hypotheses
- ❑ Communicate ideas
- ❑ Manage their time
- ❑ Monitor their understanding
- ❑ Organize information
- ❑ Persuade
- ❑ Review each other's work
- ❑ Revise their own work
- ❑ Use problem-solving strategies
- ❑ Self-evaluate
- ❑ Summarize key ideas

E

Homework and Other Out-of-Class Experiences

Examples:
- ❑ Practicing skills
- ❑ Reading with a purpose
- ❑ Working on project or performance task
- ❑ Studying and synthesizing information (e.g., create a concept map)
- ❑ Reflecting on ideas, process, or product (e.g., journal entry)
- ❑ Revising work

Templates · Stage 1 · Stage 2 · Stage 3 · Peer review · Exercises · Process sheets · Glossary

Equipping Students for Performance
Historical Role-Play

Given your overall goals (Stage 1) and the proposed assessments (in Stage 2), what knowledge and skills are needed to *equip* students for successful performance?

Performance Task or Other Evidence   **OE** **T**

Assume the role of a historical character and role-play her participation in a debate on a current issue.

To successfully perform, the student will have to **know**	**THEN**	*What teaching and learning experiences will be needed to equip her for a successful performance?*
Rules of debate		• Review the rules of debate
Debate procedure		• Show videotape excerpts of debates to illustrate the procedure and effective debating strategies
and **be able to**		
Succinctly state a position		• Teach rebuttal techniques
Use rebuttal techniques		

Equipping Students for Performance

Performance Task or Other Evidence   **OE** **T**

To successfully perform, the student will have to **know**	**THEN**	*What teaching and learning experiences will be needed to equip her for a successful performance?*
_____		_____
_____		_____
and **be able to**		_____
_____		_____
_____		_____

Templates

Stage 1

Stage 2

Stage 3

Peer review

Exercises

Process sheets

Glossary

WHERETO
Questions to Consider for *R*

The *R* in WHERETO reminds us that understanding develops and deepens as a result of *rethinking* and *reflection*. Thus, we should build in such opportunities by design. Consider the following questions as you plan learning experiences and instruction to cause students to *rethink* and *reflect* (i.e., to dig deeper into the Big Ideas), and to *refine* and *revise* their work based on feedback. Consider using the six facets of understanding to generate learning activities that require rethinking.

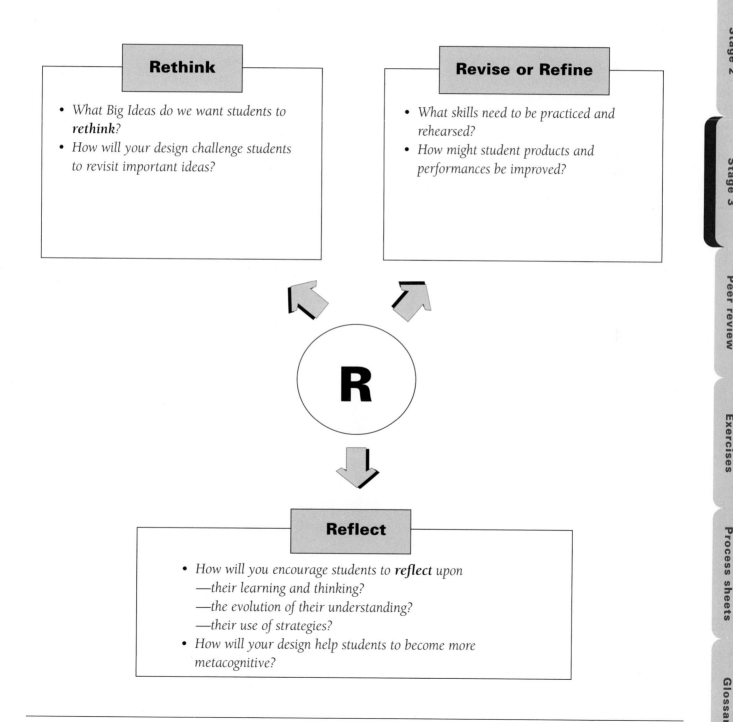

Rethink

- What Big Ideas do we want students to **rethink**?
- How will your design challenge students to revisit important ideas?

Revise or Refine

- What skills need to be practiced and rehearsed?
- How might student products and performances be improved?

R

Reflect

- How will you encourage students to **reflect** upon
  —their learning and thinking?
  —the evolution of their understanding?
  —their use of strategies?
- How will your design help students to become more metacognitive?

Templates · Stage 1 · Stage 2 · Stage 3 · Peer review · Exercises · Process sheets · Glossary

WHE**R**ETO
Examples of *R*

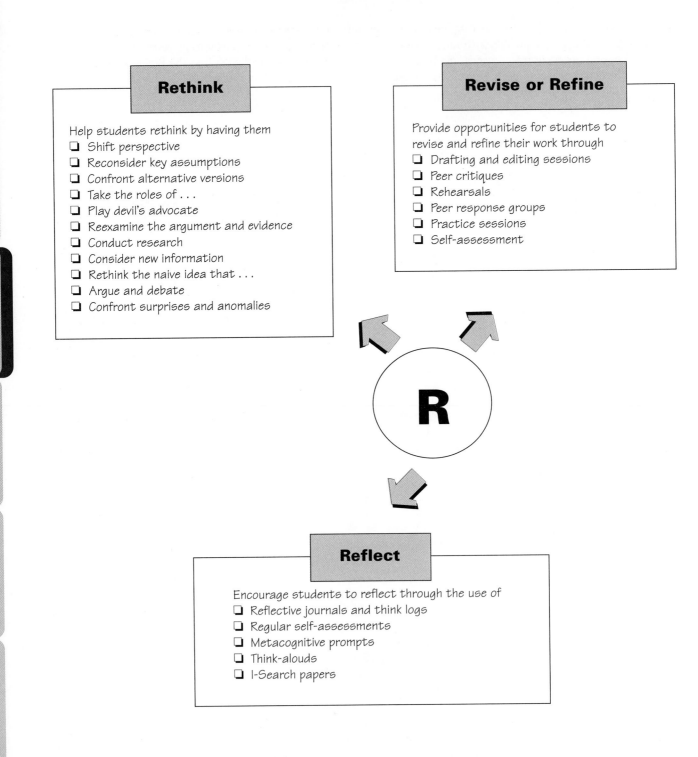

Rethink

Help students rethink by having them
- ❏ Shift perspective
- ❏ Reconsider key assumptions
- ❏ Confront alternative versions
- ❏ Take the roles of . . .
- ❏ Play devil's advocate
- ❏ Reexamine the argument and evidence
- ❏ Conduct research
- ❏ Consider new information
- ❏ Rethink the naive idea that . . .
- ❏ Argue and debate
- ❏ Confront surprises and anomalies

Revise or Refine

Provide opportunities for students to revise and refine their work through
- ❏ Drafting and editing sessions
- ❏ Peer critiques
- ❏ Rehearsals
- ❏ Peer response groups
- ❏ Practice sessions
- ❏ Self-assessment

R

Reflect

Encourage students to reflect through the use of
- ❏ Reflective journals and think logs
- ❏ Regular self-assessments
- ❏ Metacognitive prompts
- ❏ Think-alouds
- ❏ I-Search papers

Templates • Stage 1 • Stage 2 • Stage 3 • Peer review • Exercises • Process sheets • Glossary

WHERETO
Encouraging Self-Evaluation—*E*

Stage 2 of backward design specifies the assessment evidence needed for the desired results identified in Stage 1. The second *E* in WHERETO asks the designer to build in opportunities for ongoing evaluation, including opportunities for students to *self-evaluate*. The following questions may be used as prompts to guide student self-evaluation and reflection. (Note: This step connects with the *R* in WHERETO.)

E

- What do you really understand about _____?

- What questions and uncertainties do you still have about _____?

- What was most effective in _____?

- What was least effective in _____?

- How could you improve _____?

- What are your strengths in _____?

- What are your deficiencies in _____?

- How difficult was _____ for you?

- How does your preferred learning style influence _____?

- What would you do differently next time _____?

- What are you most proud of? Why? _____

- What are you most disappointed in? Why? _____

- What grade or score do you deserve? Why? _____

- How does what you've learned connect to other learnings? _____

- How has what you've learned changed your thinking? _____

- How does what you've learned relate to the present and future? _____

- What follow-up work is needed? _____

- Other: _____

_____

_____

Templates | Stage 1 | Stage 2 | Stage 3 | Peer review | Exercises | Process sheets | Glossary

Templates

Stage 1

Stage 2

Stage 3

Peer review

Exercises

Process sheets

Glossary

WHERETo
Tailoring the Design for Diverse Learners

The *T* in WHERETO refers to ways of *tailoring* the design to address student differences in background knowledge and experiences, skill levels, interests, talents, and learning styles. Designers consider ways in which lessons, activities, resources, and assessments might be personalized without sacrificing unit goals or standards. Appropriate differentiation of *content, process,* and *product* can accommodate diverse learners.

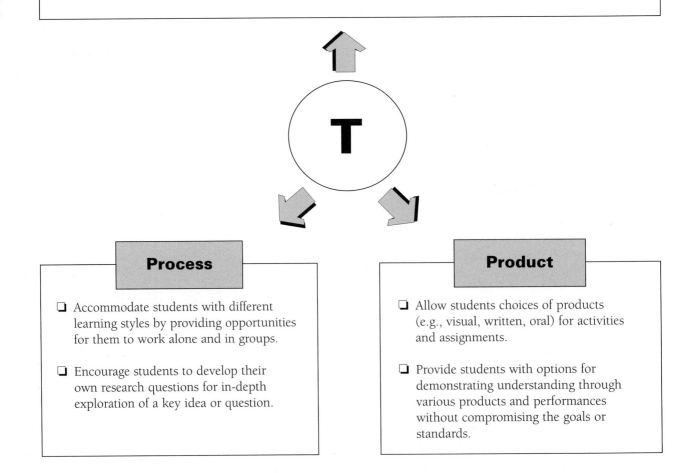

Content

❏ At the beginning of a unit, assess prior knowledge and skills, and develop differentiated activities to accommodate different knowledge and skill levels.

❏ Provide students with open-ended questions, activities, assignments, and assessments that enable students to give different but equally valid responses.

❏ Appeal to various modalities (e.g., present information orally, visually, and in writing).

❏ Use a variety of resource materials (e.g., multiple reading materials at different levels) to help students understand a difficult concept.

T

Process

❏ Accommodate students with different learning styles by providing opportunities for them to work alone and in groups.

❏ Encourage students to develop their own research questions for in-depth exploration of a key idea or question.

Product

❏ Allow students choices of products (e.g., visual, written, oral) for activities and assignments.

❏ Provide students with options for demonstrating understanding through various products and performances without compromising the goals or standards.

WHERETO
Organizing the Learning

The *O* in WHERETO relates to the organization and sequence of design. As they develop the learning plan, designers are encouraged to consider the following questions: How will the learning activities be *organized* to enable students to achieve the desired results? Given the desired results, what sequence will offer the most engaging and effective learning? How will the work unfold in a natural progression so that new teaching and activities seem appropriate, not arbitrary or meaningless, to students? Two broad organizational patterns are depicted below.

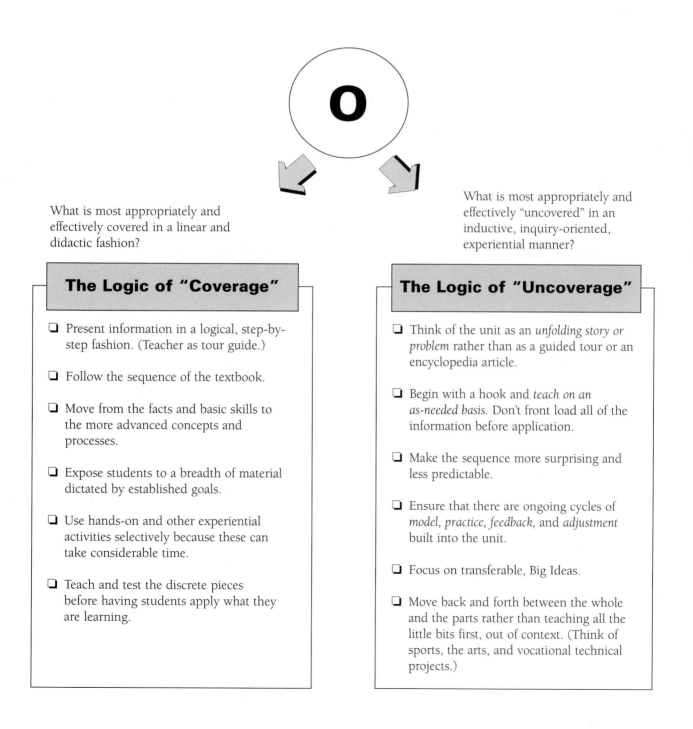

What is most appropriately and effectively covered in a linear and didactic fashion?

What is most appropriately and effectively "uncovered" in an inductive, inquiry-oriented, experiential manner?

The Logic of "Coverage"

- ❏ Present information in a logical, step-by-step fashion. (Teacher as tour guide.)

- ❏ Follow the sequence of the textbook.

- ❏ Move from the facts and basic skills to the more advanced concepts and processes.

- ❏ Expose students to a breadth of material dictated by established goals.

- ❏ Use hands-on and other experiential activities selectively because these can take considerable time.

- ❏ Teach and test the discrete pieces before having students apply what they are learning.

The Logic of "Uncoverage"

- ❏ Think of the unit as an *unfolding story or problem* rather than as a guided tour or an encyclopedia article.

- ❏ Begin with a hook and *teach on an as-needed basis*. Don't front load all of the information before application.

- ❏ Make the sequence more surprising and less predictable.

- ❏ Ensure that there are ongoing cycles of *model, practice, feedback,* and *adjustment* built into the unit.

- ❏ Focus on transferable, Big Ideas.

- ❏ Move back and forth between the whole and the parts rather than teaching all the little bits first, out of context. (Think of sports, the arts, and vocational technical projects.)

Templates | Stage 1 | Stage 2 | Stage 3 | Peer review | Exercises | Process sheets | Glossary

WHERETO—Sequencing the Learning
Nutrition

What sequence of teaching and learning experiences will equip students to engage with, develop, and demonstrate the desired understandings? Use the following sheet to list the key teaching and learning activities in sequence. Code each entry with the appropriate initials of the WHERETO elements.

1. Begin with an entry question (Can the foods you eat cause zits?) to hook students into considering the effects of nutrition on their lives. **H** **L**

2. Introduce the Essential Questions and discuss the culminating unit performance tasks (Chow Down and Eating Action Plan). **W**

3. Note: Key vocabulary terms are introduced as needed by the various learning activities and performance tasks. Students read and discuss relevant selections from the Health textbook to support the learning activities and tasks. As an ongoing activity, students keep a chart of their daily eating and drinking for later review and evaluation. **E**

4. Present concept attainment lesson on the food groups. Then have students practice categorizing pictures of foods accordingly. **E**

5. Introduce the Food Pyramid and identify foods in each group. Students work in groups to develop a poster of the Food Pyramid containing cut-out pictures of foods in each group. Display the posters in the classroom or hallway. **E**

6. Give quiz on the food groups and Food Pyramid (matching format). **E**

7. Review and discuss the nutrition brochure from the USDA. Discussion question: Must everyone follow the same diet to be healthy? **R**

8. Working in cooperative groups, students analyze a hypothetical family's diet (deliberately unbalanced) and make recommendations for improved nutrition. Teacher observes and coaches students as they work. **E-2**

9. Have groups share their diet analyses and discuss as a class. **E, E-2**
(Note: Teacher collects and reviews the diet analyses to look for misunderstandings needing instructional attention.)

10. Each student designs an illustrated nutrition brochure to teach younger children about the importance of good nutrition for healthy living and the problems associated with poor eating. This activity is completed outside of class. **E, T**

11. Students exchange brochures with members of their group for a peer assessment based on a criteria list. Allow students to make revisions based on feedback. **R, E-2**

12. Show and discuss the video, "Nutrition and You." Discuss the health problems linked to poor eating. **E**

13. Students listen to, and question, a guest speaker (nutritionist from the local hospital) about health problems caused by poor nutrition. **E**

14. Students respond to written prompt: Describe two health problems that could arise as a result of poor nutrition and explain what changes in eating could help to avoid them. (These are collected and graded by teacher.) **E-2**

15. Teacher models how to read and interpret food label information on nutritional values. Then have students practice using donated boxes, cans, and bottles (empty!). **E**

16. Students work independently to develop the three-day camp menu. Evaluate and give feedback on the camp menu project. Students self- and peer-assess their projects using rubrics. **E-2,T**

17. At the conclusion of the unit, students review their completed daily eating chart and self-assess the healthfulness of their eating. Have they noticed changes? Improvements? Do they notice changes in how they feel and their appearance? **E-2**

18. Students develop a personal "eating action plan" for healthful eating. These are saved and presented at upcoming student-involved parent conferences. **E-2, T**

19. Conclude the unit with student self-evaluation regarding their personal eating habits. Have each student develop a personal action plan for their "healthful eating" goal. **E-2, T**

WHERET**O**—Sequencing the Learning

What sequence of teaching and learning experiences will equip students to engage with, develop, and demonstrate the desired understandings? Brainstorm a list on this form. Use the following sheet to list the key teaching and learning activities in sequence. Code each entry with the appropriate initials of the WHERETO elements.

L

Templates · Stage 1 · Stage 2 · Stage 3 · Peer review · Exercises · Process sheets · Glossary

WHERETO—Sequencing the Learning
Nutrition

What sequence of teaching and learning experiences will equip students to engage with, develop, and demonstrate the desired understandings? The following calendar may be used to map the unit sequence. Use the small boxes to code each calendar entry with the appropriate initials of the WHERETO elements.

	Monday	Tuesday	Wednesday	Thursday	Friday
	1 (HW) 1. Hook students with a discussion of eating habits and zits. 2. Introduce essential questions and key vocabulary. 3. Have students begin a food diary to record their daily eating patterns.	**2** (E) 4. Present concept attainment lesson on food groups, then categorize foods accordingly. 5. Have students read and discuss the nutrition brochure from the USDA.	**3** (ET) 6. Present lesson on the Food Pyramid and identify foods in each group. 7. Read and discuss relevant selections from the Health textbook. Provide illustrated pamphlet for lower-level readers.	**4** (ET) 8. Present and discuss the video, "Nutrition and You." 9. Have students design and illustrate a nutrition brochure to teach younger children about the importance of good nutrition for healthy living.	**5** (ET) 10. Assess and give feedback on the brochures. Allow students to self- and peer-assess the brochures using a list of criteria.
	6 (E) 11. Working in cooperative groups, have students analyze a diet for a hypothetical family and make recommendations for improved nutrition.	**7** 12. Conduct a group review and give feedback regarding the diet analyses. Allow revisions.	**8** (E) 13. Have students listen to and question, guest speaker (nutritionist from local hospital) about health problems caused by poor nutrition.	**9** (ET) 14. Have students conduct research on health problems resulting from poor eating. Provide students with options for how they share their findings.	**10** (E) 15. Model how to interpret food label information for nutritional values. Have students practice interpreting food labels.
	11 (E) 16. Review the camp menu rubric so that students understand the criteria. Have them work independently to develop their three-day camp menu.	**12** (R) 17. Observe and coach students as they work on their menus.	**13** (E) 18. Evaluate and give feedback on the camp menu project. Have students self- and peer-assess their projects using the rubric.	**14** (ET) 19. Have students review their food diaries to look for changing patterns in their eating. Have each student set a personal goal for improved nutrition.	**15** (ET) 20. Conclude the unit with student self-evaluation regarding their personal eating habits. Have each student develop a personal action plan to reach his healthful eating goal.

Templates · Stage 1 · Stage 2 · Stage 3 · Peer review · Exercises · Process sheets · Glossary

WHERET**O**—Sequencing the Learning

What sequence of teaching and learning experiences will equip students to engage with, develop, and demonstrate the desired understandings? The following calendar may be used to map the unit sequence. Use the small boxes to code each calendar entry with the appropriate initials of the WHERETO elements.

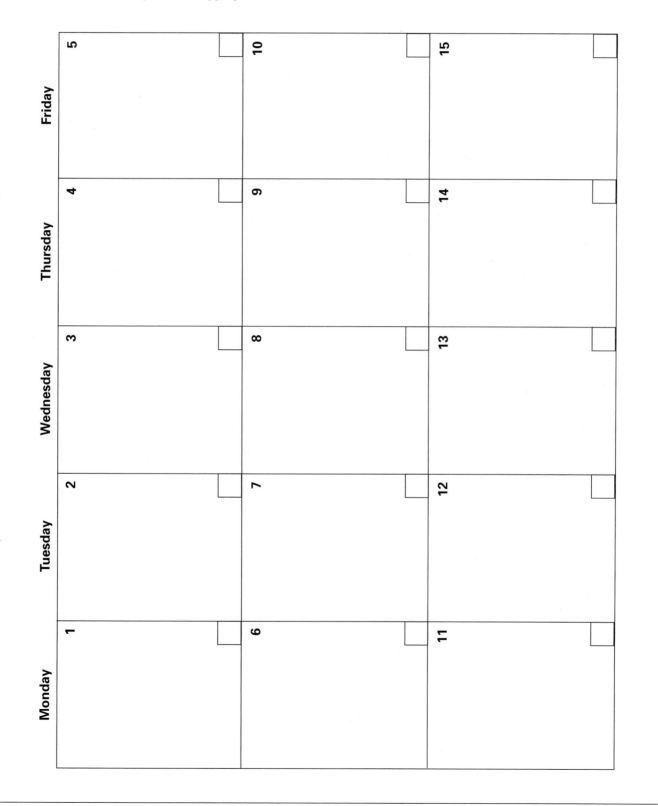

Brainstorming Learning
Using the Six Facets of Understanding
Statistics

Use the six facets of understanding to generate possible learning activities to *hook*, *engage*, and *equip* students for desired performances and *rethink* earlier ideas.

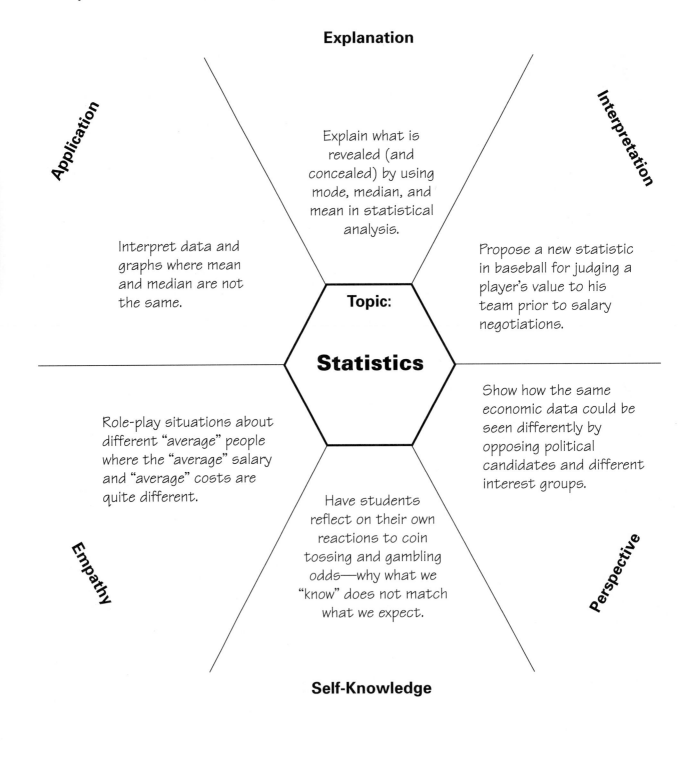

Explanation

Explain what is revealed (and concealed) by using mode, median, and mean in statistical analysis.

Application

Interpret data and graphs where mean and median are not the same.

Interpretation

Propose a new statistic in baseball for judging a player's value to his team prior to salary negotiations.

Topic:

Statistics

Show how the same economic data could be seen differently by opposing political candidates and different interest groups.

Role-play situations about different "average" people where the "average" salary and "average" costs are quite different.

Empathy

Have students reflect on their own reactions to coin tossing and gambling odds—why what we "know" does not match what we expect.

Perspective

Self-Knowledge

Templates · Stage 1 · Stage 2 · Stage 3 · Peer review · Exercises · Process sheets · Glossary

Brainstorming Learning
Using the Six Facets of Understanding
Nutrition

Use the six facets of understanding to generate possible learning activities to *hook, engage,* and *equip* students for desired performances and to *rethink* earlier ideas.

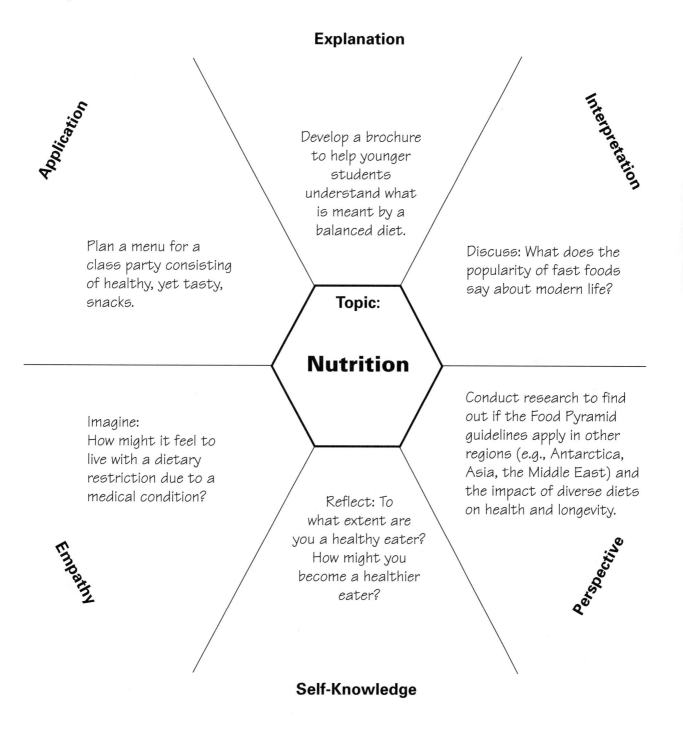

Explanation

Application

Interpretation

Develop a brochure to help younger students understand what is meant by a balanced diet.

Plan a menu for a class party consisting of healthy, yet tasty, snacks.

Discuss: What does the popularity of fast foods say about modern life?

Topic:

Nutrition

Imagine:
How might it feel to live with a dietary restriction due to a medical condition?

Conduct research to find out if the Food Pyramid guidelines apply in other regions (e.g., Antarctica, Asia, the Middle East) and the impact of diverse diets on health and longevity.

Reflect: To what extent are you a healthy eater? How might you become a healthier eater?

Empathy

Perspective

Self-Knowledge

231

Brainstorming Learning
Using the Six Facets of Understanding

Use the six facets of understanding to generate possible learning activities to *hook, engage,* and *equip* students for desired performances and to *rethink* earlier ideas.

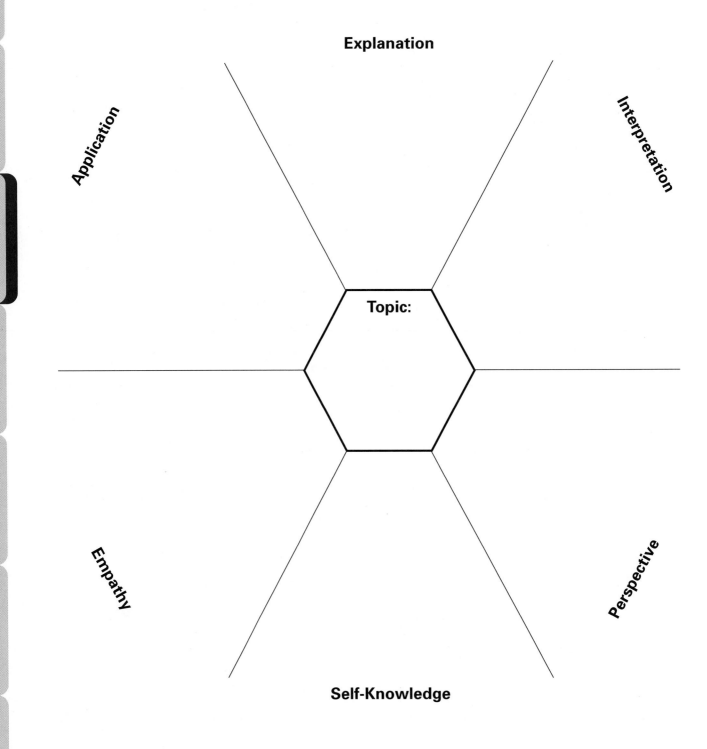

Explanation

Application

Interpretation

Topic:

Empathy

Perspective

Self-Knowledge

Templates

Stage 1

Stage 2

Stage 3

Peer review

Exercises

Process sheets

Glossary

Three Types of Classroom Assessments

Stage 3 Assessment *for* Learning		Stage 2 Assessment *of* Learning
Diagnostic:	**Formative:**	**Summative:**
Assessment that *precedes* instruction, checks students' prior knowledge and identifies misconceptions, interests, and learning-style preferences.	*Ongoing* assessments provide information to guide teaching and learning for improving learning and performance.	*Culminating* assessments are conducted at the end of a unit, course, or grade level to determine the degree of mastery or proficiency according to identified achievement targets.
Diagnostic assessments provide information to assist teacher planning and guide differentiated instruction.	Formative assessments include both formal and informal methods.	Summative assessments are evaluative in nature, generally resulting in a score or a grade.
Examples: Pretest, student survey, skills check, K-W-L	Examples: Quiz, oral questioning, observation, draft work, "think aloud," dress rehearsal, portfolio review	Examples: Test, performance task, final exam, culminating project or performance, work portfolio

Ideas for your design

_____ _____ _____

_____ _____ _____

_____ _____ _____

_____ _____ _____

_____ _____ _____

_____ _____ _____

_____ _____ _____

_____ _____ _____

_____ _____ _____

_____ _____ _____

_____ _____ _____

Templates | Stage 1 | Stage 2 | Stage 3 | Peer review | Exercises | Process sheets | Glossary

Informal Checks for Understanding

The following techniques provide efficient diagostic and formative checks of student understanding and misconceptions.

Hand Signals

Ask students to display a designated hand signal to indicate their understanding of a designated concept, principle, or process:

1. I understand _____ and can explain it (e.g., thumbs up).

2. I do not yet understand _____ (e.g., thumbs down).

3. I'm not completely sure about _____ (e.g., wave hand).

Index Card Summaries and Questions

Periodically distribute index cards and ask students to complete as follows:

Side 1—Based on our study of (unit topic), list in the form of a summary statement a Big Idea that you understand.

Side 2—Identify (as a statement or a question) something about (unit topic) that you do not yet fully understand.

Think and Draw

Ask students to create a graphic organizer or drawing to represent key ideas and their relationship. Encourage them to minimize the use of words or labels. Then, have students explain their visual.

Analogy Prompt

Periodically present students with an analogy prompt:

(designated concept, principle, or process) is like _____ because _____.

Web or Concept Map

Ask students to create a web or concept map to show the elements or components of a topic or process. This technique is especially effective in revealing the extent to which students understand the relationships among the elements.

One-Minute Essay

Periodically, have students complete a brief essay summarizing what they think they understand about a given topic.

Misconception Check

Present students with common or predictable misconceptions about a designated concept, principle, or process. Ask them to agree or disagree and explain their response. (The misconception check can also be presented in the form of a multiple-choice or true-false quiz.)

Templates

Stage 1

Stage 2

Stage 3

Peer review

Exercises

Process sheets

Glossary

Assessing and Addressing Misunderstandings

Research and experience have shown that students often harbor misconceptions about concepts and processes that they encounter in school. This is especially true for abstract, counterintuitive ideas. If these misconceptions are not identified and explicitly addressed, they will persist and interfere with the learner's understanding and performance. Use the following chart to identify potential misconceptions or predictable skill problems and plan appropriate diagnostic checks and instructional interventions.

Stage 1	Stage 3	
Identify predictable misunderstandings or errors in performance.	*Develop diagnostic and formative assessments to check for these.*	*Then, plan the needed instruction and learning activities to address them.*
Examples: ❑ Predictable misunderstandings, based on the counterintuitive or esoteric nature of the Big Idea ❑ Common performance errors, because of misunderstandings in how the skill works or how it should be used in context	Examples: ❑ Pretest ❑ K–W–L ❑ "No fault" quiz ❑ Diagnostic skills test ❑ Student-generated concept map ❑ Other: _____	Examples: ❑ Direct instruction ❑ Concept attainment ❑ Teacher modeling or "think aloud" ❑ Skill demonstration ❑ Guided practice with feedback ❑ Independent practice schedule ❑ Other: _____
Ideas for your design		

Templates — Stage 1 — Stage 2 — Stage 3 — Peer review — Exercises — Process sheets — Glossary

Addressing Misunderstandings: Assessing *for* Learning

Stage 1	Stage 3	
Identify predictable misunderstandings or errors in performance.	*Develop diagnostic and formative assessments to check for these.*	*Then, plan the needed instruction and learning activities to address them.*
Potential Misunderstanding: Many physics students think that multiple forces must be acting on an object thrown up in the air—for example, that a force must explain not only the falling but the rising. (The real answer is counterintuitive.)	☑ Pretest ☑ "No fault" quiz Use the Force Concept Inventory (multiple-choice) as a pre- and post-test, with no grade attached. Also, ask for a brief written explanation of answers to the four questions on gravitational force.	☑ Direct instruction ☑ Concept attainment Use teacher demonstrations and informal student experiments to show how change in direction or velocity is not affected by any force other than gravity.
Potential Performance Error: Swimmers learning the butterfly stroke keep their arms straight during the underwater pull phase of the stroke. This results in a visible up-and-down motion that generates waves and exhausts the swimmer.	☑ Diagnostic skills test Watch the swimmer perform the butterfly stoke and pay particular attention to the underwater pull. Look for a straight-arm pull.	☑ Skill demonstration ☑ Guided practice with feedback Demonstrate both flawed and proper stroke mechanics (e.g., "hour-glass" pull) on land and then in the water. Have swimmer practice the proper motion on land and in the water. Provide corrective feedback as needed.
Ideas for your design		
Potential Misunderstandings or Performance Errors		

Sidebar tabs: Templates · Stage 1 · Stage 2 · Stage 3 · Peer review · Exercises · Process sheets · Glossary

The Logic of Design vs. the Sequence of Teaching

Design Sequence	Instructional Sequence

Stage 1—Begin with the desired results:
• Content standards
• Big Ideas and understandings
• Essential Questions
• Knowledge and skills
 	
Stage 2—Identify assessment evidence:
• Facets of understanding
• Performance assessments and criteria
   — Authentic tasks and rubrics
   — Prompts and rubrics
• Other evidence and checklists
• Student self-assessments
 	
Stage 3—Develop the learning plan:
• Key teaching and learning activities
   — WHERETO elements
   — Sequence
• Learning materials and resources
	In the beginning
	• Introduce the topic, desired results, rationale, Essential Questions, and performance requirements
	• "Hook" the learners
	• Use diagnostic assessments for
	   — Prior knowledge and skill levels
	   — Misconceptions
	
	During the unit, provide
	• Questions, issues, and problems that stimulate students to "uncover" key ideas
	• Experiences to equip students for their final performances
	• Direct instruction (as needed)
	• Ongoing formative assessments
	• Feedback with opportunities for rethinking and revising
	
	Toward the end, include
	• Summative (culminating) assessments
	• Student self-assessments and reflections

Templates · Stage 1 · Stage 2 · Stage 3 · Peer review · Exercises · Process sheets · Glossary

Design Checklist—Stage 3

1. _____   The learning plan makes clear to students what they will be learning, what is expected of them (i.e., their performance goals) and how their work will be evaluated (W).

2. _____   Diagnostic assessments are used in the beginning to check for potential misunderstandings and predictable performance (skill) errors (W).

3. _____   The learning plan is clearly designed to engage students, with special emphasis on the opening lessons and activities (H).

4. _____   The learning plan is designed to equip learners with the prerequisite experiences necessary to understand the Big Ideas, and the needed information and skills upon which the understandings and performances depend (E).

5. _____   Opportunities are provided for students to rethink their prior and emerging understandings, and to revise their work based on feedback and guidance (R).

6. _____   Ongoing assessments of individual and group progress provide students with feedback and guidance (E).

7. _____   The learning has been personalized to accommodate the variety of learners' interests, styles, and abilities by differentiating content, process, and products (T).

8. _____   The sequence of learning activities has been organized to maximize student engagement and productivity (O).

Notes

_____

_____

_____

_____

_____

_____

_____

_____

_____

Templates | Stage 1 | Stage 2 | Stage 3 | Peer review | Exercises | Process sheets | Glossary

Frequently Asked Questions About Stage 3

1. Where do individual lesson plans fit into backward design?

Individual lesson plans are constructed within Stage 3. Although we do not expect *every* lesson to address all the Essential Questions identified in Stage 1 or involve students in a performance task from Stage 2, we (and students) should see a clear connection between particular lessons and the larger goals and assessments.

2. Over the years, our school district has conducted staff development in various instructional models, including Dimensions of Learning, writing across the curriculum, cooperative learning and the 5 E's in science. Are these approaches compatible with Understanding by Design?

Yes! These are all proven instructional models and are congruent with Understanding by Design (UbD). UbD concentrates on establishing clear content priorities in Stage 1 (i.e., What are the important Big Ideas worth understanding? What Essential Questions should be explored? What discrete knowledge and skills are needed?) and appropriate assessment in Stage 2 (i.e., What evidence of learning is needed? How will we know that students really understand?).

UbD does *not* specify any particular instructional approach or strategy in Stage 3. We believe that there are a variety of ways to teach for understanding. The selection of specific teaching methods is influenced by the intersection among variables, such as content, age and experience levels of the learners, teacher styles, and results from various achievement measures. The key questions from a backward design perspective: Is the instructional approach or model appropriate for helping students reach the desired results? Will it lead to engaging and effective learning of important ideas?

3. I have worked very hard on designing just one unit using Understanding by Design. How can I possibly plan everything I teach in this way?

Admittedly, Understanding by Design is a sophisticated and demanding planning framework (although we believe that such planning results in more effective and engaging teaching and learning). Nonetheless, the thought of planning *everything* one teaches in this manner can be daunting.

We suggest considering this challenge through a cooking analogy: UbD is to unit planning as gourmet cooking is to meal creation. Even those of us who love to cook generally do not plan gourmet meals every evening. It's too demanding. Similarly, attempting to apply the UbD framework to everything at once is not feasible. However, imagine that each teacher in a school or district (or state) had the opportunity to plan *one* "gourmet unit" a year using UbD (ideally, working with a colleague or two). Once they became familiar with the process (and it does get easier!), they would be encouraged to plan two units the following year. Then, imagine if every teacher shared their gourmet unit via the *ubdexchange.org* Web site, so that others could access their designs. By working smarter in this fashion, every teacher would have access to dozens of gourmet units for the topics they teach.

Templates

Stage 1

Stage 2

Stage 3

Peer review

Exercises

Process sheets

Glossary

240

Peer Review

Templates

Stage 1

Stage 2

Stage 3

Peer review

Exercises

Process sheets

Glossary

UbD Design Standards

Stage 1—To what extent does the design focus on the big ideas of targeted content?

Consider: Are . . .

❍ The targeted understandings enduring, based on transferable, big ideas at the heart of the discipline and in need of uncoverage?

❍ The targeted understandings framed by questions that spark meaningful connections, provoke genuine inquiry and deep thought, and encourage transfer?

❍ The essential questions provocative, arguable, and likely to generate inquiry around the central ideas (rather than a "pat" answer)?

❍ Appropriate goals (e.g., content standards, benchmarks, curriculum objectives) identified?

❍ Valid and unit-relevant knowledge and skills identified?

Stage 2—To what extent do the assessments provide fair, valid, reliable, and sufficient measures of the desired results?

Consider: Are . . .

❍ Students asked to exhibit their understanding through authentic performance tasks?

❍ Appropriate criterion-based scoring tools used to evaluate student products and performances?

❍ A variety of appropriate assessment formats used to provide additional evidence of learning?

❍ The assessments used as feedback for students and teachers, as well as for evaluation?

❍ Students encouraged to self-assess?

Stage 3—To what extent is the learning plan effective and engaging?

Consider: Will the students . . .

❍ Know *where* they're going (the learning goals), *why* the material is important (reason for learning the content), and *what* is required of them (unit goal, performance requirements and evaluative criteria)?

❍ Be *hooked*—engaged in digging into the big ideas (e.g., through inquiry, research, problem solving, and experimentation)?

❍ Have adequate opportunities to *explore* and *experience* big ideas and receive instruction to *equip* them for the required performances?

❍ Have sufficient opportunities to *rethink, rehearse, revise* and *refine* their work based upon timely feedback?

❍ Have an opportunity to *evaluate* their work, reflect on their learning, and set goals?

Consider: Is the learning plan . . .

❍ *Tailored* and flexible to address the interests and learning styles of all students?

❍ *Organized* and sequenced to maximize engagement and effectiveness?

Overall Design—To what extent is the entire unit coherent, with the elements of all three stages aligned?

Peer Review Against Design Standards

Our profession rarely subjects teacher-designed units and assessments to this level of critical review. Nonetheless, we have found structured peer reviews, guided by design standards, to be enormously beneficial—to both teachers and their designs.

The primary purpose of peer review is to provide feedback to designers for the purpose of helping them improve their designs. However, there are residual benefits. Participants in peer review sessions regularly comment on the value of the opportunity to share and discuss curriculum and assessment designs with colleagues. We believe that such sessions provide a powerful approach to professional development since the conversations focus the heart of teaching and learning: What is worthy of understanding in this unit? What counts as evidence that students *really* understand and can use what we're teaching? What knowledge and skills must we teach to enable students to achieve and apply their understandings in meaningful ways?

Peer Review Process

Begin by reviewing and discussing the Design Standards to ensure that all participants understand the unit design criteria.

Step 1—Overview of unit with designer present

a. Designer provides a brief overview of the unit and states any issues he wishes highlighted in the feedback session.

b. Reviewers ask only basic factual and contextual questions to clarify their work (e.g., When during the year does this occur, and what units precede this one?).

c. Designer leaves the review group.

Step 2—Review of unit designs without designer present

d. Establish roles (timekeeper, facilitator, reporter to designer). The facilitator's key job is to watch the time and to gently but firmly ensure that the designer listens (instead of defending) when the review is reported.

e. Reviewers silently read the unit and review materials (template, rubrics, handouts).

Individual Review

Time: ___ minutes

f. Each reviewer silently assesses strengths of design first, then weaknesses (in relation to the specific design criteria).

g. Each reviewer fills out **Individual Review Form** summarizing design's strengths and weaknesses *before* discussion of the unit by entire review group.

Templates   Stage 1   Stage 2   Stage 3   Peer review   Exercises   Process sheets   Glossary

Peer Review (continued)

Templates
Stage 1
Stage 2
Stage 3
Peer review
Exercises
Process sheets
Glossary

Step 3—Peers discuss individual reviews

```
┌─────────────────────────┐
│    Group Review         │
│  Time: ___ minutes      │
└─────────────────────────┘
```

h. Review group discusses individual reactions of strengths and weaknesses (in terms of design standards).

i. Group considers the issues highlighted by the designer.

j. Group develops a consensus on key feedback and guidance to be offered.

Step 4—Peers discuss how to frame and report feedback and guidance

k. The recorder fills out the **Group Review Form** summarizing the group's key feedback and guidance.

l. Group selects spokespersons to orally summarize the review to the designer. Also, prepare to share any reviewers' disagreements with designer.

Step 5—Peers discuss the review with the designer

m. The designer's role is primarily a listener—taking notes, asking clarifying questions of reviewers, and thinking out loud about possible revisions.

```
┌─────────────────────────┐
│   Group Discussion      │
│    with Designer        │
│  Time: ___ minutes      │
└─────────────────────────┘
```

n. The designer may respond to questions of clarification as requested, but avoids justifying the intent, history, or reasons for choice. The design must stand by itself as much as possible.

o. After feedback and guidance are offered, a general discussion of design issues or questions raised by the review may occur. (Note general design questions, issues, and dilemmas for the debriefing discussion after peer review is over.)

Tips for Effective Peer Review

1. The reviewers should be friendly, honest consultants (critical friends) to the designer. The designer's intent is the basis of the review. The aim is to improve the designer's idea, not replace it with the reviewers' teaching priorities, style, or favorite activities.

2. The designer's job in the second session is primarily to listen, not explain, defend, or justify design decisions.

3. The reviewers' job is twofold: (1) to give useful feedback (Did the effect match the intent?); (2) to give useful guidance (How might the gaps in intent vs. effect be removed? How might the design be improved, given the intent?).

4. Designers typically assume that their design is more self-evident than it is. Imagine yourself to be a naive student. Would you know what to do? Would the flow of the unit be obvious? Do you know how you will be assessed? Is the purpose of the work clear?

5. A peer review session is successful when the designer feels that the design was understood by peers and improved (or validated) by the subsequent critique and discussion.

6. Always begin by offering feedback in those areas where the design most conforms to the design criteria (i.e., strengths), describing in detail how and where the design met those criteria.

7. Reviewers give feedback, making clear the basis for the comments in the match (or mismatch) between the goals, assessments, and learning plan, in reference to the design standards. Couching feedback about possible mismatches in question or conditional form may be appropriate: "We wondered about the validity of the assessment task, in light of the specified goal." Or, "If your aim is critical thinking, then the assessments don't seem to demand more than recall."

8. Reviewers give guidance in each area where they perceive a gap between intent and effect or some confusion about the design's purpose or execution. Note that guidance should improve the designer's intent, not substitute the reviewers' goals or methods for such a unit.

Misconception Alert

A common misconception about peer review is related to the assumption that we should judge the work of others and that others will judge our design. But the goal of review is to provide helpful feedback and guidance, not a judgment.

The distinction between feedback and guidance is almost universally misunderstood. Despite common parlance, feedback merely describes what happened, not how you feel about it or what should be changed.

The most common mistake in peer review, therefore, as a result of this misconception, is to assume that the peer review process is meant to offer praise and criticism. That is far less important than accurately describing the design's strengths and weaknesses based on design standards, so that the designer will understand why advice is offered.

Templates

Stage 1

Stage 2

Stage 3

Peer review

Exercises

Process sheets

Glossary

Getting Started with Peer Review

Ideas for introducing peer review

Peer review against design standards is foreign to many teachers. Consider the following ideas for introducing design standards and the peer review process to staff in your school or district.

1. Discuss the need to walk the talk and apply standards to our own work (just as we judge student work against content and performance standards).

2. Use the Exemplary Design exercise to involve staff in generating an initial set of design standards based on their experiences. Then, ask them to revise the exercise, based on the standards they identified. Discuss the benefits of using explicitly stated standards to improve curriculum and assessment designs.

3. Introduce and discuss the UbD Design Standards. You may wish to select a subset of Standards for starters. Model their use with a sample design (e.g., *Test 4—Validity* using the "diorama" assessment task).

4. Ask staff to review a lesson, unit (such as Pioneer Life) or assessment task against the UbD Standards. Share ways to improve the design based on the standards.

5. Introduce the Peer Review process as a means of applying standards to our curriculum and assessment design work. Review the goal, structure, steps, and roles of the process.

6. Model the Peer Review process by reviewing a UbD unit. Use the nutrition unit (*You Are What You Eat*) or a unit downloaded from the ubdexchange.org Web site. Discuss the roles of reviewers and designers. (A "fishbowl" process works well to model these roles.)

7. Initially, ask for volunteers interested in having their own work (units or assessment tasks) submitted for peer review.

8. Involve more staff in peer review as people become more familiar and comfortable with the process.

Templates
Stage 1
Stage 2
Stage 3
Peer review
Exercises
Process sheets
Glossary

Individual Review Form

Design Standards	Strengths	Weaknesses
To what extent does the design • **Focus on the Big Ideas of targeted content?** • **Frame the Big Ideas around Essential Questions?**		
To what extent do the assessments provide **valid, reliable, and sufficient measures** *of the desired results?*		
To what extent is the learning plan effective and engaging?		
To what extent is the entire unit coherent, with the elements of all three stages aligned?		

Templates | Stage 1 | Stage 2 | Stage 3 | Peer review | Exercises | Process sheets | Glossary

Group Review Form

Design Standards	Feedback	Guidance
To what extent does the design • **Focus on the Big Ideas of targeted content?** • **Frame the Big Ideas around Essential Questions?**		
To what extent do the assessments provide **valid, reliable, and sufficient measures of the desired results?**		
To what extent is the learning plan **effective and engaging?**		
To what extent is the entire unit coherent, **with the elements of all three stages aligned?**		

Templates · Stage 1 · Stage 2 · Stage 3 · Peer review · Exercises · Process sheets · Glossary

Exercises

Templates

Stage 1

Stage 2

Stage 3

Peer review

Exercises

Process sheets

Glossary

What Is Exemplary Design for Learning?

1. Think back to your many experiences with well-designed learning, *both in and out of school*. What was the most **well-designed learning experience** you have ever encountered as a learner? What features of the design—*not* the teacher's style or your interests—made the learning so **engaging and effective**? (Design elements include challenges posed, sequence of activities, resources provided, assignments, assessments, groupings, site, and teacher's role.)
   Briefly describe the design.

   _____

   _____

   _____

   _____

   _____

   _____

   _____

2. In sharing your recollections and analyses with your colleagues, build **a list of generalizations that follow** from the accounts. What do well-designed learning experiences have in common? In other words, what must be built in by design for any learning experience to be maximally **effective** *and* **engaging** for students?

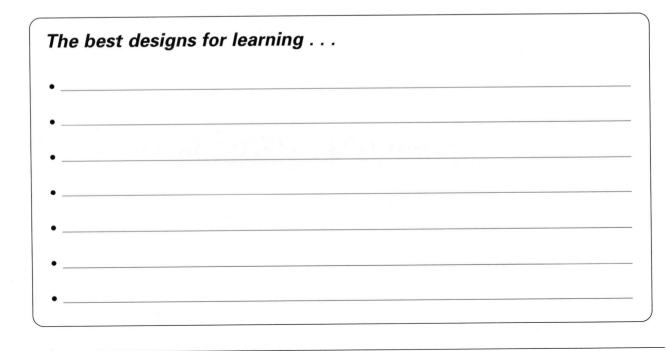

The best designs for learning . . .

- _____

- _____

- _____

- _____

- _____

- _____

- _____

What Is Exemplary Design for Learning? (continued)

3. Where in your school are the characteristics of best design most likely to be seen in action? In what programs and subject areas would we most expect to see these characteristics, compared with other programs or subjects? Are there any patterns? If so, why?

4. After a study of sample units, and one of your own designs, edit or amend your list of the characteristics of the best designs, as appropriate.

The best designs for learning . . .

-
-
-
-
-
-
-
-
-
-

Templates

Stage 1

Stage 2

Stage 3

Peer review

Exercises

Process sheets

Glossary

Characteristics of the Best Learning Designs

Use this organizer to categorize the characteristics of best design according to the three stages of backward design. What patterns do you notice?

Stage 1—Desired Results

Stage 2—Assessment Evidence

Stage 3—Learning Plan

Templates

Stage 1

Stage 2

Stage 3

Peer review

Exercises

Process sheets

Glossary

Thinking About Understanding and Design

Directions—Select one of the following quotations with which you agree or resonate. Explain why you like the quote, and, if possible, give an example to illustrate the idea.

thoughts . . .

1. "To begin with the end in mind means to start with a clear under-standing of your destination. It means to know where you're going so that you better understand where you are now so that the steps you take are always in the right direction."

    —Stephen Covey
    The Seven Habits of Highly Effective People

2. Using backward design in curriculum planning helps to avoid the twin sins of activity-oriented and coverage-oriented instruction.

3. *Understanding:* "The capacity to apply facts, concepts and skills in new situations in appropriate ways."

    —Dr. Howard Gardner

4. If the textbook presents the answers, then we should explore the *questions* that led to those answers.

5. "The *primary* purpose of classroom assessment is to inform teach-ing and improve learning, not to sort and select students or to justify a grade."

    —Jay McTighe and Steven Ferrara
    Assessing Learning in the Classroom

6. A teacher's primary job is to *uncover* the important ideas in sub-jects, not cover a textbook.

7.   "I hear, I forget.
        I see, I remember.
        I do, I understand."

    —Chinese proverb

Templates

Stage 1

Stage 2

Stage 3

Peer review

Exercises

Process sheets

Glossary

Thinking About Understanding

Directions—Select one of the following quotations with which you agree or resonate. Explain why you like the quote, and, if possible, give an example to illustrate the idea.

thoughts . . .

1. *Education:* "That which discloses to the wise and disguises from the foolish their lack of understanding."
   —Ambrose Bierce (1842–1914)
   The Devil's Dictionary

2. "We accumulate our opinions at an age when our understanding is at its weakest."
   —G. C. Lichtenberg (1742–99)
   Aphorisms, "Notebook H," aphorism 4

3. "To understand: to apprehend the meaning or import [of something]. To be thoroughly acquainted with an art . . . to be able to practice [it] . . . properly."
   —The Oxford English Dictionary

4. "Only in education, never in the life of farmer, sailor, merchant, physician or scientist does knowledge mean primarily a store of information."
   —John Dewey, *Democracy and Education*

5. "The goal of an intellectual education is not to repeat or retain ready-made truths. It is in learning to master the truth by oneself at the risk of losing a lot of time . . . an experiment not carried out by the individual himself with all freedom of initiative is by definition not an experiment but mere drill with no educational value."
   —Jean Piaget, "Mathematical Education"

6. "There are many different ways of understanding, overlapping but not reducible to one another and, correspondingly, many different ways of teaching to understand."
   —J. Passmore, *The Philosophy of Teaching*

Templates

Stage 1

Stage 2

Stage 3

Peer review

Exercises

Process sheets

Glossary

Reflecting on the Backward Design Process

1. What are the key similarities and differences between the "before" and "after" design examples?

2. To what extent does backward design as illustrated in the Template reflect the way in which people in your school or district typically plan? your own planning process?

3. Given the UbD version of backward design as illustrated in the Template, what do you predict will be challenging aspects of planning in this way?

Templates

Stage 1

Stage 2

Stage 3

Peer review

Exercises

Process sheets

Glossary

Reflecting on Backward Design—Version 2

1. List examples of backward design in various situations (e.g., *planning a trip*).

☐ _____

☐ _____

☐ _____

☐ _____

2. Consider an example where failure to plan with the end in mind led to problems or ineffective results. Briefly describe the situation.

3. Discuss the examples with members of your group. What generalizations about backward design emerge?

Templates

Stage 1

Stage 2

Stage 3

Peer review

Exercises

Process sheets

Glossary

An Exercise in Unpacking Content Standards

Reading Critically in All Content Areas   (PA 1.2.5. GRADE 5)

A. Read and understand essential content of informational texts and documents in all academic areas.

- Differentiate fact from opinion across texts.
- Distinguish between essential and nonessential information across a variety of texts, identifying stereotypes and exaggeration where present.

Types of Writing (PA 1.4.5. GRADE 5)

C. Write persuasive pieces with a clearly stated position or opinion and supporting detail, citing sources when needed.

4.9 Environmental Laws and Regulations   (PA 4.9.7. GRADE 7)

A. Explain the role of environmental laws and regulations.

- Identify and explain environmental laws and regulations (e.g., Clean Air Act, Clean Water Act, Recycling and Waste Reduction Act, Act 26 on Agricultural Education).
- Explain the role of local and state agencies in enforcing environmental laws and regulations (e.g., Department of Environmental Protection, Department of Agriculture, Game Commission).

Desired Results
List subject areas and content standard numbers.   **G**
Understandings   **U**   Students will understand that . . .
Essential Questions   **Q**

Templates

Stage 1

Stage 2

Stage 3

Peer review

Exercises

Process sheets

Glossary

Thinking About Understanding

What do we mean by "understanding"? What do we look for as evidence of understanding? Consider the various ways we use the term and list your thoughts in the space below.

- "Men just don't understand women!"

- "He knows the historical facts but doesn't understand what they mean."

- "Although I disagree, I can understand the opposition's point of view."

- "I didn't really understand it until I had to use it."

- "Does anyone here understand French?"

- "I understood exactly what she needed to hear at that moment."

- "She knows the answer but doesn't understand why it is correct."

- "Grandfather's stories about the Depression helped us to understand the importance of saving."

- "I now understand that I was mistaken."

Someone who understands . . .

_____

_____

_____

_____

_____

_____

_____

_____

_____

Templates

Stage 1

Stage 2

Stage 3

Peer review

Exercises

Process sheets

Glossary

How Do We Know Understanding When We See It?

Part 1—How would you define "understanding"? What does it mean to "really understand" or "get it"?

> **Understanding:**

Part 2—What are concrete indicators of *really* understanding a subject (vs. merely knowing important facts)? What follows from your definition for assessing understanding? What can the person with understanding do that the person with only knowledge—even lots of knowledge—cannot do?

Indicators of Understanding	Indicators of Knowledge Without Understanding

Templates

Stage 1

Stage 2

Stage 3

Peer review

Exercises

Process sheets

Glossary

Observable Indicators
of Teaching for Understanding

What would we expect to see in classrooms where teaching for understanding, rather than "coverage" or "activities," was the norm? List observable indicators ("look fors") below.

- _____

- _____

- _____

- _____

- _____

- _____

- _____

- _____

- _____

- _____

Templates

Stage 1

Stage 2

Stage 3

Peer review

Exercises

Process sheets

Glossary

UbD Indicators of Success

What would we see if teaching and assessing for understanding were the norm? What would staff now understand, and how would that understanding manifest itself? Use the spaces below to identify specific observable indicators of success or progress.

Classroom:

School:

District:

Templates

Stage 1

Stage 2

Stage 3

Peer review

Exercises

Process sheets

Glossary

Assessing Conditions for UbD Reform: Force-Field Analysis

Use the following matrix to assess those forces that support planned reforms and those that resist.

	Curriculum	Assessment	Instruction	Staff Development	Resources	Policy	Other: _____
(+) Assist							
(−) Resist							

Templates · Stage 1 · Stage 2 · Stage 3 · Peer review · Exercises · Process sheets · Glossary

Assessing Staff: Ready? Willing? Able?

Insert estimates of percentage of staff who fall into the categories below. Then, consider the different actions and strategies that may be needed for each group.

	Do they get it?	*Are they willing?*	*Are they able?*
Yes			
Not Yet			
Not Likely			

What patterns are evident?   *What are the implications?*

Possible Actions:

_____

_____

_____

_____

_____

_____

_____

_____

Templates

Stage 1

Stage 2

Stage 3

Peer review

Exercises

Process sheets

Glossary

"Yes, but . . ."—Responding to Predictable Concerns

Advocates for *Understanding by Design* often encounter predictable concerns ("yes, buts...") from colleagues. The following exercise is designed to help you prepare thoughtful responses to likely objections.

Part 1—Select one of the following concerns (or add one of your own) and generate ideas for responding to that concern. Record your ideas in the box below.

Part 2—Meet with others who have selected the same concern and share responses.

I would like to teach and assess for understanding, but . . .

1. I am expected to teach to state and district standards and benchmarks.

2. This approach takes too much time. I have too much content to cover.

3. I am being held accountable for student performance on superficial state tests.

4. I am a "skills" teacher, and students need to master the basics first.

I would like to design curriculum using the UbD framework, but . . .

5. This approach is too demanding. I couldn't possibly do this for everything I teach.

6. It's not my job to develop curriculum. Besides, I already have a textbook.

7. I don't know how to do this kind of design work.

8. I already do this.

9. Other: _____

Your response: _____

_____

_____

_____

_____

Action Planning

Desired Results	Evidence of Success	Actions	Persons Responsible	Resources Needed

Templates · Stage 1 · Stage 2 · Stage 3 · Peer review · Exercises · Process sheets · Glossary

Taking Action

Directions: *In light of this workshop, what should I . . .*

start doing: _____

_____

_____

_____

stop doing: _____

_____

_____

_____

do less of: _____

_____

_____

_____

do more of: _____

_____

_____

_____

266

Templates

Stage 1

Stage 2

Stage 3

Peer review

Exercises

Process sheets

Glossary

Characteristics of the Best Learning Designs
(Based on surveys of K–16 faculty throughout the United States)

Expectations

- Provide clear learning goals and performance expectations.
- Cast learning goals in terms of genuine and meaningful performance.
- Frame the work around genuine questions and meaningful challenges.
- Show models and exemplars of expected performance.

Instruction

- The teacher serves as a facilitator or coach to support the learner.
- Targeted instruction and relevant resources are provided to equip students for expected performance.
- The textbook serves as one resource among many (i.e., text is resource, not syllabus).
- The teacher "uncovers" important ideas and processes by exploring essential questions and genuine applications of knowledge and skills.

Learning Activities

- Individual differences (e.g., learning styles, skill levels, interests) are accommodated through a variety of activities and methods.
- There is variety in work methods and students have some choice (e.g., opportunities for both group and individual work).
- Learning is active and experiential to help students construct meaning.
- Cycles of model-try-feedback-refine anchor the learning.

Assessment

- There is no mystery as to performance goals or standards.
- Diagnostic assessments check for prior knowledge, skill level, and misconceptions.
- Students demonstrate their understanding through real-world applications (i.e., genuine use of knowledge and skills, tangible product, target audience).
- Assessment methods are matched to achievement targets.
- Ongoing, timely feedback is provided.
- Learners have opportunities for trial and error, reflection and revision.
- Self-assessment is expected.

Sequence and Coherence

- Start with a hook, and immerse the learner in a genuine problem, issue, or challenge.
- Move back and forth from whole to part, with increasing complexity.
- Scaffold learning in doable increments.
- Teach as needed; don't overteach all of the basics first.
- Revisit ideas; have learners rethink and revise earlier ideas and work.
- Be flexible (e.g., respond to student needs; revise plan to achieve goals).

267

Templates · Stage 1 · Stage 2 · Stage 3 · Peer review · Exercises · Process sheets · Glossary

Observable Indicators of Teaching for Understanding

What does "teaching for understanding" look like? What would we expect to see in an Understanding by Design classroom? The following list of observable indicators includes items developed by Grant Wiggins, Jay McTighe, and Elliott Seif.

The Unit and Course Design

- Units and courses reflect a coherent design. Big Ideas and Essential Questions clearly guide the design of, and are aligned with, assessments, teaching, and learning activities.

- In the design, clear distinctions are made between Big Ideas and Essential Questions, and clear indication is given of knowledge and skills necessary for learning the Big Ideas and answering the Essential Questions.

- Multiple forms of assessment allow students to demonstrate their understanding in various ways.

- Instruction and assessment reflect the six facets of understanding. The design provides opportunities for students to explain, interpret, apply, give perspective, empathize, and examine their own self-knowledge.

- Assessment of understanding is anchored by authentic performance tasks calling for students to demonstrate their understanding and apply knowledge and skills.

- Teacher, peer, and self-evaluations of student products and performances include clear criteria and performance standards.

- The unit or course design enables students to revisit and rethink important ideas to deepen their understanding.

- A variety of resources are suggested. The textbook is only one resource among many (instead of the syllabus).

The Teacher . . .

- Informs students of the Big Ideas and Essential Questions, performance requirements, and evaluative criteria at the beginning of the unit or course.

- Hooks and holds students' interest while they examine and explore Big Ideas and Essential Questions.

- Uses a variety of strategies and interacts with students so as to promote deeper understanding of subject matter.

- Facilitates students' active construction of meaning (rather than simply "telling").

- Promotes opportunities for students to unpack their thinking—to explain, interpret, apply, give perspective, empathize and examine self-knowledge (incorporates the six facets of understanding).

Templates   Stage 1   Stage 2   Stage 3   Peer review   Exercises   Process sheets   Glossary

Observable Indicators of Teaching
for Understanding (continued)

The Teacher (continued)...

- Uses questioning, probing, and feedback to stimulate student reflection and rethinking.

- Teaches basic knowledge and skills to help students uncover Big Ideas and explore Essential Questions.

- Uses information from ongoing assessments to provide feedback for guiding rethinking and revising instruction.

- Uses information from ongoing assessments to check for understanding and misconceptions along the way.

- Uses a variety of resources (more than the text) to promote understanding.

The Learners...

- Can describe the goals (Big Ideas and Essential Questions) and performance requirements of the unit or course.

- Can explain what they are doing and why (i.e., how today's work relates to the larger goals).

- Are hooked at the beginning and engaged throughout the unit.

- Can describe the criteria by which their work will be evaluated.

- Are engaged in activities that help them to learn the Big Ideas and answer the Essential Questions.

- Are engaged in activities that promote explanation, interpretation, application, perspective taking, empathy, and self-knowledge (the six facets).

- Demonstrate that they are learning the background knowledge and skills that support the Big Ideas and Essential Questions.

- Have opportunities to generate relevant questions.

- Are able to explain and justify their work and their answers.

- Are involved in self- and peer assessment based upon established criteria and performance standards.

- Use the criteria and rubrics to guide and revise their work.

- Set relevant goals based on feedback.

Templates Stage 1 Stage 2 Stage 3 Peer review Exercises Process sheets Glossary

Process Sheets

Self-Assessment for UbD

1. Directions: Check the appropriate box to indicate your degree of expertise with each of the following elements.

	Novice			Expert
Content Expertise	❑	❑	❑	❑
Using Concept-Based, Inquiry Curriculum	❑	❑	❑	❑
Designing Concept-Based, Inquiry Curriculum	❑	❑	❑	❑
Using Essential Questions	❑	❑	❑	❑
Designing Essential Questions	❑	❑	❑	❑
Using Performance Tasks	❑	❑	❑	❑
Designing Performance Tasks	❑	❑	❑	❑
Using Scoring Rubrics	❑	❑	❑	❑
Designing Scoring Rubrics	❑	❑	❑	❑

2. Directions: Place a mark along the continuum to reflect your preferences.

Learning and Design Preferences

design collaboratively --- work alone

follow a structured, sequential process --- move back and forth in a nonlinear fashion

seek feedback from experts and peers ------------------------------------ trust my own instincts about my work

Templates | Stage 1 | Stage 2 | Stage 3 | Peer review | Exercises | Process sheets | Glossary

Participant Self-Assessment—Part 1

Position: _____ **Grade and Department:** _____

Profile

1. Years of professional experience:

   ❏ 0–5   ❏ 6–12   ❏ 13–20   ❏ > 20

2. Self-assessment—your skills as a designer:

   a. I am skilled at designing informative and meaningful teacher-directed lessons/lectures/discussions.

      ❏ highly skilled   ❏ very skilled   ❏ somewhat skilled   ❏ minimally skilled

   b. I am skilled at designing engaging, self-directed, and effective activities for students to learn from.

      ❏ highly skilled   ❏ very skilled   ❏ somewhat skilled   ❏ minimally skilled

   c. I am skilled at designing valid and reliable assessments of my goals.

      ❏ highly skilled   ❏ very skilled   ❏ somewhat skilled   ❏ minimally skilled

3. I have the expertise to design my courses to make the elements (goals, assessments, lessons) fully aligned and understanding-focused.

   ❏ strongly agree   ❏ agree   ❏ disagree   ❏ strongly disagree

4. I seek feedback on my teaching by soliciting written student reactions to the activities, lessons, and work.

   ❏ weekly or more   ❏ every few weeks   ❏ a few times per year   ❏ once per year   ❏ never

5. I adjust my teaching by using the results from student assessment and student feedback to modify the design of upcoming work.

   ❏ weekly or more   ❏ every few weeks   ❏ a few times per year   ❏ once per year   ❏ never

6. I am aware of what constitutes "best practice" locally (via staff sharing, curriculum map).

   ❏ very aware   ❏ aware   ❏ somewhat aware   ❏ unaware

7. I am aware of what constitutes "best practice" in the profession for my area of responsibility.

   ❏ very aware   ❏ aware   ❏ somewhat aware   ❏ unaware

8. I am interested in what constitutes "best practice" in education.

   ❏ very interested   ❏ interested   ❏ somewhat interested   ❏ uninterested

Participant Self-Assessment—Part 2

Your Views on Design

1. It is not all that important to be a great designer if you know your subject and your students and you are a skilled classroom teacher.

    ❏ strongly agree   ❏ agree   ❏ unsure   ❏ disagree   ❏ strongly disagree   ❏ no opinion

2. Most teachers are not highly skilled as designers: the twin sins of design (cute activities with little intellectual value, and content coverage with no clear purpose or priorities) are common.

    ❏ strongly agree   ❏ agree   ❏ unsure   ❏ disagree   ❏ strongly disagree   ❏ no opinion

3. External mandates (tests, accountability systems) limit our ability to design well and teach for understanding.

    ❏ strongly agree   ❏ agree   ❏ unsure   ❏ disagree   ❏ strongly disagree   ❏ no opinion

4. There is a strong belief among educators that external mandates limit our design options and teaching, but it isn't clear if that belief is grounded in fact.

    ❏ strongly agree   ❏ agree   ❏ unsure   ❏ disagree   ❏ strongly disagree   ❏ no opinion

5. Our time is limited for collaborative design work, study groups and action research—but most educators just do not safeguard and use the time available to ensure that good planning, design, and action research get done.

    ❏ strongly agree   ❏ agree   ❏ unsure   ❏ disagree   ❏ strongly disagree   ❏ no opinion

6. The characteristics of good designs identified in the exercise provide a solid basis for self-assessment and peer review of designs locally.

    ❏ strongly agree   ❏ agree   ❏ unsure   ❏ disagree   ❏ strongly disagree   ❏ no opinion

7. I am here because I really want to be here. I expect to learn something of value.

    ❏ strongly agree   ❏ agree   ❏ unsure   ❏ disagree   ❏ strongly disagree   ❏ no opinion

8. Whether I am thrilled to be here, I see the need for professional development in curriculum and assessment design.

    ❏ strongly agree   ❏ agree   ❏ unsure   ❏ disagree   ❏ strongly disagree   ❏ no opinion

---

Templates

Stage 1

Stage 2

Stage 3

Peer review

Exercises

Process sheets

Glossary

The UbD Workshop Roadmap

The labeled boxes below (such as **U**, **Q**) refer to the boxes on the UbD Template. The concepts in each oval represent some Big Ideas for that stage of design. Thus, the visual provides a map for the work we will do.

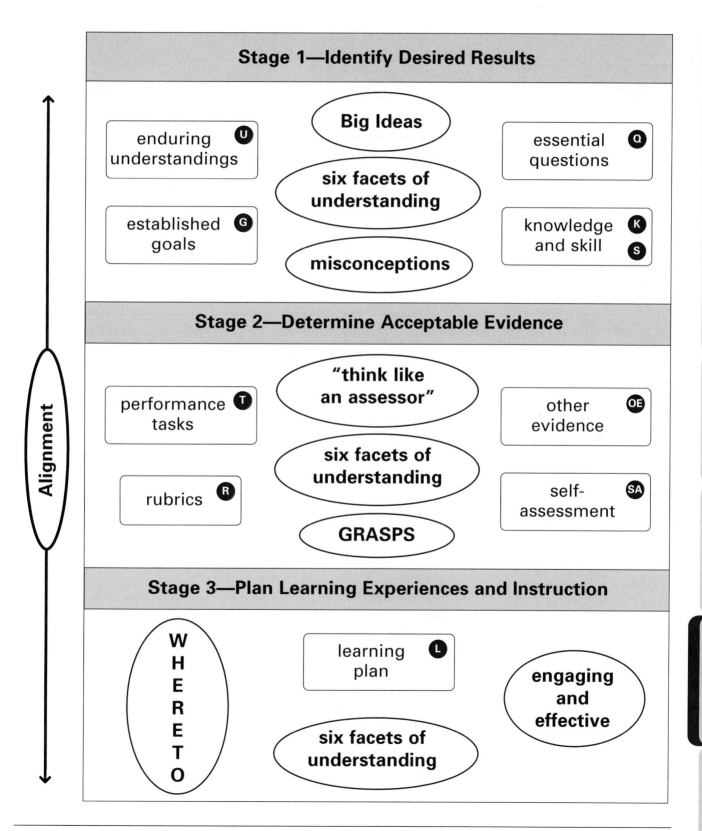

Entry Points for the Design Process

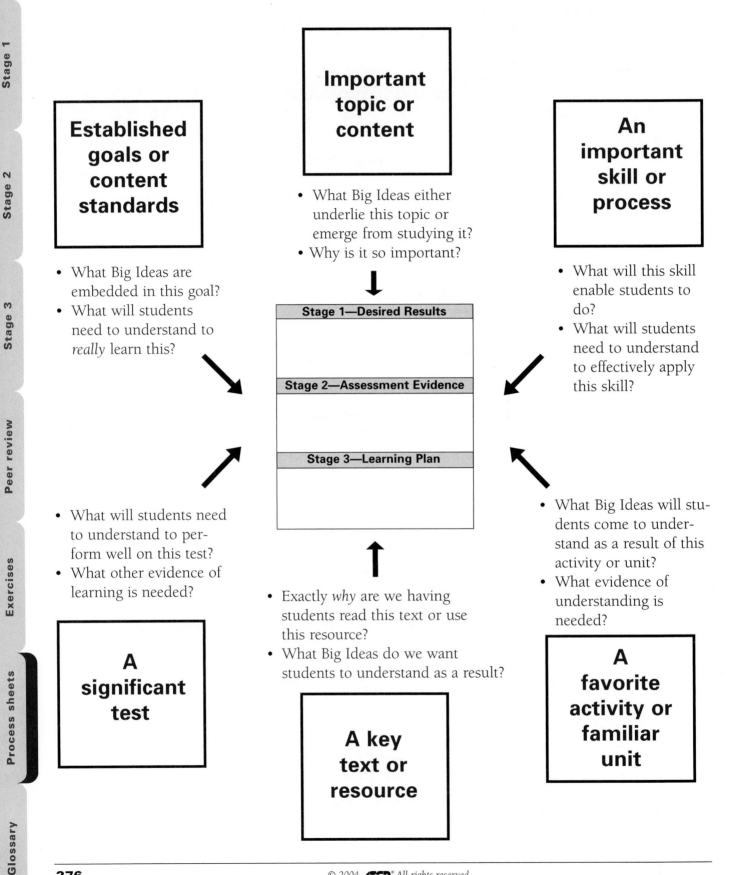

Important topic or content

- What Big Ideas either underlie this topic or emerge from studying it?
- Why is it so important?

Established goals or content standards

- What Big Ideas are embedded in this goal?
- What will students need to understand to *really* learn this?

An important skill or process

- What will this skill enable students to do?
- What will students need to understand to effectively apply this skill?

Stage 1—Desired Results

Stage 2—Assessment Evidence

Stage 3—Learning Plan

- What will students need to understand to perform well on this test?
- What other evidence of learning is needed?

A significant test

- Exactly *why* are we having students read this text or use this resource?
- What Big Ideas do we want students to understand as a result?

A key text or resource

- What Big Ideas will students come to understand as a result of this activity or unit?
- What evidence of understanding is needed?

A favorite activity or familiar unit

Templates | Stage 1 | Stage 2 | Stage 3 | Peer review | Exercises | Process sheets | Glossary

Clarifying Understanding by Design

Directions: Add specifics within the two columns below to reflect your understanding of what UbD is and is not.

Understanding by Design IS	Understanding by Design IS NOT

277

Templates

Stage 1

Stage 2

Stage 3

Peer review

Exercises

Process sheets

Glossary

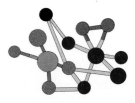

Connecting Big Ideas in UbD

Directions: Draw connecting lines to show the links among the Big Ideas in Understanding by Design. Be prepared to explain your connections.

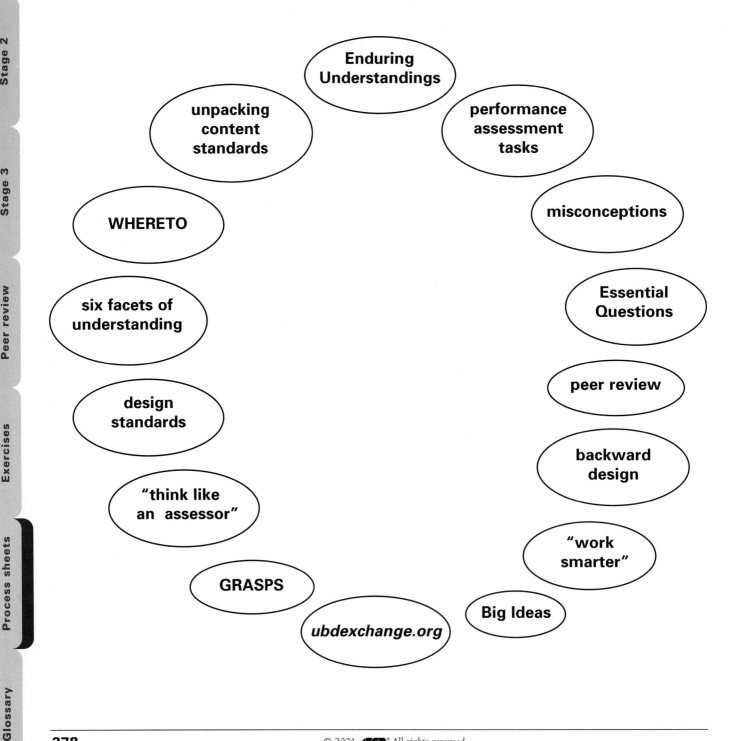

Enduring Understandings

performance assessment tasks

unpacking content standards

misconceptions

WHERETO

Essential Questions

six facets of understanding

peer review

design standards

backward design

"think like an assessor"

"work smarter"

GRASPS

Big Ideas

ubdexchange.org

Templates · Stage 1 · Stage 2 · Stage 3 · Peer review · Exercises · Process sheets · Glossary

Understanding by Design Tic-Tac-Toe

Directions: Select three in a row. Then use those ideas to form generalizations about UbD. Record them in the space below. **Variation:** Select *any* two or three ideas.

Big Ideas	**Enduring Understandings**	**Essential Questions**
GRASPS	**Backward Design**	**Six Facets of Understanding**
Design Standards	*ubdexchange* **Web site**	**WHERETO**

Generalizations: _____

_____

_____

_____

Templates · Stage 1 · Stage 2 · Stage 3 · Peer review · Exercises · Process sheets · Glossary

Give One, Get Many

Directions: In the first box, briefly summarize an idea for _____.
Then, meet with others to share ideas. Record other ideas in the blank boxes.

Templates

Stage 1

Stage 2

Stage 3

Peer review

Exercises

Process sheets

Glossary

UbD Comparisons

Directions: Use the Venn diagram to compare, for example, the six facets of understanding with Bloom's Taxonomy, or UbD with other frameworks, such as Dimensions of Learning.

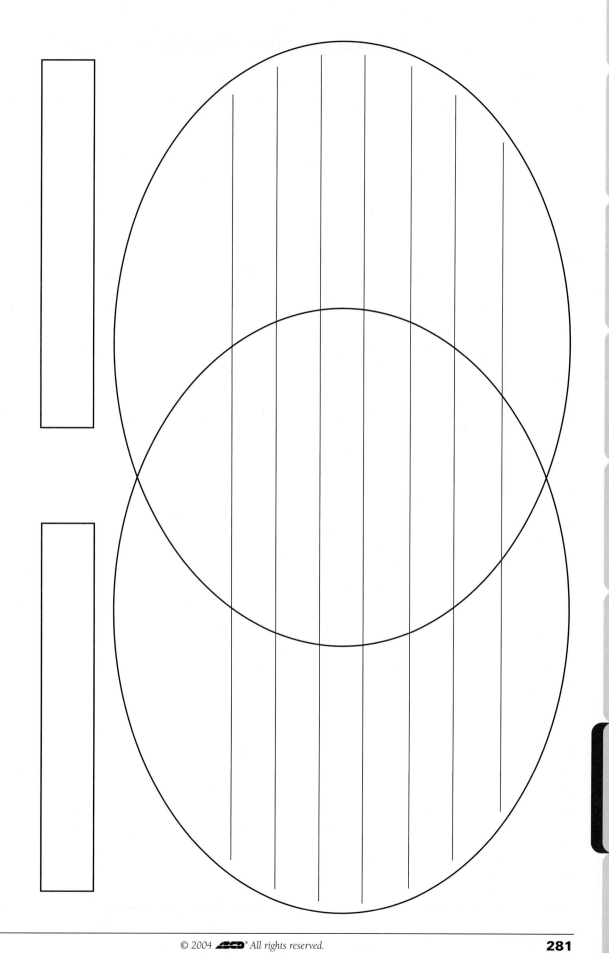

281

Assessing Your Understanding

Directions: Use the following prompts to periodically assess your understanding of the workshop content.

STAGE 1

I really understand _____

_____

_____

I do not yet understand _____

_____

STAGE 2

I really understand _____

_____

_____

I do not yet understand _____

_____

STAGE 3

I really understand _____

_____

_____

I do not yet understand _____

_____

Templates

Stage 1

Stage 2

Stage 3

Peer review

Exercises

Process sheets

Glossary

Reflecting on UbD—Version 1

What Big Ideas have I gained?

What new questions were raised?

What feelings have I experienced?

What actions do I plan to take?

283

Templates

Stage 1

Stage 2

Stage 3

Peer review

Exercises

Process sheets

Glossary

Reflecting on UbD—Version 2

What questions or concerns do you have?

What are implications for your work?

What were the key points or Big Ideas of the session?

What do you better understand?

284

Templates

Stage 1

Stage 2

Stage 3

Peer review

Exercises

Process sheets

Glossary

Reflecting on UbD—Version 3

What existing resources will support UbD?

What important questions need to be answered?

What do I already have in place that supports UbD?

What next steps can I take?

Templates

Stage 1

Stage 2

Stage 3

Peer review

Exercises

Process sheets

Glossary

Synthesizing Activity

Directions:

1. Individually—Review your handouts, notes, and questions. Identify two or three useful or interesting ideas gained as a result of attending this session.

2. With Your Group—Share your ideas with group members and listen to theirs. Add to your list in the space below.

Templates | Stage 1 | Stage 2 | Stage 3 | Peer review | Exercises | Process sheets | Glossary

Action Planning

Desired Results	Evidence of Success	Actions	Persons Responsible	Resources Needed

287

Templates

Stage 1

Stage 2

Stage 3

Peer review

Exercises

Process sheets

Glossary

Taking Action

Directions: In light of this workshop, what should I . . .

➡️ ***start doing:*** _____

_____

_____

_____

🛑 ***stop doing:*** _____

_____

_____

< ***do less of:*** _____

_____

_____

_____

> ***do more of:*** _____

_____

_____

_____

Templates | Stage 1 | Stage 2 | Stage 3 | Peer review | Exercises | Process sheets | Glossary

Glossary

Glossary
A more detailed glossary is found in *Understanding by Design*.

analytic rubric   Analytic-trait scoring of performance involves the use of separate criteria in scoring work (as opposed to **holistic** scoring and rubrics), typically involving separate rubrics for each key criterion. In effect, a performance is assessed numerous times, using the "lens" of a separate criterion each time. For example, when using an analytic rubric to evaluate essays, a teacher might evaluate five traits: organization, use of detail, attention to audience, persuasiveness, and conventions. Analytic-trait scoring is thus in contrast with holistic scoring whereby a judge forms an overall impression about a performance.

application   One of the six facets of understanding. Evidence of understanding is the ability to apply knowledge and skill in new situations and diverse contexts.

assess, assessment   To assess is to thoroughly and methodically analyze student accomplishment against specific goals and criteria. Assessment techniques include tests, exhibits, interviews, surveys, and observation. Effective assessment requires a balance of techniques because each technique is limited and prone to error.

    Assessment is sometimes viewed as synonymous with "evaluation" though there is a subtle difference. We might well assess a student's strength and weaknesses without placing value or a grade on that performance.

authentic assessment   An authentic assessment task is designed to simulate or replicate important, real-world performances. Authentic performance tasks establish a realistic context with genuine purposes, audiences, and constraints. Thus, the context of the assessment, not just the task itself (e.g. "messiness" of problem, ability to seek feedback and revise, and access to apt resources), is what makes the work authentic, not merely whether it is performance-based or hands-on.

backward design   A process to designing curriculum by beginning with the end in mind and designing toward that end. Why is such a view "backward" when it seems so logical? Because many teachers *begin* their unit design with textbooks, favored lessons, and time-honored activities rather than deriving those from targeted goals or standards. In backward design, one starts with the end—the desired results (goals or standards)—and identifies the evidence necessary to determine that the results have been achieved, that is, the assessments. With the results and assessments clearly specified, one can determine the necessary (enabling) knowledge and skill, and the teaching needed to equip students to perform.

Big Idea   A Big Idea refers to transferable concepts, principles, and theories that should serve as the focal point of curricula, instruction, and assessment. Big ideas help connect the discrete facts and skills. They are typically revealed through one or more of the following forms: a concept (e.g., adaptation), a theme (e.g., man's inhumanity to man), an issue or debate (e.g., liberal vs. conservative), a paradox (e.g., poverty amidst plenty), a process (e.g., writing process), an authentic problem (e.g., voter apathy), a theory (e.g., Manifest Destiny), an underlying assumption (e.g., the markets are rational), or differing perspectives (e.g., terrorist vs. freedom fighter).

criteria   The qualities that must be met by performances and products for work to measure up to a standard. To ask *What are the criteria?* amounts to asking Where should we look in examining students' products or performances to know if they were successful? What should we look for? How will teachers identify acceptable work?

    Four different types of criteria are often at play in any complex performance: *Content* refers to the aptness, adequacy, or accuracy of the knowledge and skills used. *Process* refers to the means, processes, attitude, or approaches taken in [per]formance or in preparation for performance. Was the work efficient? Was the manner fluid and poised? Was the per[son] dedicated? *Quality* refers to the attention to detail, polish, and craftsmanship. Was the paper organized? Was the [...] well-delivered? Was the lab write-up error-free and done according to proper format? *Impact* is clearly at the heart [of what we] mean by performance, for example, did the performance work? What was its effect, its result, its outcome, [regardless] of effort, attitude, and approach? Criteria may be weighted to signal relative importance.

[...] explicit and comprehensive plan developed to honor a framework of standards as outlined in a [...] [m] is thus a course of study or complete program, composed of numerous units.

Templates

Stage 1

Stage 2

Stage 3

Peer review

Exercises

design   To design is to plan the form and structure of something, or the pattern or motif of a work of art. In education, teachers are designers in both senses, aiming to develop purposeful, coherent, effective, and engaging lessons, units, and courses of study and accompanying assessments to achieve desired results.

diagnostic assessment   Assessments that precede instruction to check students' prior knowledge and identify misconceptions, interests, or learning-style preferences. Diagnostic assessments provide information to assist teacher planning and guide differentiated instruction.

Enduring Understanding   Refers to the important ideas or core processes that are central to a discipline and transferable to new situations and that have lasting value beyond the classroom. In thinking about the Enduring Understandings for a unit or course, teachers are encouraged to ask, "What do we want students to understand and be able to use several years from now, after they have forgotten the details?"

empathy   One of the six facets of understanding. The ability to "walk in another's shoes," to escape one's own emotional reactions to grasp another's.

Essential Question   Essential Questions reflect the most historically important issues, problems, and debates in a field of study. For example, Is history inevitably biased? What is a proof? Nature or nurture? By examining such questions, students are engaged in thinking like an expert (i.e., "doing" the subject). Essential questions are open-ended with no single, correct answer. They are meant to stimulate inquiry, debate and further questions, and can be reexamined over time. They are designed to be thought provoking to students, engaging them in sustained, focused inquiries, culminating in meaningful performances.

explanation   One of the six facets of understanding, calling for sophisticated and apt explanations and theories that provide knowledgeable and justified accounts of events, actions, and ideas. Student explanations need to be in their own words to reveal their understanding.

facets of understanding   The six different kinds of understanding identified in Understanding by Design: explanation, interpretation, application, perspective, empathy, and self-knowledge. Understanding (or lack of it) reveals itself in different mutually reinforcing ways. In other words, the more we see a student able to explain, apply, and offer multiple points of view on the same idea, the more likely that the student understands that idea.

formative assessment   Ongoing assessments that provide information to guide teaching and learning for improving learning and performance. Formative assessments include both formal and informal methods, such as quizzes, oral questioning, observations, and reviews of draft work.

guiding question   an engaging and focusing question that frames a particular topic or unit of study. It represents a more narrowly focused and content-specific form of an essential question.

holistic rubric   A rubric used to obtain an overall impression of the quality of a performance. Typically, a holistic evaluation yields a single score. Holistic scoring is distinguished from analytic trait scoring, where separate rubrics are used for each separate criterion that makes up an aspect of performance.

interpretation   One of the six facets of understanding involving interpretations, narratives, and translations that provide meaning.

iterative approach   A process that continually revisits earlier work. Synonyms include recursive, circular, and spiral. The curricular design process is always iterative: Teachers keep revisiting their initial ideas about what they are after, how to assess it, and how they should teach to it as we keep working on each element of the design.

leading question   A question used in teaching to teach, clarify, or assess for knowledge. Unlike essential questions, leading questions seek straightforward, correct answers.

performance standard   A performance standard describes a specific result or level of achievement that is deemed exemplary or appropriate. Content standards specify *what* students should know and be able to do, performance standards identify *how well* students need to perform.

Templates   Stage 1   Stage 2   Stage 3   Peer review   Exercises   Process sheets   Glossary

Templates

Stage 1

Stage 2

Stage 3

Peer review

Exercises

Process sheets

Glossary

perspective   One of the six facets of understanding referring to critical and insightful points of view. When one understands, one can get at a distance from what is known and avoid getting caught up in the views and passions of the moment.

prerequisite knowledge and skill   The knowledge and skill required to achieve a targeted understanding or successfully complete a culminating performance.

prompt   An academic prompt is a form of assessment somewhere between an authentic performance task and a short-answer test or quiz. Academic prompts are open-ended, paper-and-pencil tasks, such as a timed essay question. By definition, such prompts are not authentic because they are bound by school constraints, including access to resources, time allotted, limits on talking to others.

quiz   Any selected-response or short-answer test (oral or written) where the sole purpose is to assess for discrete knowledge and skill.

reliable, reliability   Reliability in measurement and testing refers to the accuracy of the score. Is it sufficiently free of error? What is the likelihood that the score or grade would be constant if the test were retaken or the same performance were scored by someone else? Error is unavoidable; all tests, including the best multiple-choice tests, lack 100 percent reliability. The aim is to minimize error to tolerable levels.

In performance assessment the reliability problem typically occurs in two forms: (1) To what extent can we generalize from the single or small amount of performances to the student's likely performance in general? Is the score truly representative of the student's general capacities and patterns of results? and (2) What is the likelihood that different judges will see the same performance in the same way (inter-rater reliability)?

rubric   A rubric is a scoring guide that enables judges to make reliable judgments about student work and students to self-assess. A rubric is based on a continuum of performance quality, built upon a scale of different possible score points to be assigned; identifies the key traits or dimensions to be examined and assessed; and provides key features of performance for each level of scoring (descriptors) which signify the degree to which the criteria have been met.

self-knowledge   One of the six facets of understanding pertaining to the accuracy of self-assessment and awareness of the biases in one's understanding brought about by favored styles of inquiry, habitual ways of thinking, and unexamined beliefs. A learner with self-knowledge understands what he does and does not understand.

task, performance task   A task is a complex assessment challenge that requires the use of one's knowledge and skill to effectively perform or create a product to reveal one's understanding or proficiency.

template   A guide or framework for designers. In Understanding by Design, we use a planning template to address the various elements of backward design in the development or refinement of a unit. Each page of the template contains key questions, prompting the user to consider particular elements of backward design, and a graphic organizer containing frames for recording design ideas.

transfer, transferability   Refers to the appropriate and fruitful use of knowledge in a new or different context from that in which it was initially learned.

uncoverage   To go in depth using an inquiry-based approach whereby meaning is discovered, constructed, or inferred by the learners with the aid of the teacher and well-designed learning experiences. Uncoverage is required to develop understanding of ideas that are abstract and possibly counterintuitive.

unit   Short for a unit of study. Though there are no hard and fast criteria, a unit focuses on a major topic (e.g., the Civil War), process (e.g., research), or resource (e.g., a novel), and typically lasts a few days to a few weeks.

valid, validity   The inferences one can confidently draw about student learning from the results of an assessment. Does the test measure what it purports to measure? Does the assessment correlate with other performance results that educators consider valid? Does the small sample of questions or tasks accurately correlate with what students would do if tested on everything that was taught? Do the results have predictive value, that is, do they correlate with likely future success in the subject? Some or all of these questions must have a "yes" answer for an assessment to have validity.

Acknowledgments

Many individuals, far too numerous to mention, have helped us develop and refine the ideas and materials in the *Understanding by Design Professional Development Workbook* over the last few years. Nonetheless, a few are deserving of special acknowledgment. First, we owe a debt of gratitude to the members of the Understanding By Design Training Cadre— John Brown, Ann Cunningham-Morris, Marcella Emberger, Judith Hilton, Catherine Jones, Everett Kline, Ken O'Connor, Jim Riedl, Elizabeth Rutherford, Janie Smith, Elliott Seif, Michael Short, Janie Smith, Joyce Tatum, and Allison Zmuda. Their helpful feedback and guidance, based on extensive experience conducting professional development in *Understanding by Design* (UbD), has resulted in greater precision of language, clarity of examples and supportive scaffolding. We especially appreciate the helpful advice of Elliott and Allison over the course of countless hours of review and conversation.

We offer heartfelt thanks to the thousands of educators who have participated in UbD workshops and conferences. Their helpful feedback, penetrating questions, and design struggles helped us shape and sharpen the materials in this *Workbook*.

Like the book, *Understanding by Design*, this book would never have come about had it not been for the support and enthusiasm provided by Sally Chapman at ASCD. Sally was the first to have the vision of a comprehensive set of resources and services for *Understanding by Design*, and the confidence in the authors to undertake the journey. We are very grateful.

We are also thankful to Darcie Russell, lead editor, and Reece Quinones, graphic designer, for their ability to fashion an unwieldy manuscript into a well-designed final product. Darcie and her editorial colleagues deserve a special commendation for their patience and good-natured understanding in dealing with the unending changes and refinements that are the hallmarks of the authors. The manuscript is the better for their flexibility and talents.

Finally, we once again thank our families for tolerating the endless phone calls, trips back and forth between Maryland and New Jersey, and the hours spent on the road using and refining these materials. We trust that they again—understand.

About the Authors

Jay McTighe brings a wealth of experience developed during a rich and varied career in education. He served as director of the Maryland Assessment Consortium, a state collaboration of school districts working together to develop and share formative performance assessments. Prior to this position, McTighe was involved with school improvement projects at the Maryland State Department of Education. He is known for his work with thinking skills, having coordinated statewide efforts to develop instructional strategies, curriculum models, and assessment procedures for improving the quality of student thinking. McTighe also directed the development of the Instructional Framework, a multimedia database on teaching. In addition to his work at the state level, McTighe has experience at the district level in Prince George's County, Md., as a classroom teacher, resource specialist, and program coordinator. He also served as director of the Maryland Summer Center for Gifted and Talented Students, a statewide residential enrichment program held at St. Mary's College.

McTighe has published articles in leading journals and books, including *Educational Leadership* (ASCD), *Developing Minds* (ASCD), *Thinking Skills: Concepts and Techniques* (National Education Association), and *The Developer* (National Staff Development Council). He coauthored three books on assessment, *Assessing Learning in the Classroom* (NEA), *Assessing Outcomes: Performance Assessment Using the Dimensions of Learning Model* (ASCD), and *Evaluation Tools to Improve as Well as Evaluate Student Performance* (Corwin Press). He is coauthor, with Grant Wiggins, of two recent, best-selling publications, *Understanding by Design* and *The Understanding by Design Handbook* (ASCD).

Jay has an extensive background in staff development and is a regular speaker at national, state, and district conferences and workshops. He is also a featured presenter in four videotape programs, *Performance Assessment in the Classroom* (Video Journal of Education), *Developing Performance Assessments*, and *Understanding Understanding* (ASCD).

Jay received his undergraduate degree from The College of William and Mary, earned a masters degree from The University of Maryland and has completed post-graduate studies at The Johns Hopkins University. He was selected to participate in The Educational Policy Fellowship Program through the Institute for Educational Leadership in Washington, D.C. He served as a member of the National Assessment Forum, a coalition of education and civil rights organizations advocating reforms in national, state and local assessment policies and practices. McTighe also completed a three-year term on the ASCD Publications Committee, serving as committee chair during 1994–95. He can be reached at 6581 River Run, Columbia, MD 21044-6066, USA. Phone: 410-531-1610. E-mail: jmctigh@aol.com.

Grant Wiggins is president of Grant Wiggins & Associates in Monmouth Junction, N.J. He consults with schools, districts and state education departments on a variety of reform matters; organizes conferences and workshops; and develops print materials and Web resources on curricular change, based on Understanding by Design. Wiggins's work has been supported by the Pew Charitable Trusts, the Geraldine R. Dodge Foundation, the National Science Foundation, and the Education Commission of the States, among other organizations.

Over the past fifteen years, Wiggins has worked on some of the most influential reform initiatives in the country, including Vermont's portfolio system and the Coalition of Essential Schools. He has established a statewide Consortium devoted to assessment reform, and designed a performance-based and teacher-run portfolio assessment prototype for the states of North Carolina and New Jersey.

Wiggins is the author of Educative Assessment and Assessing Student Performance. His many articles have appeared in such journals as *Educational Leadership* and *Phi Delta Kappan*.

His work is grounded in 14 years of secondary school teaching and coaching. Wiggins earned an Ed.D. from Harvard University and a B.A. from St. John's College in Annapolis. Wiggins taught English and electives in philosophy, coached varsity soccer, cross country, junior varsity baseball, and track and field. Recently he has coached his two sons in soccer and baseball. In 2002, Wiggins was a Scholar in Residence at the College of New Jersey. He also plays guitar and sings in the Hazbins, a rock band. He can be reached at Grant Wiggins & Associates, 4095 Route 1, Box 104, Monmouth Junction, NJ 08852, USA. Phone: 732-329-0641. E-mail: grant@grantwiggins.org.

Related ASCD Resources: Understanding by Design

At the time of publication, the following ASCD resources were available; for the most up-to-date information about ASCD resources, go to www.ascd.org. ASCD stock numbers are noted in parentheses.

Audiotapes

Applying Understanding by Design to School Improvement Planning by Jay McTighe and Ronald S. Thomas (#202143)

Structures That Support Understanding by Design by Fran Prolman and Grant Wiggins (#299321)

Understanding by Design: Structures and Strategies for Designing School Reform by Jay McTighe and Grant Wiggins: (#202189)

Walking the Talk: Applying Standards to Our Own Work by Jay McTighe and Grant Wiggins (#200334)

What Does Understanding by Design Have to Do with Professional Development by Harolyn Katherman and others (#202137)

Working Smarter in Curriculum Design by Jay McTighe and Grant Wiggins (#20114)

Networks

Visit the ASCD Web site (www.ascd.org) and click on About ASCD. Under the header of Your Partnership with ASCD, click on Networks for information about professional educators who have formed groups around topics, including "Arts in Education," "Authentic Assessment," and "Brain-Based Compatible Learning." Look in the Network Directory for current facilitators' addresses and phone numbers.

Online Courses

Understanding by Design: An Introduction (register for these online or by calling ASCD)
Understanding by Design: Six Facets of Understanding
Understanding by Design: The Backward Design Process

Print Products

Understanding by Design
by Grant Wiggins and Jay McTighe (#198199)

The Understanding by Design Handbook
by Jay McTighe and Grant Wiggins (#199030)

Understanding by Design Study Guide (#100246)

Understanding by Design Bundle for Study Groups, includes 10 copies of Understanding by Design and 1 copy of the Study Guide (#100245)

Understanding by Design, 2nd edition, is expected off press in late 2004.

Training

The ASCD Understanding by Design Faculty: ASCD will arrange for a UBD expert to deliver onsite training tailored to the needs of your school, district, or regional service agency. Call (703) 578-9600, ext. 5677.

Videotapes

The Understanding by Design Video Series, three tapes (#400241)

Web Products

Professional Development Online, at http://pdonline.ascd.org, features several UbD-related online study courses.

The UbD Exchange, at http://www.ubdexchange.org/, features a database of units designed using the Understanding by Design framework. It contains short tutorials and self-checks to guide designers through the electronic unit template as they build units and assessments to store in the database. Users of the Exchange can interact with others by giving and receiving feedback on curriculum units using the design standards.

Exemplars of essential questions, enduring understandings, performance tasks, rubrics, and learning activities are highlighted with blue ribbons and trophies awarded by the authors and other expert UbD trainers.

For additional resources, visit us on the World Wide Web (http://www.ascd.org), send an e-mail message to member@ascd.org, call the ASCD Service Center (1-800-933-ASCD or 703-578-9600, then press 2), send a fax to 703-575-5400, or write to Information Services, ASCD, 1703 N. Beauregard St., Alexandria, VA 22311-1714 USA.